"What Stephen Rhodes has given us is a vision of the church rooted in the gospel and yet as widely welcoming as there are cultures on earth. He has gone beyond the old terms *liberal* and *conservative* to fresh biblical resources."

WILLIAM MALLARD
Candler School of Theology
Emory University

"Stephen Rhodes's book has been written out of his own real-life experience. . . . I highly commend this book to any person who is interested in a congregation which reflects both the diversity and the unity of the Christian church."

BISHOP JOE E. PENNEL JR.
Virginia Conference
United Methodist Church

Where *the* Nations Meet

The Church in a Multicultural World

Stephen A. Rhodes

InterVarsity Press
Downers Grove, Illinois

InterVarsity Press
P.O. Box 1400, Downers Grove, IL 60515
World Wide Web: www.ivpress.com
E-mail: mail@ivpress.com

InterVarsity Press® is the book-publishing division of InterVarsity Christian Fellowship/USA®, a student movement active on campus at hundreds of universities, colleges and schools of nursing in the United States of America, and a member movement of the International Fellowship of Evangelical Students. For information about local and regional activities, write Public Relations Dept., InterVarsity Christian Fellowship/USA, 6400 Schroeder Rd., P.O. Box 7895, Madison, WI 53707-7895.

ISBN 0-8308-1936-3

Printed in the United States of America ♻

Library of Congress Cataloging-in-Publication Data

Rhodes, Stephen A.
    Where the nations meet : the church in a multicultural world / Stephen
A. Rhodes.
        p.   cm.
    Includes bibliographical references.
    ISBN 0-8308-1936-3 (pbk. : alk. paper)
    1. Multiculturalism—Religious aspects—Christianity.
2. Christianity and culture. 3. Christianity and the world.
4. Church—Marks. 5. Mission of the church—Biblical teaching.
6. Christianity—20th century.   I. Title.
BR115.C8R56   1998
261.8'348—dc21   98-17881
                                                                          CIP

21 20 19 18 17 16 15 14 13 12 11 10 9 8 7 6 5 4 3

16 15 14 13 12 11 10 09 08 07

I dedicate this book to
my wife, Lynn, without whose love, friendship and shared calling in ministry
none of this would have been possible;
our precious children: Cora, Hannah, Sarah, Gabriella and Abraham,
my pastor and missionary mentor, Robinson McAden;
and my friend and lifelong spiritual guide, Charles Neal,
who first helped me to "hear and to obey."

Acknowledgments

As the writer of the book of Hebrews recognizes, "Since we are surrounded by so great a cloud of witnesses, let us also lay aside every weight and the sin that clings so closely, and let us run with perseverance the race that is set before us" (Hebrews 12:1). No passage from Scripture better describes the obstacles and hindrances to writing a book than this one. There were moments when I certainly felt as though I were carrying a number of weights as I slowly made my way toward the finish line of completing this project. I believe that, if nothing else, one learns humility in the process of writing. I have certainly learned my own limitations. What possessed me to write a book just after Lynn and I had our fifth child, not to mention continuing to pastor full time, is beyond me. So, I wish to thank the great "cloud of witnesses" who have stood with me in this process, encouraging me by shouting from the sidelines until I completed the race.

First, I would like to thank the readers who were willing to endure my many draft manuscripts, both faxed and mailed, and who spoke truth with love: Monte Campbell, Tom Elliot, Bishop Kern Eutsler, Dr. Stanley Hauerwas, Al Horton, Dr. James Logan, Mark Lykins, Dr. Bill Mallard, Bob McAden, Jim Noland, Jose Palos, Bishop Joe Pennel, Doug Ruffle, Dr. Kendall Soulen, Bishop Tom Stockton and Rachel Ye.

Second, I want to thank those congregations that welcomed me on the seven-thousand-mile trek during my sabbatical and openly shared the joys and struggles of multicultural churches. In particular, I want to thank several of the pastors and staff members who helped by telling their stories: Austin Armistead, Sung Jun Yoo, Bill Bryan, Marta Burke, Clarke Campbell-Evans, Jerome Hamm, Mark and Pat Lykins, Doug Ruffle, Jose Palos, Joseph Lee and Conrado Saltero.

Third, I want to thank many of the friends who have endured with me by listening to my thoughts and ideas concerning this manuscript: Helen Casey-Rutland, Tim Gerde, Dr. Barry Penn Hollar, Janet Horman, Won-

Hee Kang, Seon-Young Kim, Larry Lenow, Jim Noland, Carol Ploch, Ileana Rosas, Allison Rutland-Soulen and Ted Smith.

Fourth, I want to thank Lee Sheaffer, Bob McAden, Bishop Tom Stockton and Bishop Ray Chamberland for encouraging me to take the leap of faith in coming to Culmore as pastor. They saw something that I had not yet seen.

Fifth, I want to thank my secretary, Pat Shattuck, who faithfully read through every jot and tittle of this manuscript before its first submission.

Sixth, I want to thank the members of my church, Culmore United Methodist, for their graciousness of spirit, first for granting my sabbatical three years ago, and second for modifying my schedule at church so that I could complete this book.

Seventh, I want to thank my editor, Rodney Clapp, who enthusiastically embraced this book while it was still just an idea in my head, and who willingly took a risk with this first-time author.

Finally, I want to thank my wife, Lynn Rasor, who believed in both me and this project when my own enthusiasm sometimes waned, and with whom I have shared the dream and the reality of serving in a church of all nations. She is my dearest, truest friend, and I give thanks to God every day that I have been blessed in sharing my life with her. Now that the book is complete, I must fulfill my promise of more family time.

Introduction
What Does
This Mean?

••

When the day of Pentecost came, they were all ... filled with the Holy Spirit and began to speak in other tongues as the Spirit enabled them. ... A crowd came together in bewilderment, because each one heard them speaking in his own language. Utterly amazed, they asked, ... "What does this mean?" ACTS 2:1-7, 12 NIV

On the first Pentecost, believers in the resurrected Jesus were gathered, waiting and praying in an upper room in anticipation of whatever it was that God had in store. For their fifty days of prayerful watchfulness, the disciples were rewarded with an awesome display of celestial fireworks. On Pentecost all heaven broke loose, and the Holy Spirit descended upon the cacophonous humanity gathered in Jerusalem, transforming their dissonant voices into holy harmony. The fiery Spirit fell upon persons "from every nation under heaven" (Acts 2:5). Those who had previously been separated by geography, culture and language suddenly found themselves speaking with, hearing, and understanding others with whom they had nothing in common save that they were all descendants of Abraham. Called and blessed by God, Abraham was exclusively chosen from among all the peoples of the earth for the specific purpose of God's inclusive mission. God promised Abraham that through his descendants *all* the nations of the earth would be blessed. The believers who gathered in Jerusalem on Pentecost believed this promise was fulfilled in Abraham's descendant, Jesus of Nazareth. As Scripture reminds us, of course, not all who witnessed the events of that day understood. Many were utterly bewildered by what they saw. Many onlookers who saw believers proclaiming the mighty works of God in many languages and tongues asked themselves, *"What does this mean?"*

That is precisely the question I find myself asking again and again. As a pastor serving a congregation where each Sunday believers from over 30 different countries gather to worship and praise God in many tongues, but with one heart; as a Christian claiming the Pentecost promise that God has broken down every dividing wall (Eph 2:14); as a father longing for his children to grow up believing and living out the conviction that race does not *have* to matter, I find myself also asking, What does it mean for the church of Jesus Christ to live and make its witness in a multicultural world?

Our world, our nation and our communities are rapidly changing around us. Leonard Sweet, in his book *FaithQuakes*, says that Americans now eat more tortillas for breakfast than bagels or biscuits or pita bread; more salsa is sold now than ketchup. The year 2056 is the magic date cited by sociologists as the moment when the majority of the US American population will be nonEuropean, nonwhite. As it is now, Asians, Africans and Hispanics make up one-fourth of the population.[1]

And the church now finds itself as the bewildered cultural bystander to this multicultural change, asking, What does this mean?

Why bewildered? If the truth be told, most Christian congregations are still homogeneous and ethnocentric. The staggering diversity being embraced by the postmodern world overwhelms our theological senses. Now should be a time for rejoicing: the Pentecost nature of Christian mission can create new paradigms for witness and evangelization. Instead of rejoicing, we find ourselves threatened and defensive, wondering whether all this heterogeneity is not merely the babblings of a world falling apart, rather than the blessing of a world to which God is giving birth. One of the questions facing the church is this: Do congregations see themselves as the last line of defense in a siege by a pluralistic and skeptical age, maintaining the status quo down to the last member, or do they have the willingness to adapt for missionary ministry in this postmodern setting?

A World and a Lifetime Away

The congregation I have served for the past seven years has had to confront the dilemma of choosing between siege or mission. Culmore United Methodist Church, five miles from the nation's capital, is celebrating its forty-fifth year in ministry. For over twenty of those years, the church has been intentionally embracing the diversity of God's people in the international community. We have chosen to serve the community that surrounds us, and as that community has changed, so have we.

In the past decade the population of "new" Americans in northern Virginia has risen dramatically. *U.S. News & World Report* has declared our county, Fairfax, to be "America's most diverse community."[2] The largest ethnic group is Asian, and in our neighboring county, Arlington, the largest is Latin American. In much of northern Virginia, a language other than English is spoken in one out of every four homes. The immediate community in which our church is located is seventy percent Latin American and twenty percent Asian.

My oldest daughter, Cora, is a student at Bailey's Elementary, our neighborhood school. While most of her subjects are taught in English, each afternoon she spends two and a half hours learning math, science and health with her teacher, Señora Armengol, who teaches only in Spanish. When Cora graduates from fifth grade, she will speak Spanish fluently, and with a Cuban accent! More than 90 percent of the students in Cora's school are non-Anglo, and 85 percent speak English as a second language. Over forty different languages are represented in the student body. The country represented by the most students is El Salvador. The PTA newsletter is written in English, Spanish, Vietnamese, Khmer, Somali and Farsi. It is a world and a lifetime away from when I went to elementary school.

Considering these demographics, it should not be surprising that if you were to worship at Culmore on any given Sunday, you would find a congregation primarily made up of immigrants: approximately forty percent are Anglo,[3] but thirty percent are Filipino; fifteen percent are African; ten percent are Latin American; and five percent are of other nationalities, including Jamaican, Cambodian, Korean, Indonesian, and Asian Indian. You would also see a young congregation. The majority of those attending worship are in their forties or younger. These are interesting demographic facts, considering that our denomination, the United Methodist Church, is more than 95 percent Anglo and is aging rapidly. Our congregational diversity includes language, culture, race, class, educational level, theology, and worship style, but the glue that holds all of us together is the theological conviction that our center is Jesus Christ. We are *many* nations, but together we serve *one* Lord.

Of course, you *might* be surprised at the composition of our congregation, even given the diversity of our community. One of the questions I am asked most frequently is, "Does it really work?" People seem genuinely perplexed at the viability of a multicultural church. The question reflects less a sense of whether multicultural churches *ought* to exist, than whether, in fact, they *can* exist. Christian idealism has given way to Christian pragmatism on issues of racial harmony in the body of Christ. In the thirty years since the American church made a very public stand on the issue of racial segregation in our society, its own congregations still move with glacial speed toward their own integration. Although we now find nothing exceptional in a president promising that his cabinet appointees will look like America, we are still skeptical when a Christian congregation seeks to look like the kingdom of God.

Culture Wars

Our uncertainties over the practicality of crosscultural and crossracial ministry are caused, in part, by the church's dismal record to date. Those uncertainties, however, are affected even more by our country's current divisive debate over race, ethnicity and culture.

Presidential candidate Patrick Buchanan sounded a call to arms in his keynote speech at the 1992 Republican Convention when he declared that America was engaged in nothing less than a "cultural war," fighting for the heart and soul of the nation. His populist rhetoric touched a deep cord within our country: the increasing diversity of American society threatens to unravel America's cultural and social fabric.

The 1990s have seen America's multicultural melting pot come to a boil. Tom Sine, in his book *Cease Fire: Searching for Sanity in America's Culture Wars,* writes:

> People everywhere are building more walls. Skinheads are holding more rallies. Californians passed Proposition 187, denying welfare, public education, and nonemergency medical care to illegal aliens. White Howard Beach teenagers used baseball bats on black teenagers who made the mistake of wandering into their neighborhood.[4]

Hostility or Hospitality?

Arthur Schlesinger, in his thoughtful book *The Disuniting of America,* asks:

> What happens when people of different ethnic origins, speaking different languages and professing different religions, settle in the same geographical locality and live under the same political sovereignty?

Unless a common purpose binds them together, tribal hostilities will drive them apart. Ethnic and racial conflict, it seems evident, will now replace the conflict of ideologies as the explosive issue of our times.[5] Schlesinger quotes *The Economist:* "The virus of tribalism . . . risks becoming the AIDS of international politics—lying dormant for years, then flaring up to destroy countries."[6]

Lest we think only of Bosnia, Liberia, Chechnya or Rwanda, our own nation is not immune. Adding to the already heated diversity debate is the whole issue of immigration. Arguably a land of immigrants, this country today is considerably less hospitable toward international neighbors who are coming to make a home here than it was even a year ago. It is hostility, not hospitality, that most aptly characterizes the current climate of our culture. A *USA Today*/CNN/Gallup poll revealed that anti-immigrant sentiment was "as high as it's been at any time since World War II."[7] Two-thirds of those persons polled wanted decreased immigration, 64 percent said that immigrants hurt the economy, and 55 percent said that the racial and ethnic diversity of immigrants threatens U.S. culture. In addition, two presidential candidates in the 1996 primaries ran on isolationist platforms, advocating not only a decrease in immigration levels, but zero immigration.

One of the reasons for this xenophobia is the magnitude of recent immigration. From 1980 to 1990, the United States experienced the largest amount of immigration since the turn of the century, as well as the most racially and ethnically diverse ever. In that decade 9.5 million documented and undocumented immigrants arrived in the U.S. Those 9.5 million immigrants represent almost one-fifth of the 54 million immigrants who have come to the United States since 1820. The foreign-born population is 7.9 percent of the total, which is still smaller than in 1900, when it was 15 percent. In describing this new immigrant population, Ruben Rumbaut observes that

today's new and rapidly accelerating immigration to the United States is extraordinary in its diversity of color, class, and national origins. The 1990 census counted 19.8 million immigrants, an all-time high. In terms of color, most new immigrants reported themselves to be nonwhite in the census. . . . In terms of class, today's immigrants include by far the most educated groups (Asian Indians, Taiwanese) and the least educated groups (Mexicans, Salvadorans) in American society, as well as the groups with the lowest poverty rates in the United States (Filipinos) and the highest (Laos and Cambodians)—a reflection of polar-opposite types of migration embedded in very different historical and structural contexts.[8]

Though still a primarily urban phenomenon, the new immigrant population is also finding its way to suburbia and the rural heartlands. When I went home recently to visit my parents in upper east Tennessee, I found that what had been a very homogeneous company town[9] in the heart of Appalachia has now blossomed into a virtual cosmopolitan crossroads. When I ate lunch at a local fast-food restaurant, I sat across from four Korean businessmen on a lunch break from the local paper plant. When I went to the mall, I spotted four separate Asian families shopping. When I went to visit my mother, who was in the hospital, I noticed that not only were several of the physicians Indian, but more than a few of the nurses were African or Filipino. My daughter, Cora, is growing up in a world far different from the one I grew up in, but even if I had never left home, it seems that the ends of the earth still would have converged in no less likely a place than Kingsport, Tennessee.

Stanley Grenz, in his book *A Primer on Postmodernism*, writes:

The advent of the global village has produced seemingly self-contradictory effects. The mass culture and global economy that the age of information is creating are uniting the world into what one droll observer has called "McWorld." But at the same time that the planet is coming together on one level, it is falling apart on another. The advent of postmodernity has fostered both a global consciousness and the erosion of national consciousness. Nationalization has diminished in the wake of a movement toward "retribalization," toward increased loyalty to a more local context. This impulse is found not only in the countries of Africa but also in such unlikely places as Canada.[10]

The result is that the postmodern ethos puts far more emphasis on *pluribus* than it does on *unum*. The affirmation of our plurality comes easily, but defining what now unites us is a far more difficult task.

Is it any wonder then that people are skeptical of the plausibility of multicultural congregations? Not only are complications inherent in congregations that seek to embody so much diversity, but we live in a polarizing period in history in which we are not afforded the luxury of cultural stability to work out our differences. We are challenged from within and from without. How the church of Jesus Christ deals with the rapidity and the complexity of this multicultural, postmodern ethos will tell the world whether or not it has a reason to listen to the message we proclaim.

Let me say that as Christians, we should not pursue racial or cultural diversity simply because it is politically correct (or incorrect, as the case may now be), or because it is the latest theological fad, or even because it is a good conservative or liberal idea. We should do it because it is the gospel. We are called to welcome the world because it is God's mandate for evangelism: "Go therefore and make disciples of *all nations*" (Mt 28:19). I believe that our multicultural congregations are in a unique position to reach the rich diversity of God's people who live in our communities, and also to model for our culture what it means to live in unity amid diversity. Right now our culture wants to show that multicultural congregations do not work. We must witness that they do.

Peter Berger and other sociologists have contended that our world is governed by what they call *plausibility structures*. These are institutions, organizations and communities that, in their life together, create the "plausibility" that the worldview they inhabit is true. The church may also be considered a plausibility structure in the sense that, through its congregational life, the church creates the plausibility of Christian truth claims. It has been said that the church in its mission has sought in many ways to engage the world and its culture in order to present the truthfulness of the gospel. We now live in a world, says Grenz, that has rejected "the Enlightenment quest for universal, supracultural, timeless truth in favor of searching out truth as the expression of a specific community."[11] A world suspicious of any grand narratives having global implications "replaces these with a respect for difference and a celebration of the local and particular at the expense of the universal."[12] In this world, before the church can tell the world that Christianity is true, the church must demonstrate in its common life the plausibility that it *might* be true.

In the civil rights struggle, the church in essence said to our culture, "Do as we say, not as we do." We said to culture that it was a moral imperative to integrate our schools, workplaces and neighborhoods while simultaneously preserving the segregation that we practice in services of worship. By refusing to embody the truth claims of the gospel that we preached to our culture, we lost our credibility. If we cannot be trusted on an issue such as with whom we are willing to share the body and blood of Jesus, why should our culture believe anything else we have to say? I am convinced that the advent of the postmodern world has given the church a new opportunity to engage our culture. I also believe that multicultural congregations are the new plausibility structures in this environment that will create the possibility of the world considering the gospel's plausibility. Before the church can ask our culture to believe the gospel, we must show our culture that *we* believe it by how we live together.

In Search of an Answer

This book has its roots in the sabbatical I took in 1994. During the summer of that year, I visited or contacted approximately fourteen multicultural or homogeneous ethnic congregations in metropolitan Washington, D.C., New York, New Jersey, Texas, Florida, Georgia and North Carolina. I went with one question in mind: "What is 'normal' in a multicultural congregation?" I went in search of practical help.

As a pastor of a multicultural church, I found that precious few resources provided insight into the work of ministry in this setting. Much of the first three years at Culmore I spent trying to figure out what, indeed, was normal in a multicultural church. I felt that I was flying by the seat of my pants more often than not, basing ministry on hunches, intuitions, and not a little help from the Holy Spirit. What frustrated me most was that I had so little to go on in terms of previous experience—from myself or from others who had gone before me. My hope for the sabbatical was that I would find others who understood the unique stresses, demands and opportunities for this pastoral ministry.

In my journey of seven thousand miles by minivan with my wife and four children, I found all of this and more. I met pastors and laity doing extraordinary things that witnessed to God's reign. The relationships and collegiality created by that sojourn have continued these past four years. It was out of conversations with the clergy and laity of these congregations that the parameters and commonalities of this ministry have begun to emerge.

Since that sabbatical I have felt called to share what I have learned about multicultural ministry, both from my own experience at Culmore and from the churches I visited. As this book developed, however, I realized that it would be inadequate simply to tell the stories of one or more congregations apart from their implications for the church universal. While it is important to bring to light particular truths of congregational life, these truths, in the end, must illuminate the greater Truth in the metanarrative of the gospel of Jesus Christ. Put differently, unless a multicultural congregation locates itself with the story of God's salvation of humanity, it has nothing more to offer than its own particularity, however interesting that may be.

This reality came home to me when I was talking with Kendall Soulen, associate professor of systematic theology at Wesley Theological Seminary in Washington, D.C., who attends Culmore. Kendall posed a question: "Can a church which is all white, in a rural or suburban area, where everyone has a similar educational level, income level and ethnic background, be considered a multicultural church?" Kendall provided his own answer: "Yes, I believe it can, because each Sunday that congregation worships a Jewish Messiah, reading holy Scriptures originally written by Jews in Hebrew, Aramaic and Greek, but whose readership was found all across the Roman Empire. In this sense every congregation is a multicultural congregation." What I have learned over the past year years, I believe, applies not only to churches in a multicultural setting but what it means to be *the church* in a multicultural world.

About This Book

Each book is written for a particular audience. I have written this book with not one but three audiences in mind:

1. Christians who have grown skeptical of, and possibly hostile toward, the issues of inclusivity and diversity, as a result of the current debates on race, ethnicity and immigration, but who may be open to the biblical teachings related to these issues.

2. Christians who are currently supportive of multicultural issues but whose views are based on political or philosophical categories more than on theological ones. This book is an invitation to rethink the whole concept of multiculturalism from a postmodern, evangelical point of view.

3. Pastors and congregations who are already involved in multicultural ministries, or who have the possibility of doing so, to affirm the importance of this ministry as the model of the church in this post-Enlightenment era, to present its theological underpinnings, to outline the basic principles of this ministry and to illumine this ecclesiology through the narrative life of one such congregation.

This book is divided into three sections. Section one (chapters one through four) addresses the biblical dilemma of diversity by developing a trinitarian ecclesiology of the multicultural church. Section two (chapters five through eleven) addresses the more practical ministry-related issues of the multicultural church. Section three (chapter twelve) presents the eschatology of hope that the multicultural church embodies.

Where the Nations Meet focuses on the biblical teachings and narratives that have particular significance for crosscultural ministry, and will explore what their implications for the nature of the church in a multicultural world are. From a postmodern, evangelical point of view, I will maintain that the multicultural church is not only one valid option for the church of Jesus Christ, but is, in truth, its normative model. This position will become even more apparent as we enter the ethnically heterogeneous culture of the twenty-first century, in which traditional racial categories of *majority* and *minority* become obsolete. Not only is a multicultural approach to ministry a practical necessity for the survival of local congregations, but I will contend that, according to Scripture, God's intention has always been that the church be a multicultural, multinational community—a church of all languages, ethnicities, nationalities and peoples. And yet for all of this diversity, this church proclaims its unity through common faith in Jesus Christ. I will argue that, in order to realize this state, we must discard much of the current theological arguments on multiculturalism because of the inherent political and philosophical assumptions on which they are based. Thereby can we reclaim the universalizing metanarrative of Scripture.

"In the beginning," we are told, the God whom we worship is a God who loves and values diversity. Scripture tells us that God created *both* the heavens *and* the earth; God created *both* the sun to rule the day *and* the stars to rule the night; God created *both* the sky above our heads *and* the earth beneath our feet; God created *both* the wet, roaring seas teeming with life *and* the dry, fertile land covered with luscious vegetation; God created *both* great sea creatures roaming the ocean depths *and* winged birds of every kind soaring to the highest heights; and last but surely not least, God created humankind in God's own image—*both* male *and* female God created us. You see, our God is not an either-or God; rather, our God is a both-and God. After all, God's creational design is not exactly what one would ever call uniform. In the melodious mélange of Genesis 1, it seems apparent that God delights in creating opposites—but opposites that complement, not clash, opposites that harmonize, not antagonize. Following each day of the creational activity of pairing thesis with antithesis, God pronounces the benediction of synthesis: "And God saw that it was good." To this sacred synthesis of unity and diversity we now turn.

1
With Their Own Languages, Families & Nations

•••

PRINCIPLE: God's intention for creation has always been multicultural.

Now the whole earth had one language and the same words. And as they migrated from the east, they came upon a plain in the land of Shinar and settled there. . . . Then they said, "Come, let us build ourselves a city, and a tower with its top in the heavens, and let us make a name for ourselves; otherwise we shall be scattered abroad upon the face of the whole earth." GENESIS 11:1-4

*S*unday. Today is "*International Heritage Sunday.*" More than two hundred fifty people gather to worship, many dressed in clothes that reflect their cultural traditions. The choral anthem is sung in both English and Zulu; the Scripture is read in Spanish, Indonesian and Korean; the offertory and the prayer of dedication are in Tagalog; and the Lord's Prayer is prayed in unison in each person's native language. The congregational luncheon that follows includes empanadas de navidad, kimchi, pulgugee, pancit and sticky rice.

Monday. I meet with an immigration attorney, a translator and three of the families in my congregation who are concerned about their immigration status. They want to know what they can do to be sponsored by an employer. The meeting is a result of my growing awareness that it is impossible to do pastoral care in this congregation without also addressing issues of legal status, permission to work and the fear of deportation.

Tuesday. I counsel a bicultural couple preparing for marriage. The key issue for them is racism, specifically the racism of the woman's immigrant family. Her father has asked her: "Why do you want to marry an Anglo? Don't you know how *they* are? They're lazy, they cheat on their wives, you can't trust them. Why don't you marry someone like *us*?"

Wednesday. A Cambodian woman in her late thirties comes to the church, accompanied by a parent volunteer from a local school. The volunteer has encouraged her to come to Culmore for spiritual support in her role as a single parent of six children. The two oldest children are involved with gangs. She wants to keep from losing her other four children to gangs. I ask her if she is a Christian.[1] She answers that she did not worship Jesus in Cambodia. The parent volunteer explains that in Cambodia she had been Buddhist, but after she arrived in the United States she was evangelized by the Mormons. She has since left the Mormon church and now wants to worship with us. I tell her how glad we are to have her and her children come, and I will see them on Sunday. A Buddhist, Mormon, Cambodian family with ties to local youth gangs—I muse to myself, *Well, Steve, welcome to the world of multicultural evangelism!*

Thursday. I am to give the devotional in our English as a second language (ESL) classes in the evening. While I wait in the church office before class, I meet a Bolivian man about my own age. As we talk through a translator, he shares that his wife recently has died after a four-year battle with breast cancer. He has a two-year-old daughter but no other relatives here. With little knowledge of English and no family support, he talks about how alone he feels. We pray together, and I encourage him to seek counseling with our pastor for Latin American ministries. Our ESL principal also invites him to the revival service we are having Friday night.

Friday. Our All Nations Youth Choir and Praise Band leads a special service of our Friday-night praise celebration. Hands are lifted high, and people pray aloud as the congregation stands and sings praise choruses. Our pastor for Filipino ministries, Max Francisco, leads testimony time. Gil Fernandez, a Filipino young adult, testifies to how Christ has changed his life and saved him from sin. He wears a tattered, dirty T-shirt with the words *sin* and *the old Adam* written on it. Suddenly he tears off his shirt, revealing a clean, white T-shirt underneath with the words *Jesus Is Lord* printed above his heart. Our Liberian lay leader, Esther Jones, stands and shares the joy of her daily prayer life, assuring the congregation that God is the friend who will never leave them.

After two hours of singing, praying, testifying and preaching, the call to discipleship is given. Anyone who wishes to do so may come to the altar and have someone pray with him or her. Near the back of the sanctuary, a young couple invited by our Korean choir director, Won-Hee Kang, are quietly praying. They are Vietnamese and Buddhist. The young Bolivian man from ESL has come to the service also. He and his two-year-old daughter walk down to the altar to pray for God's healing in their lives. Meanwhile I am kneeling at the altar with the six-year-old grandson of the matriarch of our African ministries, Ms. Fanny, who is from Sierra Leone. She is Christian. Her daughter, who also has come with her tonight, is Muslim. As I pray with Fanny's grandson, I ask his name. "Mohamed," he responds.

Babel or Blessing?

Over the years I have shared stories of Culmore and our international ministry with folks outside our congregation. To my surprise I have received a rather common response: "Oh, that sounds so *interesting*. . . . I'm sure ministry there must be very *challenging*. . . . It must be very *demanding* of you as a pastor."

Being a pastor of a multicultural church *is* interesting, challenging and demanding, but not necessarily in the way that people usually mean. Serving this congregation has been the most exhilarating period of my ministry. Because of the unique demands and challenges, I have grown both as a Christian and as a pastor in ways that might not have been possible in a homogeneous congregation.

Yes, there are times when finding common ground in so much diversity is just plain difficult and painful. (I say more about that in chapters nine through eleven.) I suspect, however, that the seemingly sympathetic reactions I have received to what it means to be a church in a multicultural setting have more to do with a subtext of suspicion than with an empathy of hope.

The church's ministry in a multicultural world may seem to many as more "Babel-ing" than blessing, more a problem than an opportunity. Besides simple discomfort in racial or ethnic diversity, it may represent a sense that, in the words of a recent bestseller, this is "not the way it's supposed to be."

Should Christians be surprised at such a sentiment? In the opening chapters of Scripture, we are told that once "the whole earth had one language and the same words," but because of human disobedience, God confused their speech so that they could not understand one another, then scattered them abroad across the face of the earth (Gen 11:1-9). Given the story of Babel, might we not infer that human differences, language, cultures—even nations themselves—are the result of God's judgment? Might we not also infer that the continuing diversity of the human race is simply a residue of this curse? This chapter addresses that question.

God's Intention Has Always Been Multicultural

In Genesis 10, immediately preceding the story of Babel, the writer records the descendants of Noah through his three sons: Shem, Ham and Japheth. It is the story of the reestablishment of humanity following the flood. What is unusual about this genealogy is the comment the writer makes following the lineage of Japheth: "From these the coastland peoples spread . . . in their *lands*, with their own *language*, by their *families*, in their *nations*" (Gen 10:5). In fact, Noah's sons' descendants are described by their lands, languages, families and nations. In all, seventy people are named, symbolizing what was thought to be the number of known nations,[2] constituting a veritable "verbal 'map' of the world."[3] In addition to this heterogeneity, the writer speaks positively of the spreading of these descendants into new lands as a sign of obedience to God's commandment—first to Adam and Eve, then to Noah—that humanity should "multiply, and fill the earth" (Gen 1:28; 9:1).

Seen in this context, linguistic, familial and national diversity are not curses of divine wrath but fulfillment of the blessing of creation. A multilingual and multinational humanity was God's intention all along. What is more, amid this growing diversity in humanity is a fundamental unity based on the relational nature of God's people. This is, after all, a genealogy—it is about who is related to whom. Even with the acknowledgment of differences, the writer of Genesis focuses not on what separates humanity but on what unites human beings: family. Lesslie Newbigin, a noted missiologist, has said:

> The Bible does not speak about "humanity" but about "all the families of the earth" or "all the nations." It follows that this mutual relatedness, this dependence of one on another, is not merely part of the journey toward the goal of salvation, but is intrinsic to the goal itself. . . . There is, there can be, no private salvation, no salvation which does not involve us with one another.[4]

The theme of family occurs not only in Genesis 10—11 but also in the calling of Abram the Chaldean, through whose descendants God promises "all the families of the earth shall be blessed" (Gen 12:3). Throughout Scripture the importance of family is emphasized in our relationship with God, culminating in the eschatological family reunion anticipated in Revelation 7, which describes the "great multitude that no one could count, from every nation, from all tribes and peoples and languages, standing before the throne and before the Lamb, robed in white, with palm branches in their hands. They cried out in a loud voice, saying, 'Salvation belongs to our God who is seated on the throne, and to the Lamb!'" (vv. 9-10). The unity found in creational diversity, the Bible says, will be nothing less than salvation itself.

So if God's intention for creation has always been multicultural, what should we make of the story of Babel? If God intended diversity, why depict its divine implementation as judgment?

We Shall Not Be Moved
Babel has often been portrayed as a parable of human hubris. Although pride is certainly one aspect of this tale, it must also be viewed in its context: wedged between the emergence of the nations in chapter 10 and the calling of Abraham the patriarch in chapter 12. In chapter 10 the writer of Genesis tells us that from "their lands, with their own language, by their families, in their nations" humanity has regathered, and settled on the plain of Shinar. Rejecting the pluriform nature of creation that God has willed, the people impose a self-styled unity.

Scholars have noted that understanding Babel lies less in knowing *what* they built than in knowing *why* they built—that is, the motivation for their actions. The people say to each other, "Come, let us build ourselves a city, and a tower with its top in the heavens, and let us make a name for ourselves; otherwise we shall be scattered abroad upon the face of the whole earth" (Gen 11:4). Although many interpretations have focused on the presupposed pride of "making a name," note what motivates this need for power and recognition: the fear of being *scattered* across the earth. Afraid of once again being separated and differentiated from one another, humanity presents God with a common front and a unifying purpose— self-preservation on their own terms.

Walter Brueggemann, in his commentary on Genesis says, "There are two kinds of unity. On the one hand, God wills a unity which permits and encourages scattering. The *unity willed by God* is that all of humankind shall be in covenant with him (9:8-11) and with him only, responding to his purposes, relying on his life-giving power."[5] Then there is the unity suggested by this passage: "a different kind of unity sought by fearful humanity organized against the purposes of God. This unity attempts to establish a cultural, human oneness without reference to the threats, promises, or mandates of God. This is a self-made unity in which humanity has a 'fortress mentality.' It seeks to survive by its own resources."[6] The focus of humanity is on self-interest, not on obedience to God. What would normally be considered a worthy goal, human unity, now serves as a supreme act of defiance.

Babel plays itself out over and over again in the lives of congregations. A new church is formed with excitement, energy and vision. As the years pass, however, the church functions less to introduce Jesus Christ to nonbelievers than to provide a safe, secure and familiar environment to those who already believe and belong. As the congregation ages, the church finds that it has few if any bridges to the community that it is supposed to serve. Jesus' words "Those who want to save their life will lose it" (Mt 16:25) have special significance for such congregations. Terence Fretheim, in the *New Interpreter's Bible*, writes that

> the unity of the church is not to be found by focusing on unity, building churches and programs that present a unified front before the temptations of the world. We receive true unity finally as a gift . . . [and it] will be forged most successfully in getting beyond one's own kind on behalf of the word in the world.[7]

That is exactly what God does in Babel: God forces humanity out beyond itself and into the world on behalf of the Word!

God's judgment on Babel is the fulfillment of what humanity hoped to prevent: its scattering. In Genesis 11:7-8 God says, "'Come, let us go down, and confuse their language there, so that they will not understand one another's speech.' So the LORD scattered them abroad from there over the face of all the earth, and they left off building the city." The judgment is twofold: (1) the diversity of languages is restored as God had originally intended; and (2) humanity is again spread across the earth so that the people may "multiply, and fill the earth." God's judgment in Babel may not be seen solely as punishment, for in the divine act of scattering humanity,

God's original intention for humanity and creation is fulfilled. Stanley Hauerwas says, "God's confusing the people's language as well as his scattering of them was meant as a gift. For by being so divided, by having to face the otherness created by separateness of language and place, people were given the resources necessary to recognize their status as creatures."[8] Of this scattering, Fretheim has said that "God . . . promotes diversity at the expense of any form of unity that seeks to preserve itself in isolation from the rest of the creation."[9]

We should also remember that human beings had scattered previously, of their own accord. Genesis 10 uses virtually the same word for scattering, but there the word is translated as "spreading abroad," and it is mentioned positively. God the heavenly parent, whose children have been on their own, grown afraid, and tried to come home, now must push them back out into the world.

Before leaving our brethren at Babel, note that Brueggemann offers a new twist on the interpretation of linguistic diversity, which may serve our purposes here. He says that although verse 7 is most frequently translated "that they may not understand each other," another rendering may also be "that they do not listen to each other." Brueggemann says that "if the word is rendered 'understand,' it may reflect only a verbal, semantic problem. But if translated as 'listen,' the text may pose a covenantal, theological issue."[10] Thus the sin of Eden continues: human beings refuse to listen—to each other or to God. This Frank Sinatra theology ("I'll do it my way") gets them exactly what they got in Eden—eviction! God the heavenly parent separates his children until such time as they are prepared to listen, hear and obey.

Diversity Versus Pluralism

How we view diversity—as bane or blessing—may well be determined by the vocabulary we use. Our words shape both the way we perceive something and the meaning we attach to it. Therefore we must be very careful and use the words that most precisely reflect what we are trying to say.

I became aware of just how important it is to choose the right words during the course of a church-planning retreat during my first summer at Culmore. I was asked to begin the retreat with a devotional. The gist of my devotion was how the Bible affirms diversity. Unfortunately, my words were not well chosen. In my excitement and exuberance over being a pastor of such a diverse church, I went on at length about how "different" we were and how that was a good thing.

Those attending the retreat were very polite, but I could tell that something was not quite right. Either I had not been very clear in my devotional, or I had been all too clear and they were not particularly happy about what I had to say.

Finally, after a few anxious moments, Maxine, a warm-hearted evangelical Anglo, spoke up: "Steve, I'm not quite sure I agree with your point. Yes, we are a congregation made up of many different people from many different places, but what is important to know about us is not how *different* we are from each other but how much we have in common with one another. We are from different cultures, but we are united through the same Lord."

Although I had been trying to say something similar to what Maxine said, my choice of words led my hearers to understand something quite the opposite.

Words are important in how we discuss diversity. For example, people often use the words *diversity* and *pluralism* interchangeably, as if they meant the same thing. In fact, they have quite different meanings. Using the wrong word may cause you to express something entirely different from what you intend.

In his essay "The Christian Citizen and Democracy," George Weigel writes that people frequently confuse the terms *plurality* and *pluralism*. For example, he says, we "are used to thinking of 'pluralism' as a demographic fact." But as Weigel notes, the "demographic fact is plurality." *Plurality* is the acknowledgment that a large number of differences are present. As Weigel goes on to say, "*pluralism*, genuine pluralism, is never just a sociological fact."[11] Pluralism is not simply something that one can discern by examining the latest census report. Pluralism is far more complex than the simple acknowledgment of distinct ethnic, religious or cultural groups. Rather, the pluralism of which Weigel speaks also includes the coexistence of differing worldviews, value systems and the like.

Diversity assumes that we hold a common truth but express it in different ways. Diversity presupposes unity. We may not always agree in diversity, but we are committed to working toward the underlying unity amid our differences. Pluralism, on the other hand, assumes that we cannot agree on the common truth, that in effect we have agreed to disagree. Pluralism rejects any notion of an underlying unity. Pluralism may hold mutually incompatible positions or truth claims based on either tolerance or indifference. In pluralism we really do not care if we ever agree or not.

So, for example, when we refer to the diversity present in the Genesis account of creation, we may freely refer to the plurality of God's endeavors. That is, in the act of creation God did in fact make things different from one another: God created both men and women, day and night, heaven and earth, and so on. Hence the *demographic fact* of creation was *plurality:* it is the simple acknowledgment that differences were present.

What this account does not do is present many different possibilities for how the world came to be. The story is not a subjective account of a personal truth. No, objectively speaking, the heavens and the earth were created by the Lord God for a common purpose—"the praise of his glory" (Eph 1:12). There is a fundamental unity in creation, and even the most diverse dimensions of creation are united for a common purpose.

The psalmist reveals a deep understanding of the diversity of God's creation and how it is united by the praise given to God.

Hallelujah!
Praise GOD from heaven,
    praise him from the mountaintops,
Praise him, all you his angels,
    praise him, all you his warriors,
Praise him, sun and moon,
    praise him, you morning stars;
Praise him, high heaven,
    praise him, heavenly rain clouds;
Praise, oh let them praise the name of God—
    he spoke the word, and there they were! . . .

Praise GOD from earth,
    you sea dragons, you fathomless ocean deeps;
Fire and hail, snow and ice,
    hurricanes obeying his orders;
Mountains and all hills,
    apple orchards and cedar forests;
Wild beasts and herds of cattle,
    snakes, and birds in flight;

Earth's kings and all races,
  leaders and important people,
Robust men and women in their prime,
  and yes, graybeards and little children.

Let them praise the name of GOD—
  it's the only Name worth praising. (Ps 148:1-5, 7-13 *The Message*)
Now *this* is diversity—but diversity united in the service of praising God's name.

Multicultural America and the Cult of Ethnicity

In the past thirty years in American society we have seen the advent of not one but many ideologies of pluralism. With roots in the struggle over civil rights and embodied now in the debates concerning curricular reforms, philosophical dogmas have emerged that focus on the particularization of our cultural lives, emphasizing group, ethnic and tribal identity over any other unifying social or national identity.

A *Doonesbury* cartoon a few years ago portrayed an embattled university president saying to a group of protesting black students, "Look, I let you have your own African-American studies program and your own black student union, but I draw the line at letting you have your own drinking fountain."[12] As this cartoon cynically reflects, there is a sense of disillusionment over the direction that multiculturalism and the ideal of a racially inclusive society have taken. Sometimes appeals to multiculturalism look more like a de facto resegregation of American life than a transcendence of racism.

Two of the premier critics of multiculturalism in America, Arthur M. Schlesinger Jr. and Michael Lind (the former with roots in Democratic liberalism and the latter with roots in Republican conservatism) have reached astonishingly similar conclusions on the inherent difficulties posed by the fragmentation and separatism represented by these ideologies of pluralism.

Schlesinger, in his book *The Disuniting of America*, argues that multiculturalism in America has produced a "cult of ethnicity [which] has reversed the movement of American history, producing a nation of minorities."[13] The problem, of course, is not with minority *or* majority status, but the perception that "membership in one or another ethnic group is the basic American experience." As such, the purpose is now not to find common ground with the majority culture but to declare one's experience of "alienation from an oppressive, white, patriarchal, racist, sexist society."[14] While Schlesinger strongly defends the importance of claiming pride in one's ethnic heritage or the contributions made to the American present, he does argue that the cult of ethnicity further isolates us in our ethnic enclaves and "nourishes a culture of victimization and a contagion of inflammable sensitivities."[15] Implicit in this worldview, Schlesinger argues, "is the classification of all Americans according to ethnic and racial criteria. . . . Instead of a nation composed of individuals making their own unhampered choices, America increasingly sees itself as composed of groups more or less ineradicable in their ethnic character."[16] Whereas America once celebrated the great "melting pot" of Israel Zangwill's play, it now praises "the unmeltable ethnics."[17] Whereas multiculturalism as ideology is seen as a defensible reaction against the ethnocentrism of the majority culture with Anglo-European heritage, Schlesinger asks, "At what point does it pass over into an ethnocentrism of its own? The very word [multiculturalism] . . . has come to refer only to non-Western, nonwhite cultures."[18]

Michael Lind, in *The Next American Nation*, says that there have actually been three American nations since our founding: Anglo America, which lasted from the Revolutionary War until the Civil War; Euro-America, which followed the Civil War and lasted until the civil rights movement; and Multicultural America, the period in which we now live. This third American republic began in the civil rights period (1950s-1970s), and with it was born an idealism of an integrated society. Yet many of those who led the first part of the civil rights struggle to overcome legal segregation, Lind says, lost control in the second half, "which saw the triumph of group consciousness and racial preference programs."[19] As a result, Lind argues, "multicultural America is not the Third Republic that the color-blind liberals intended in the early sixties; it is the Third Republic that emerged later, from the intersection of black-power radicalism and white-backlash conservatism."[20]

Lind says that one of the consequences of the ideologies of pluralism in multicultural America is that "there is no coherent American national community, but rather five national communities, defined by race—white, black, Hispanic, Asian and Pacific Islander, and Native American."[21] Like Schlesinger, he believes that the melting-pot image of assimilation has been rejected. One of the images touted to replace it, he says, is America as "mosaic," merging the five national communities without assimilating any. Again in agreement with Schlesinger, Lind says:

> These races are not mere ingredients to be blended in a future unity, but permanently distinct communities. . . . Each of the five American races has its own distinct culture, to which immigrants belonging to that race are expected to assimilate. . . . Moreover, each race, in addition to preserving its cultural unity and distinctness, should act as a mono- lithic political bloc. . . . Those who criticize the fivefold race-culture- political bloc scheme are, by definition, racists who wish to turn back the clock to the era of white supremacy.[22]

Lind argues that the preservation of culture is taken one step further in Multicultural America. Great value is placed on the ideal of authenticity with regard to one's identity. Lind believes that authenticity in Multicul- tural America actually means cultural and racial conformity to one's appropriate subculture: "To find yourself, you need only to find your ghetto, and adopt its politics, its style of dress, and its approved beliefs about the world and humanity. Having done so, you can then demand that society at large recognize your individuality—that is to say, your abject conformity."[23] One must conform "politically, psychologically, and cultur- ally"[24] in order to be seen as an authentic person. Assimilation is still accepted in Multicultural America, but only insofar as it takes place within the confines of one's own racial grouping. Lind says:

> It is unacceptable for Hondurans to be expected to assimilate to a generic American identity; but they are expected and encouraged to submerge their Honduran national identity in a new Hispanic American identity unique to the United States. Similarly, Czech and Norwegian immigrants will assimilate to White America, Ibo and Jamaican and Zulu immigrants to Black America, Indian and Chinese and Filipino immigrants to Asian America. Historian David A. Hollinger calls this the theory of the quintuple melting pot.[25]

Lind concludes his book with a descriptive walk through three metaphori- cal museums, representing each of the three republics. When he comes to the third and last, he describes a museum that has many beautiful and ornate rooms, each celebrating a distinct heritage and culture but with no entrance or exit to any of the other rooms. In order to go to another room, you first must go into the main gallery. But when you come to the main gallery, to which all of the rooms are connected, there is nothing at all—it is absolutely empty, much in the way there is nothing at the center of Multicultural America to unite it.[26]

The Towers of Babel

In many ways Lind brings us back to where we started, the story of Babel. But now, instead of just one walled city and one tower, there are many. Human beings are once again afraid of being scattered, so we are busily erecting our cities, our towers, our walls to prevent this scattering. To protect our linguistic, cultural and racial identities, we are sealing ourselves off and imposing a self-styled uniformity to ensure homogeneous purity. Once again we seek to speak the same language, but only within our tribal confines. As the T-shirt says: "It's a Black [or Anglo, Latino, Asian] Thing. You Wouldn't Understand."

As in Babel, once more we refuse to listen to one another. In fact, we no longer care whether others understand the idiosyncratic nature of our cultural and linguistic communities, just so long as the members of the tribe do. Much has been written about the perceived threat of the "balkanization" of American life, but in actuality it is the "Babelization" of our society that we must worry about: each group shouts more and more loudly, seeking to make a name for itself. This chorus of angry, defensive voices has no harmony, much less melody. The only sound to be heard is babble. There is speaking, but there is no listening. There is ideology, but there is no understanding.

The Promise of a Great Name

As with Babel, we construct our realities in this postmodern world based on racial, ethnic or group identity because we are afraid. Our pride reveals our deepest insecurities. As in all times of rapid change, we are clinging to what we know, what we have experienced. God, however, calls us to live not in fear but in faith. God accepts each one of us, as the hymn says, "just as I am," but God does not leave us where God found us. To live by faith is to go on a journey, to intentionally leave behind what we have known, what we have come to put our trust in, and to move out beyond our field of vision. Like Babel, we also can respond by saying, "We shall not be moved," but that is no guarantee that we will not be moved.

God invites each one of us to respond in faith by traveling to a new land and being given a new identity, an identity that honors who we have been—and also transcends the limitations of our past and enables us to embrace God's future. We can still spend our lives vainly seeking to make a name for ourselves, only to see our projects, our agendas, our plans end as the construction project at Babel ended—in failure. Or we can receive the promises of God, who is committed not to giving us just any name, but a "great name" that will be a blessing to "all the families of the earth."

2
To Bless
the Nations

••

PRINCIPLE: A multicultural church is a fulfillment of God's promise to bless all the nations.

Now the LORD said to Abram, "Go from your country and your kindred and your father's house to the land that I will show you. I will make of you a great nation, and I will bless you, and make your name great, so that you will be a blessing. I will bless those who bless you, and the one who curses you I will curse; and in you all the families of the earth shall be blessed." GENESIS 12:1-3

It is Christmas Eve, and we are celebrating the birth of our Savior through the service of lessons and carols. In this service we use Scriptures and hymns to remember the story of God's faithfulness from creation to the new creation. Representatives from the various ethnic communities in our congregation read the lessons. As is common at Culmore, each reader is invited to greet the congregation in his or her own language before the lesson.

One of our young adults, Dan Roth, stands to read the second lesson. Dan first came to Culmore as a volunteer teacher in our English as a second language (ESL) program. He had just returned from a five-month mission to Ghana and wanted to continue his crosscultural experience at home by teaching English to immigrants. Dan's lesson is from Genesis 22:15-18, in which "God promises to Abraham that by his descendants all the nations of the earth shall obtain blessing." He greets the congregation, saying: "Baruch ata Adonai, Eloheinu melech ha-olam, shehecheyanu, vekiye-manu, vehigiyanu, lazman hazeh"—"Blessed is the Lord our God, Ruler of the universe, for giving us life, for sustaining us, and for enabling us to reach this season." Dan, a descendant of Abraham—Jewish by birth, Christian by conversion—blesses God's name and thereby blesses this congregation of many nations.

When God called Abraham, inherent in God's promise to bless this one person was also the promise that, through him, God would also bring blessing upon all the nations of the earth. Terence Fretheim has written that "God's choice of Abram serves as an initially exclusive move for the sake of a maximally inclusive end. Election serves mission (in the broadest sense of the term)."[1] If indeed that is the case, then God chose Israel to bear God's message of blessing and salvation not just to the covenant people, but to every nation. This chapter explores how multicultural congregations are a fulfillment of God's promise of blessing to Abraham.

From Curse to Blessing

Scholars describe Genesis 12:1 as a kind of fulcrum text. Whereas Genesis 11:32 and the chapters that lead up to it are concerned with the history of all humankind and our disobedience and rebellion toward our Creator, Genesis 12:1 begins the story and history of Israel, as well as the creation of a covenantal relationship with God. Some have described this dramatic break at 12:1 as the canonical distinction of the "history of the curse and the history of the blessing,"[2] the history of expulsion and the history of anticipation.[3] Stanley Hauerwas puts it this way:

> Babel is the climax of the primeval history, as after scattering human-kind over the face of the earth God no longer acts toward humankind as a unity. Rather, he calls Abraham out of his tribe and makes covenant with him to be a great people. In Abraham, God creates a rainbow people so that the world might know that in spite of our sinfulness, God has not abandoned us.[4]

In his commentary on Genesis, Walter Brueggemann says that Genesis is clear about two things:

> First, the God who forms the world is the same God who creates Israel. It is the same God who calls creation and who calls the community of faith. . . . The call to Sarah and Abraham has to do not simply with the forming of Israel but with the re-forming of creation, the transforming of the nations. . . . Second, it is clear that Abraham and Sarah, in contrast to the resistant, mistrustful world represented in Gen. 1-11 . . . are responsive and receptive. They fully embrace the call of God.[5]

The story of Abraham and Sarah is therefore a story of life out of death. It is no wonder, then, that Paul, in his letter to the Galatians, refers to the story of Abraham as "the gospel beforehand."[6] In the face of the curse of Eden and the confusion of Babel, God's promise to Abraham is one of hope: it announces good news "to those who despair . . . that what the world has thought impossible is possible by the power of God."[7] In his book *The Land*, Brueggemann says that Abraham and Sarah shared the futility and hopelessness marked by the old history of Genesis 1-11 in their inability to have children. Genesis 12:1, however, marks the beginning of a new history, a history of hope based on nothing less than the promises of God. Abraham and Sarah are lifted up in Scripture because they leave their "secure barrenness" on the invitation of God to a "risky" future, but one which promises life.[8] God promises not just a child but descendants "as numerous as the stars of heaven" (Gen 26:4). God promises that out of Abraham's obedience will emerge not only a new people and nation but many peoples and nations. God promises not only blessing for Abraham and Sarah but that through them all the families of the earth will be blessed.

The Scandal of Particularity

Stanley Hauerwas and Will Willimon, in their book *Resident Aliens*, say that in the story of "Abraham and Sarah . . . what we have is not first of all heroic people, but a heroic God who refuses to abandon God's creation, a God who keeps coming back, picking up the pieces, and continuing the story: 'And then . . .' 'And next . . .' "[9] Immediately following the debacle at Babel, what does God do? God calls Abraham to help continue God's heroic story of salvation. Though humanity is confused and scattered, God does not give up. Instead God chooses one person, Abram of Ur, to bring true unity to humanity.

Abraham's calling is essential for understanding the nature of the church in a multicultural world. The story of Abraham is first and foremost a story about God's mission to the world. God indeed has chosen one nation, but God intends salvation to be available to all. Throughout Scripture God reminds the people of Israel of their sacramental nature: "I am the LORD. . . . I have given you as a covenant to the people, *a light to the nations,* to open the eyes that are blind, to bring out the prisoners from the dungeon" (Is 42:6-7). "May God be gracious to us and bless us and make his face to shine upon us, that your way may be known upon earth, *your saving power among all nations*" (Ps 67:1-2). "To him was given dominion and glory and kingship, *that all peoples, nations, and languages should serve him*" (Dan 7:14). And in Jesus of Nazareth, descendant of Abraham and Son of God, this mission was reaffirmed: "All authority in heaven and on earth has been given to me. Go therefore and *make disciples of all nations,* baptizing them in the name of the Father and of the Son and of the Holy Spirit" (Mt 28:18-19).

Leonard Sweet notes that many missiologists have pointed out the theological misnomer of the church's "having a mission": "The church does not have a mission. . . . It is God who has a mission, and the missionary of God is the Holy Spirit. The question is whether the mission of God has a church."[10] The question before the church today is indeed just that— whether we as the church will be faithful to God's mission in the world. Will we be bearers of God's universal metanarrative of salvation and blessing to people of all nations, languages and cultures? Or are we more concerned with resurrecting the specter of religious imperialism, that in this postmodern world of pluralistic realities we might inadvertently impose *our* truth upon others? After all, how can the church have the audacity to proclaim that it holds the one truth at a time when most people understand truth at best as relative, personal and provincial? (What Tip O'Neill once said of politics now appears to apply to truth: "All truth is local.") To answer these questions, we first must understand that the God revealed in Scripture is a God revealed in particularity, but for universal purposes.

Lesslie Newbigin says, "The Christian tradition affirms that God has made his mind and purpose known to some (not to all) people through events in history—not all events but some. . . . This affirmation is a cause of scandal, what is sometimes called the scandal of particularity."[11] This scandal, Newbigin says, has become the stumbling block for Christian missions. After all, "Why should God not speak his own word to every soul and to every culture?"[12] But, Newbigin says, "that is to do violence to the nature of human beings as the Bible reveals it . . . the heart of the biblical story is in God's choosing, God's election of one people among all the peoples, and finally of one man among all people, to be the bearer of the secret of his saving purpose for all."[13] It is a secret, he says, because, "it contradicts human ideas about world dominion. A man nailed to a cross does not look like the one to unify the world."[14]

One can argue that Israel's election through Abraham's promise, instead of being an election to privilege and position, was an election to service. That is, Israel was called "to be the particular, historically conditioned vessel chosen to mediate a universal story of the healing of the world. As a servant of Yahweh, Israel exists for the sake of other nations."[15] Put another way, "The well-being of Israel carried potential for the well-being of other nations. Israel is never permitted to live in a vacuum. It must always live with, for and among the others."[16] Missiologist Charles Van Engen takes it one step further in saying that Israel had no special merit or significance in and of itself:

> Its uniqueness did not stem from its ancestry, nor its history, race, culture, or language. It stemmed from YHWH's unique call. Yet precisely because of YHWH's unique purpose, Israel considered itself different, having a special destiny, a unique mission which set it apart from all other races, cultures, tribes, families, and nations.[17]

Israel was special only because it was given a universal concern as a nation. Unlike other nations that could and would live for self-interest and self-preservation, Israel would always be a nation set apart for the blessing of all.

The same may be said of the church. Christians have been chosen and set apart, not to segregate themselves from the world, but that they might engage the world on behalf of God's promises. It has been said that the church does not need to worry so much about whether it is in the world, "but how, in what form, and for what purpose."[18] That purpose is nothing less than fidelity to God's promises. Stanley Hauerwas says that the church's first task in any society is to be itself. What this means, according to Hauerwas, is serving as "a 'contrast model for all polities that know not God. Unlike them, we know that the story of God is the truthful account of our existence, and thus we can be a community formed on trust."[19] If the church is called to be a people of blessing to all the nations, to all the polities of the earth, we cannot be such if we are always seeking to conform to their values and expectations rather than to God's call. To discern how the church may live out this contrast model of blessing and promise, let us look more closely at the Abrahamic narrative.

Go from Your Country

God's first words to Abraham were "*Go* from your country" (Gen 12:1).

Jesus' first words to many of his disciples were "*Come,* follow me" (Mt 19:21). Zan Holmes has described Christianity as a "Come and Go" affair. We *come* to see and experience God. Then we are to *go* and tell others.[20] Abraham became the prototype of all disciples who would follow him, when he was willing to pick up all that he had and follow God. The writer of Hebrews says, "By faith Abraham obeyed when he was called to set out for a place that he was to receive as an inheritance; and he set out, not knowing where he was going" (11:8). Unlike his forebears at Babel, Abraham listened to God and obeyed God. His very first act of obedience was his willingness to be intentionally "scattered," sent abroad and sent away from everything with which he was familiar: country, kindred and home.

Abraham was a person of hope and conviction who was willing to walk by faith, even when he had nothing but the promises of God to go on—even when there was no visible evidence that any of these promises would be fulfilled. By faith Abraham left his home, his country, for the promise of a new one, a home he had never seen, and even after he had seen it, never really possessed.

In the book of Hebrews, obedience is an integral part of faith. Faith is not mere belief but the willingness to act on that belief. For Abraham to live by faith meant first believing in God's character, that God is who God says he is, and second, believing in God's promises, that God will do what God says he will do. Abraham Lincoln once said that "faith is not [only] believing that God can, but that God will!"[21] Father Abraham's obedience was his willingness to live as if God's promises already had been fulfilled.

The church in a multicultural world witnesses theologically to "living by faith" in its own willingness to follow Abraham's example of leaving home. For many in the church, leaving home is a literal act of leaving one's town or even country and emigrating to another. For others, leaving home is a more metaphorical journey, signifying one's willingness to live faithfully even when everything seems to change around you. You do not have to actually move to leave home. Many of the long-time members in my congregation have lived here for thirty or forty years. In that time Culmore has changed from a homogeneous, suburban church to an urban, multiethnic one. In a very real sense, these long-time members have "left home."

Retired colonel H. G. MacDaniel joined Culmore in the early sixties, when he moved to northern Virginia to serve a "short" stint at the Pentagon. He has been here ever since. Mac, as he is affectionately known, is one of the strongest supporters of Culmore's multicultural approach to ministry. Given his background, it is clear that Mac has made a long journey to be where he is spiritually. He grew up in Alabama during the Great Depression, when legal segregation was the norm. By his own efforts, he worked and put himself through the University of Alabama. There on the football field he met the legendary Coach Bear Bryant—not as a coach but as a teammate. No doubt about it, Mac was southern-born and southern-bred.

When Mac came to Culmore, it was an all-Anglo congregation in what was then considered the outer suburbs of Washington, D.C. Much has changed in these last three decades, but Mac's commitment to this congregation and the mission it has received from God is one thing that has not changed. When Mac was a lay leader and proud octogenarian, he would stand and greet the congregation each Sunday with his Alabama accent: "Welcome to Culmore United Methodist Church, an international Christian congregation. I like the sound of that! Don't you?"

To be people of the promise means to be willing to risk leaving home, whatever or wherever that may be, and to be willing to walk with God toward what we cannot yet fully see. Leonard Sweet, in an article on Abraham, discussed the problem of myopia, or nearsightedness. Spiritually speaking, we are nearsighted when we focus only on our own comfort level: our needs, our wants, our desires. This nearsightedness can lead to shortsightedness in ministry. The church that focuses only on its own comfort level is a church that inevitably will have no mission. Mission always involves change—in us, in the church and in others.

The opposite of myopia, Sweet points out, is hyperopia, or farsightedness. He says Scripture suggests that God has a tendency to deal with human beings when we become "farsighted."[22] God came to Abraham when he was seventy-five years old to give him the promise, and at age one hundred, when the child of promise, Isaac, was born. In order for us to live faithfully, perhaps we need the ability to see from a distance, to have perspective—that is, "to see through" the present circumstances and to live as if God's promises were a present reality.

The first Sunday I arrived at Culmore was Communion Sunday. Although I had been told of the ethnic diversity of the congregation, what I had imagined paled in comparison to the reality. Words can never describe the overwhelming joy and humility I felt to share the body and blood of

Jesus amid the international body of Christ gathered there.

I am still in awe. Yet I now realize that even with this incredible diversity, it is but a foretaste of that heavenly feast that awaits us. The writer of Hebrews says, "Now faith is the assurance of things hoped for, the conviction of things not seen" (Heb 11:1). This passage also can be translated "faith is the *substance* of things hoped for." Faith gives our hopes real substance and tangibility. God's promises are not idle speculation or insubstantial dreams that evaporate with waking; they are confident expectations of a faithful people. Each Sunday as I gather with brothers and sisters from around the world, I realize that I am given hope to live as though God's kingdom were a fully present reality, even while I make my way through this life toward the eternal city.

Blessed in Order to Bless

Abraham was called to leave home for a purpose. That purpose was both to receive and to give a blessing. The term *to bless* occurs 88 times in the book of Genesis alone, and 400 times in the Old Testament. As Gary Smalley and John Trent point out in their book *The Blessing,* the word translated *to bless* literally means to "bow the knee."[23] Even more significant, however, is that it means to highly value someone or something. Fretheim says:

> Blessing stands as a gift of God . . . that issues in good and well-being in life. It involves every sphere of existence, from spiritual to more tangible expressions. Blessing manifests itself most evidently in fertility and the multiplication of life, from herds and flocks, to field and forest, to new human life; it embraces material well-being, peace, and general success in life's ventures.[24]

Although most often understood in terms of the benefits it conveys, what is more important about blessing is the relationship it establishes between the one who blesses and the one who is being blessed. The Bible mentions three types of blessing: (1) God's blessing humankind, (2) human beings' blessing each other and (3) humankind's blessing God. In the Bible, by blessing humankind, God is telling us how highly he values us. When we bless one other, we remind one another how important and significant our lives are to each other. And when we bless God, as in worship, we are telling God how important God is to us—God is that to which we ascribe our ultimate worth.

One of the more memorable Scripture passages about blessing is

Numbers 6:24-26: "The LORD bless you and keep you; the LORD make his face to shine upon you, and be gracious to you; the LORD lift up his countenance upon you, and give you peace." Blessing is not only bowing the knee, but as Smalley and Trent note, it can also mean "shining the face." To bless someone is to look upon him or her with favor, to notice that person, to recognize the person with familiarity.

The church in a multicultural world is called to bless the nations by valuing persons and cultures in their particularity. God calls us to remind the world of the high value and worth God has placed not only on each person, but on each family, ethnicity, tribe, tongue and nation. We not only pray for the well-being of persons, but we also seek to be in relationship with them. Therefore the ministry of blessing can never be an ethnocentric affair; it must be a family affair, as in "all the families of the earth."

Abraham reminds us that the point of our being blessed is to bless others; that is, having discovered how highly the Creator values us, we are in turn to value God's creation. The ministry of blessing reminds us of the essential connectedness of the Christian life. It reminds us that we were created to live in relationship. We cannot live alone, counting our own blessings. Rather, the act of blessing reaffirms God's multicultural intention for creation. In blessing and being blessed, we discover the reestablishment of the true unity willed by God.

A Great Name

As noted in chapter one, the people of Babel sought to "make a name" for themselves—to create their own identity by trying to secure the future on their terms. When God approached Abram, God promised him not just a name, but a great name. Signifying the change that living by the promises of God would entail, God gave Abram of Ur a new name: "No longer shall your name be Abram, but your name shall be Abraham; for I have made you the ancestor of a multitude of nations" (Gen 17:5).

Our identities are gifts from God, and our names are especially significant in understanding who we are. Our names mark us, label us, even brand us. They tell others to whom we belong and to whom we are related. Although our names are not the sum total of our lives, they are important—if for no other reason than to remind us that we are not self-made persons. We receive our names as gifts, which reminds us that our very lives are themselves gifts.

In giving Abram a new name, God reminded him of the importance of relying completely on God for his identity. God called Abraham out of his own racial and cultural identity, not to discard it but to transform and to transcend it. Abraham would secure the future only by letting go and trusting the grace of God.

The church in a multicultural world means receiving a new identity, whose basis can be God alone. For the multicultural congregation, it is immediately apparent that cultural conformity is not the answer. As discussed in chapter one, the current "cult of ethnicity" demands that we place supreme importance on our ethnic heritage. To be an authentic person in our current context, one must conform culturally and racially to one's particular subculture. This attitude, however, is not just near-sighted or shortsighted, it is backward-looking. The God of Abraham calls us to be forward-looking. Appeals to identity as a right to be defended, as opposed to a gift to be guarded, will never get us any further than ourselves. Who we are right now, as well as who we have been, biblically speaking, is much less important than who we will be.

Authenticity in the Christian life is not cultural conformity but conformity to the promises of God. Living by faith, in this context, means trusting God alone for our identity and worth, especially when following God puts us at odds with our culture.

What was authentically radical about Abraham was that he trusted God alone for his identity. This trust allowed him, in the language of *Star Trek*, "to boldly go where no one has gone before!" Trusting God is exactly the opposite of the ideologies of pluralism, which call us to trust no one outside our racial or ethnic heritage and from whose tribal confines no one is willing or able to go.

Holding On to What Really Matters

Paul addresses these issues of faith and identity in Galatians 3 by appealing to the example of Abraham. The Christians in Galatia had been having a serious debate concerning spiritual maturity. A majority of the Christians in this congregation were converted Gentiles—that is, they were not Jews before becoming Christians. A small but significant group in this congregation argued that in order for one to be a good and mature Christian, one must follow the Jewish law in addition to believing in Christ. They argued that one could not be a Christian if one did not obey the law. In some ways this faction represented the traditionalists of the congregation, those who wanted to retain the best of their heritage; for them the best was the law revealed by God and given to Moses. For all their lives and from generation to generation, they had understood that spiritual maturity was measured in one's ability to keep the law.

Paul, himself a Pharisee, trained under the greatest teacher of the Jewish law in his day, Gamaliel. More important, Paul was a missionary for Jesus Christ to the Gentiles, the nations—one who had loved the law but who had also seen its limitations; he was just the person to address this controversy. Paul begins by reminding the Galatians that before God gave Moses the commandments, God gave Abraham a promise, that through him God would raise up a people, God's own people, who would bless all the nations of the earth. In essence Paul said to them, "If you want to hold on to your tradition, hold on to the one that really matters. In Abraham a promise was made, and in Christ Jesus a promise was kept. And now all who bear the name of Jesus are God's people, and it is through us that God will bless all the nations of the earth."

As for the law, Paul argues it was at best a temporary guardian until the promise made to Abraham was fulfilled. Paul argues that though the law was good, it was limited. In the end simply obeying laws could not produce a spiritually mature son or daughter of God. Only Christ, the Son of God, could do that. With the coming of Christ, Paul says, the law was discharged of its duties. Through the coming of faith in Christ, the very character of Christ, of God, clothed those who believed. Unlike the law, which defined who could be included in or excluded from God's family, when faith came, all the barriers that divided us came tumbling down. Paul says, "There is no longer Jew or Greek, there is no longer slave or free, there is no longer male and female; for all of you are one in Christ Jesus" (Gal 3:28).

Spiritual maturity is to be "clothed with Christ," to take on the character and identity of God. To be a son or daughter of God is to be a person who believes in the promises of God, who keeps the promises of God, and who trusts in the promises of God.

The multicultural church is a constant reminder that spiritual maturity is to be clothed with Christ. The multicultural church understands that it is important to let go of the traditions that have now become stumbling blocks to Christian unity. The multicultural church is willing to hold on to the one tradition that matters—new life in Jesus Christ.

Identity based on cultural or racial origin will never be sufficient to make us spiritually mature or whole persons. The multicultural church, although not demeaning or negating culture, does call us to a transcendent identity in Jesus Christ, as well as a transformational citizenship that lies in the reign of God. As the Scripture reminds us, our identity has been given by God: "You are a chosen race, a royal priesthood, a holy nation, God's own people, in order that you may proclaim the mighty acts of him who called you out of darkness into his marvelous light" (1 Pet 2:9).

Abraham's Offspring

Paul also tells the Galatians that spiritual maturity means that there can be no distinction in the body of Christ. He says, "And if you belong to Christ, then you are Abraham's offspring, heirs according to the promise" (Gal 3:29). Our family inheritance, of course, is the gift of faith—the ability to believe what we have yet to see.

When I think of the story of Abraham and of Paul's admonition to hold on to what really matters, I am reminded of the spiritual pilgrimage of Seon-Young Kim, our associate pastor for evangelism. Seon-Young is a first-generation Christian from Korea. She grew up in a family where religion was not considered important. She was in college in Seoul, pursuing a degree in physics, before she was exposed for any length of time to the Christian community. Seon-Young had a cousin who was active in a Christian student association and a local Baptist church. Her cousin frequently invited her to Bible studies and prayer meetings. Seon-Young politely refused each time. She was not so much averse to the Christian faith as uninterested. It did not seem relevant to her life at that point—but this attitude was soon to change.

In her senior year, Seon-Young experienced a profound crisis that prompted a reconsideration of her cousin's invitation. Seon-Young was president of the student body in her physics department at a time when many students were politically active in the prodemocracy movement in Korea. On the one hand, she began to feel pressure from her peers to take a more political stance, to be overt in her support for the prodemocracy movement. On the other hand, pressure also began to mount from her professors and the school administrators for her to "do something" about her fellow students. As the president of the student body, she was expected to hold the other students in check.

For weeks the tension increased, until she came to a breaking point. Not knowing where to turn, she remembered her cousin's invitations. She called her cousin and asked her to pray for her. Her cousin immediately reached out, comforting her, sharing her own faith with Seon-Young and praying for her. She invited Seon-Young to go to church with her. For the first time, Seon-Young agreed.

They went to a Sunday worship service at the Baptist church. For two hours Seon-Young prayed, tears streaming down her cheeks. That very day she accepted Jesus Christ as her Savior, and received the assurance that not "death, nor life, nor angels, nor rulers, nor things present, nor things to come, nor powers, nor height, nor depth, nor anything else in all creation, will be able to separate us from the love of God in Christ Jesus our Lord" (Rom 8:38-39).

Following her conversion, Seon-Young felt a strong calling to leave Korea and emigrate to the United States. She wanted to go to graduate school in computer science. Her one prayer to God was that she would glorify God in her vocation. Friends and family alike advised her against this plan. One of her friends even took her to a fortuneteller, who predicted that Seon-Young was destined to live in Korea all her life. None of this changed her conviction that she was called to go to America—that God's purpose for her life lay in that distant land. Finally, her fiancé, Nam-sub Lee, whom she had personally led to the Lord, agreed that they should follow her calling. Shortly after their wedding they moved to Iowa City, Iowa.

In Iowa they both attended the University of Iowa, Nam-sub for a degree in political science and Seon-Young for a master's degree (and later a doctorate) in computer science. She was halfway through the coursework for her doctorate when another crisis emerged. The professor with whom she was working—and on whom she was dependent for her research project—announced he was leaving the university and could not take her with him. This situation meant that she would have to find another professor and begin a new research project—a setback of two years.

She began the search for a new professor, a search that lasted more than six months. Seon-Young had reached a low point in her life. If God had brought her to America to study, why was this happening? She wanted to glorify God in her studies and her career, but how could she if she was unable to find the right research partner to continue?

One night when she was very frustrated, Seon-Young turned to God in prayer, asking for guidance. She asked God to give her an answer about her future. She says she heard an inaudible voice speaking to her, telling her that there was another path for her life. She would indeed glorify God in her studies and her career—but instead of computer science, she should go to seminary to become a pastor. God indeed had a plan for her life in this distant land, but it lay in a direction she had not imagined.

Once more Seon-Young's calling seemed to test her and her husband's faith. Seon-Young, a first-generation Korean woman halfway through a doctoral program that would open a door to a lucrative career in computer science, was now called to give it all up to begin another three-year master's degree program so that she could serve as a pastor in a predominantly non-Korean, English-speaking denomination. What was God doing?

The Bible tells us that living on the promises of God means being willing to be surprised by God. We are to expect the unexpected, imagine the unimaginable, conceive the inconceivable. Needless to say, sometimes that can be hard to do. Even Abraham, long before Sarah's chuckle, "fell on his face and laughed" (Gen 17:17) when God revealed his promise of a son. The promises of God can appear hilarious, if not downright ludicrous, even to those who walk by faith.

But like Abraham before her, Seon-Young listened to God and obeyed. She is now a student at Wesley Seminary and pastoring in this multicultural parish. In her spiritual journey Seon-Young has had to decide which traditions were most important; she has had to decide what to hold on to and what to let go of. By faith alone Seon-Young has followed God to a new land, and here she has been given a new name: Seon-Young the computer scientist is now Seon-Young the pastor, a woman called by God to bless the nations.

A Better Country

Augustine said that "faith is to believe what we do not see; and the reward of this faith is to see what we believe."[25] Year after year, Abraham lived in the Promised Land, pitching his tent among the Canaanites but never owning a square foot of ground until he bought a plot in Hebron in which to be buried. Although living as a stranger in a strange land, a land promised to him and to his descendants, Abraham did not grow impatient.

What was the secret of Abraham's patience? Scripture says that it was his ability to keep his eyes fixed on the heavenly country, the eternal city, "whose architect and builder is God" (Heb 11:10). He never forgot that Canaan, though promised to him, still would never be his true home. For as Paul says in Philippians, "our citizenship is in heaven" (3:20). We are but pilgrims here. Canaan was not the final goal of Abraham nor the fulfillment of the Abrahamic promise. Faith is a forward-looking endeavor that realizes the ultimate fulfillment of God's promise is not to be found in any of our building projects—not the Tower of Babel, not the royal city of Jerusalem, and not even in the most diverse multicultural congregation. God's promise will be fully realized only in the city "not made with hands, eternal in the heavens" (2 Cor 5:1).

The Christian life has an essential incompleteness. No matter how much we accomplish in our spiritual journeys and in our ministries, fulfillment of God's promises lies just past life's horizon. The writer of Hebrews, while celebrating that many peoples and nations were born from Abraham, nonetheless notes that Abraham and other faithful pilgrims "died in faith without having received the promises, but from a distance they saw and greeted them. They confessed that they were strangers and foreigners on the earth" (Heb 11:13).

The church in a multicultural world is composed of a pilgrim people: we are making our way as immigrants in this world, even as we long for the "better country" (Heb 11:16). Obedience to the promises of God does not guarantee success, but it does give us victory. As Christians, we can live in the secure trust that God is indeed who God says he is, and that God will indeed do what God has promised he will do. And because of the humble admission that so much of life is beyond our grasp and that we can live only by faith alone, the writer of Hebrews says, "Therefore God is not ashamed to be called their God; indeed, he has prepared a city for them" (Heb 11:16).

3
Just Give
Them Jesus

••

PRINCIPLE: A multicultural church is under the lordship of Jesus Christ.

*Then Peter, filled with the Holy Spirit, said to them, "Rulers of the people and elders,
if we are questioned today because of a good deed done to someone who was sick
and are asked how this man has been healed, let it be known to all of you, and to all
the people of Israel, that this man is standing before you in good health by the name
of Jesus Christ of Nazareth, whom you crucified, whom God raised from the dead.
This Jesus is*
   'the stone that was rejected by you, the builders;
      it has become the cornerstone.'
*There is salvation in no one else, for there is no other name under heaven given
among mortals by which we must be saved." ACTS 4:8-12*

*D*uring *Lent of 1994 I spoke with members of Culmore about the possibility*
of forming an outreach ministry to new immigrants from Africa. I spoke
with Benoni Johnson, who is from Sierra Leone, and Esther Jones, who is
from Liberia. One of the issues both Benoni and Esther raised was that
most of the African members had joined Culmore not because they were
Africans or because a specific ministry targeted them, but because they
had been accepted as individuals. They easily could have joined
homogeneous churches where most of the congregants came from their
home countries, but they had chosen Culmore instead. Their acceptance
as individuals was the primary reason they were hesitant to form an African
ministry. The other major reason they cited was that the African
membership at Culmore represented many different countries and tribes,
sharing neither common culture (as did the Filipino Fellowship) nor
language (as did the Latin American Fellowship). They wondered what
would serve as the common denominator of this ministry. In a very real
sense, they argued that "African" identity is nonexistent. One's identity is

determined by country, village or tribe. An all-inclusive African identity doesn't exist.

After much prayer and discussion, we decided that any African ministry we might create would have to be based on something besides culture, language or tribe. If we were to form a ministry directed toward new immigrants from Africa, we would have to form a multicultural, multitribal, English-speaking African ministry. And most important, such a ministry would have to receive the blessing of one of the elders, one of the older African members.

One day Esther and I went to visit Fanny George,[1] an older woman from Sierra Leone. Fanny came to the United States to help her daughter, Hosanatu, care for her two sons, Mohamed and Yassa. The past few years have been difficult ones for Fanny. Because she cares for the children and has severe arthritis in her hip, she stays in her apartment most of the time. And since many of her relatives and friends frequently work long hours, sometimes holding down two or more jobs, they do not have time to come and visit with her.

Esther explained as we drove to Fanny's apartment that this is a very different life from the one Fanny would have had in Sierra Leone. There, as a village elder, Fanny would have been treated with great respect and honor. People from the village would have come regularly to her home to ask her advice and seek her wisdom. She would have been consulted on major decisions in both the lives of the people and the village itself. And she never would have been alone. There always would have been someone to stay with her and look after her. In going to Fanny to consult her about whether we should establish an African ministry, we were helping Fanny reclaim her position and authority as an elder.

After we presented the idea of an African ministry to Fanny, she enthusiastically "blessed" it. Not only that, but she proposed that she become the encourager, calling members and African visitors who come to worship to ask how they are doing, to encourage them spiritually and encourage them to attend worship regularly.

On our way back to the church after visiting Fanny, Esther and I still were struggling with the central focus of this new ministry. We were vaguely aware that we did not simply want to minister to those who were already active in the church, but to reach new people. The question was, how do we do it?

I began to talk to Esther about my experiences with many Africans whom I had met and their struggles with survival and adapting to a new culture. I was concerned particularly with many families that separated after arriving. When husbands and wives arrive, one of the biggest issues they face is how they will relate as men and women. By virtue of the economic difficulties in the immigrant experience and, more important, the radically different message concerning women and culture in America, conflict occurs around role definition in marriage, status and power. I shared with Esther that I thought one way we might reach the African community was through support ministries for single women and their children.

Esther paused in silent contemplation for several moments. Then she said, "Pastor, for years I have been helping people with their problems. I listen to them, I pray for them, I help them financially. And sometimes their problems are so big that I feel that my own shoulders will break by helping to carry their burdens. Pastor, I think we should help people with their problems, but that is not where we should begin. You asked me, 'What do we have to offer them?' Pastor, just give them Jesus. We can't solve all their problems, but we can point them to the One who can!"

As Stanley Hauerwas and Will Willimon have argued, the church is misguided when it assumes its first task is to "help people." First, this approach puts the focus on our efforts and our power instead of God's. And second, it assumes we know what people really need. To begin ministry by trying to help people is to admit defeat to the forces of secularization from the outset. It is to admit that nothing truly differentiates us from other so-called helping professions. The church thus loses it raison d'être and gives up its unique identity for an ephemeral substitute. As Hauerwas and Willimon put it, "we are *not* called to help people. We are called to follow Jesus, in whose service we learn who we are and how we are to help and be helped."[2]

The Chief Cornerstone
Multicultural ministry is Christ-centered ministry. Nothing else, in heaven or on earth, can hold such diversity together. The church of Jesus Christ is not a mere collection of individual cultures, races or ethnic groups that are separate, but equal. Rather, the church is the body of the risen Christ. In the midst of our cultural diversity, Christ stands at the center to bridge

and yet transcend our differences. In Acts 4, preaching to the temple authorities, Peter proclaimed that Jesus, whom they ("the builders") rejected, had become the chief cornerstone. Like the cornerstone of a building that joins two separate walls, without which the walls would never be united and therefore could not stand, so too Jesus unites the separate and diverse factions of the church. In another possible translation, Jesus is likened to the keystone, the wedge-shaped stone that unites and holds together the various parts of an arch. Suffice it to say that in either image, Jesus is the indispensable center of God's building project, without whom the church cannot stand. As the psalmist says:

Unless the LORD builds the house,
  those who build it labor in vain. (Ps 127:1)

As mentioned earlier, Michael Lind, in his book *The Next American Nation*, argues that the most problematic part of multiculturalism as a worldview is that multiculturalists attempt to reduce the sense of self to its most elemental origins. In other words this worldview says that who one is may be defined as what one is ethnically, racially and sexually. Lind says that this worldview has resulted in the unintended consequence of conformity. One is urged to conform to the culture of one's official subculture—politically, psychologically and socially.

In adopting the nomenclature of political multiculturalism, the church risks the same unintended consequence of de facto resegregation by overemphasizing one's culture of origin to the exclusion of the transcendent and transcending Christ. As Christians, we are called to value our own culture as well as those of other persons, not because of a culture's inherent worth but because of the incarnation of God in Jesus Christ. When God revealed God's self to the world, that revelation was in cultural and ethnic particularity—a first-century, Middle Eastern Jewish male. Thus, we may see our own cultural heritage as a gift from God. (I may therefore take pride in the fact that I am a twentieth-century white male from rural Appalachia! This was God's gift to me.) As Christians, however, we also must remember that what we have in common and what we have to offer is not our own cultural particularity but Jesus Christ. In the words of Stanley Hauerwas:

The most striking . . . fact about the church is that the story of Jesus provides the basis to break down arbitrary and false boundaries between people. The church is an international society only because we have a story that teaches us to regard the other as a fellow member of God's Kingdom. Such regard is not based on facile doctrines of tolerance or equality, but is forged from our common experience of being trained to be disciples of Jesus. The universality of the church is based on the particularity of Jesus' story and on the fact that his story trains us to see one another as God's people.[3]

That They Might Be One

In the high priestly prayer of John 17, Jesus prays: "And now I am no longer in the world, but they are in the world, and I am coming to you. Holy Father, protect them in your name that you have given me, so that they may be one, as we are one" (v. 11). Jesus prays for all who follow him, that we may find the same unity that he and God the Father have found. Jesus' prayer is for us to experience the same acceptance, love and friendship that Jesus shares with God the Father.

Note that the unity Jesus prays for is not one of conformity. Jesus doesn't pray for us to look alike, dress alike or speak alike. Jesus' prayer is not about fitting in. It is not about accommodating ourselves to others. Nor is his prayer about giving up who we are to meet someone else's expectations—at least as far as the world is concerned. If we have learned anything as Jesus' disciples, it is that following God always puts us out of step with the status quo. We march to the beat of a different drummer. Paul, in his letter to the Romans, says, "Do not be conformed to this world," or, as it might also be translated, "Don't even try to fit in," but rather "be transformed by the renewing of your minds" (Rom 12:2). The unity that Jesus prays for is not uniformity but oneness in spirit, a oneness in love, a oneness of mission.

If we are to live and practice the unity that Jesus prayed for us, we need to talk about friendship. No metaphor better describes the meaning of Christian unity than friendship. In fact, earlier in John, Jesus even tells his disciples, "I do not call you servants any longer . . . but I have called you friends" (Jn 15:15). To be one in God is to be friends of God.

We can view friendship as a direct manifestation of our call to be people of blessing. Friendship with each other and with God is the direct way we convey how much we value, appreciate and respect each other. Roberta Bondi, in an article entitled "Friendship with God," says that one characteristic of friendship is to want the same things, to share a common purpose, a common goal. Thus, to be friends with God is to share God's concern for people. It is to share God's purpose—salvation to and for all his children. To be a friend of God is to love the people God loves. Bondi says, "If we desire to become all flame, we must also come to yearn for the things God yearns for, including the well-being of the people with whom, left to ourselves, we would rather not share the kingdom."[4] Jesus' prayer in John 17 concludes with Jesus' appeal that we who are his disciples witness our faith to the whole world by means of our unity. Put plainly, if the church has any hope of sharing the faith with those in the world who do not believe, we must first practice what we preach. We must learn to be friends with each other before our friendship to the world will be credible. Friendship, unity, means to love those whom God loves.

In 1991 I led a short-term Volunteers in Mission team to Seaforth, Jamaica, to help rebuild a church destroyed by Hurricane Gilbert. We were not the first mission team from Virginia to work on this church; three other teams had preceded us. These short-term mission teams usually consist of ten or twelve people who give up two weeks of vacation time, paying their own way to go serve as missionaries for Jesus Christ. Though most of our work involves building churches, parsonages and schools, just as important is our work of building up the global body of Jesus Christ by working side by side with Christians in other countries. Such was the case in Seaforth: we went to build a church, but we also found ourselves uplifted by the witness of the Jamaican Methodist church in that community.

On this trip something happened to me that reinforced my conviction that Christian unity and evangelism are inseparable. The day our team arrived in Seaforth, we were welcomed by the members of the church. While we were getting acquainted, a woman wearing a Virginia United Methodist T-shirt approached me. She asked me if I knew Roy Creech. Roy is a pastor in Virginia and a long-time friend. He also just happened to be the leader of one of the preceding teams. I told her that I knew Roy. She went on to tell me that Roy had introduced her to Jesus Christ. She had not been a member of the church in Seaforth, but she lived in the community. Each night Roy, his team and people from the church gathered on the front lawn of the home of one of the members to sing, pray and share their faith with each other. She was so intrigued by this that she came to join with them. Through that time of sharing the unity of Christian fellowship, she accepted Jesus Christ into her life—all because Roy and others were willing to witness what God was doing in their lives through

Christ. "As you, Father, are in me and I am in you, may they also be in us, so that the world may believe that you have sent me" (Jn 17:21).

Unity, Not Uniformity

Unity as a biblical concept does not mean uniformity. Christian unity assumes diversity. It is a sense of oneness that surpasses that which separates us. The most common word in the New Testament in referring to unity is *heis*, which means *one*; it is used over 337 times. The New Testament addresses the concept of unity in two different ways: (1) the unity of humanity and (2) the unity of the church itself.[5]

The New Testament understanding of a unified humanity has its origins in the primordial history of Genesis 1—11. Humanity is God's creation, intended from the beginning for unity in relationship to God. Ontologically, we were created as one. We have a unified anthropology. Even the name used for the first human being, Adam, also refers to *man*, or *humanity*. The genealogy of Genesis 10 underscores that the nations of the earth have their foundation in the lineage of Adam. In Judaism human unity was vividly portrayed through the image of Adam. Rabbinic Judaism expressed this idea by depicting Adam as a giant, encompassing the world, and hence encompassing all people. Adam was seen as the prototype of all human beings.[6]

In his letters Paul picks up on this theme of anthropological unity in two ways: (1) humanity is united in its opposition to God—that is, sin; and (2) humanity is united in death.[7] Adam most certainly, according to Paul, is a prototype of humanity in that his sin has affected each of his descendants: "Therefore, just as sin came into the world through one man, and death came through sin, and so death spread to all because all have sinned" (Rom 5:12). In Romans 1—3 Paul develops a systematic argument that humanity was united by its refusal of friendship with God: "They exchanged the glory of the immortal God for images . . . the truth about God for a lie and worshiped and served the creature rather than the Creator" (Rom 1:23, 25). Humanity seeks to know God on its own terms, through its own categories, in its own particular truths. We are united in our tendency to turn away from the universal truth of God's salvific story and turn toward our own personal understanding of truth as we see it, and each time we do so the result is idolatry—we worship the creature instead of the Creator. Consequently Paul says, "There is no distinction, since all have sinned and fall short of the glory of God" (Rom 3:22-23).

If, then, what unites us as a human race is rebellion and spiritual death, we might ask, Is there any hope? Yes, says Paul, there is hope: "For if the many died through the one man's [Adam] trespass, much more surely have the grace of God and the free gift in the grace of the one man, Jesus Christ, abounded for the many" (Rom 5:15). According to Paul, if Adam served as the prototype for all of humanity in sin and death, then Jesus Christ serves as the prototype for faith and life. Through Jesus Christ, God has intervened in human affairs and broken the cycle of our union in disobedience. Through the life, death and resurrection of Jesus, God has created the possibility for the potential unity of all humankind: "Therefore just as one man's trespass led to condemnation for all, so one man's act of righteousness leads to justification and life for all" (Rom 5:18). Paul believed the *telos*, the goal of creation itself, was the restoration of the children of God in friendship and unity with the Creator. This restoration is the very purpose of the metanarrative of God's salvation. Hauerwas puts it this way: "The church must be a universal community capable of showing forth our unity in our diversity. Such unity comes not from the assumption that all people share the same nature, but that we share the same Lord."[8]

No Other Name

As I drive to the church each day, I pass by the only mosque in northern Virginia. I make sure to take the back way home on Friday afternoons, lest I get caught in the traffic congestion of afternoon prayers.

In the summer months I take my daughters, Hannah and Cora, to the 7-Eleven a block away from the church for a seasonal treat—Slurpees! The 7-Eleven is operated by a family of Sikhs.

One day I had lunch at the home of a church member who is from Cambodia. She was entertaining two out-of-town guests. These travelers turned out to be Buddhist monks from Europe, attending the funeral of an important American Buddhist priest in Maryland. They were friends of this woman's uncle, who also was a Buddhist monk and scholar living in Bangkok.

A group of ethnic Gypsies bought the house directly across the street from our church. Soon a giant blue neon hand appeared in the window, along with a red neon sign that read *Spiritual Guidance—Inquire Inside.* (I have been trying to convince the congregation that we should put a large neon sign in front of the church, one that shows two hands clasped in prayer and reads *Spiritual Guidance Also Offered Here! Inquire Inside.*)

The church in a multicultural world faces not only the demographic fact of ethnic and cultural pluralism, but also the increasing presence of religious pluralism. For the American church, such encounters with world religions were once reserved for the mission field, but now these experiences are not uncommon for many Christians in urban parishes.

A carpet retailer came to the church recently to give an estimate on recarpeting the sanctuary. He was a devout Muslim from India. He gave us the best bid. When I asked him why his bid was so low, he said that he liked to help religious institutions, so he always gave them a special discount. "After all," he said, "we all worship the same God, don't we?"

Though I was very grateful for the discount, I could not help thinking, *Do we? Do we worship the same God?* In the case of my Muslim brother, scripturally speaking, a case can be made that we do worship the same God, for Islam traces its spiritual heritage back to Ishmael, the first son of Abraham. Yet the question remains for the religious pluralism of the postmodern world: Do we all worship the same God? I think not.

Lesslie Newbigin, in his book *The Gospel in a Pluralist Society,* says that there is a distinction to be made between cultural and religious pluralism. Whereas cultural pluralism embraces the wide diversity of cultures and lifestyles, religious pluralism seeks to embrace and yet downplay the distinctions between the various religious worldviews. He says religious pluralism argues that our differing views of the transcendent are less a matter of truth and falsehood than simply "different perceptions of the one truth . . . [that] religious belief is a private matter. Each of us is entitled to have . . . a faith of our own."[9] Furthermore, he says that the "relativism which is not willing to speak about truth but only about 'what is true for me is an evasion of the serious business of living. It is a mark of a tragic loss of nerve in our contemporary culture. It is a preliminary symptom of death."[10]

Allan Bloom made the argument that openness has become a cultural and religious virtue in and of itself.[11] As a result, says William Craig,

Religious diversity thus calls for a response of openness, and a necessary condition of openness is relativism. Since religious relativism is obviously incompatible with the objective truth of Christianity, religious diversity implies that normative Christian truth claims can neither be made nor defended. Thus, we are led to the paradoxical result that in the name of religious diversity traditional Christianity is delegitimated and marginalized.[12]

Newbigin also notes that this postmodern tendency to blur the distinction between *facts* and *values* further complicates the issue of religious truth. In the world of values, we are pluralists because, after all, values are a matter of personal opinion and choice. But in the world of facts, Newbigin says, we are not pluralists. For example, the "teacher who asks her class whether Paris is the capital of France or of Belgium will not appreciate the child who tells him that he has an open mind on the matter."[13] When it comes to religious belief, Newbigin says, this is usually assigned to the realm of values, rather than facts. Therefore, "in this cultural milieu, the confident announcement of the Christian faith sounds like an arrogant attempt of some people to impose their values on others."[14] Therefore, Newbigin concludes,

> if what matters about religious beliefs is not the factual truth of what they affirm but the sincerity with which they are held; if religious belief is a matter of personal inward experience rather than an account of what is objectively the case, then there are certainly no grounds for thinking that Christians have any right—much less any duty—to seek the conversion of these neighbors to the Christian faith.[15]

Although I deeply respect and appreciate the religious devotion of my Buddhist, Islamic and Sikh neighbors, I must admit nevertheless that the Christian faith that informs my belief and my life *does* make universal claims. J. Richard Middleton and Brian Walsh put it this way: "It is difficult to find a grander narrative, a more comprehensive story anywhere. Christianity is undeniably rooted in a grand narrative that claims to tell the true story of the world from creation to eschaton, from origin to consummation . . . the Christian faith rooted in a metanarrative of cosmic proportions."[16] To give up the universal implications of this biblical metanarrative for a more "local story," they argue, would not only be tragic, it would also not be the gospel.

Many argue that the universal claims of the Christian metanarrative are yet another manifestation of the religious imperialism of Western Christianity. And it is true that Christianity has indeed been co-opted by culture at various times in its history as a tool of imperialism. But, Newbigin says, at the heart of Christianity "is the denial of all imperialisms. . . . The very heart of the biblical vision for the unity of humankind is that at its center is not an imperial power but the slain Lamb."[17]

In the passage from Acts 4 cited earlier in this chapter in which Peter preaches to those with power and position, he proclaims to them that "There is salvation in no one else, for there is no other name under heaven given among mortals by which we must be saved" (Acts 4:12). In the very next verse, the writer notes the reaction of the temple authorities: "Now when they saw the boldness of Peter and John and realized that *they were uneducated and ordinary men,* they were amazed and recognized them as companions of Jesus" (Acts 4:13). Newbigin says it is worth noting that the most energetic evangelistic outreach being done at the present time is not by the wealthy and well-positioned churches of the First World but by Third World churches, which lack both power and privilege.[18] Ordinary people still proclaim with boldness an extraordinary Lord.

Finally, says Newbigin,

> the essential contribution of the Christian to the [interfaith] dialogue will simply be the telling of the story, the story of Jesus, the story of the Bible. . . . The Christian must tell it, not because she lacks respect for the many excellencies of her companions—many of whom may be better, more godly, more worthy of respect than she is. She tells it simply as one who has been chosen and called by God to be part of the company which is entrusted with the story.[19]

Susanne Hargrave, in an article in *Missiology* entitled "Culture, Abstraction and Ethnocentrism," explains how many in the church have called for a new missiology in which that missiology would downplay "the truth claims of the gospel and . . . accept uncritically the use of a people's myths and metaphors without considering their cultural and historical context."[20] In this understanding the contribution of the Christian is to be less interested in fidelity to the story of Jesus than it is to be accepted by cultures and theologies. Its main thrust is to jettison Christianity of its "Western imperialism and ethnocentrism." While Hargrave acknowledges the importance of the Western church's moving away from an "attitude of cultural superiority . . . even these changes," she says, "remind us how much we are influenced by our own context."[21]

"Furthermore," says Hargrave, despite our progress, "we can never assume we are free from ethnocentrism." In fact, she says,

> in the desire to have done away with the ethnocentrism of the past, current missiology may easily substitute a more subtle ethnocentrism.

The missionaries of yesterday who boldly stated, "Christ is the only way to God; repent and follow him," may have had little interest in or appreciation of the beliefs and values of those to whom they spoke. . . . But they made it clear to their audiences that what they preached was "news," something radically different. . . . I believe that it is a more honest and respectful approach than one that reduces others' religions to a version of one's own. It is a subtle ethnocentrism that says, "Your religion is essentially another way of worshiping the same God I worship." What purports to be a humbler acknowledgment of others' insights and grasp of truth may be but a reduction of all religions, in their rich variety of beliefs and practices, to variations on the same theme.[22]

"We cannot escape ethnocentrism," concludes Hargrave. "We will continue to judge, value, and relate to others based on our cultural values."[23] But more dangerous than open disagreement of truth claims is co-optation "of another religion so that [it] become[s] Christianity in another garb."[24]

In Him We Live and Move and Have Our Being

Hauerwas asserts that

Christians are forbidden to despair in the face of the dividedness of the world. On the contrary, we are commanded to witness to others that there is a God that overcomes our differences by making them serve his Kingdom. The task of the Christian is not to defeat relativism by argument but to witness to a God who requires confrontation.[25]

The task of the church is not to prove that everyone else's story is wrong, but to live as though the Christian story is true.

Pluralism—religious, cultural or otherwise—is not necessarily bad news for the postmodern church. If nothing else, it may awaken the church to how culture-bound its proclamations of the gospel have become. As Bernard Adeney points out in his book on crosscultural ethics, *Strange Virtues,* "No one culture contains a universal system of values that is universally valid."[26] Furthermore, Adeney says that "in a crosscultural situation we are often forced to see, for the first time, that our way of living in the world is not the only way. Our glasses are not the only glasses."[27] Crosscultural encounters can liberate Christians from their own ethnocentrism. The pluralistic world in which we now find ourselves is a constant reminder that even under the best of circumstances our thoughts, as Isaiah says, are not the same as God's thoughts, our ways are not the same as God's ways (Is 55:8). The church's presence in a multicultural world results not only in epistemological humanity but in ecclesiological humility as well. Newbigin says that

> every church is . . . tempted to become the domestic chaplain to the nation instead of being the troublesome, prophetic, missionary voice to the nation—challenging all its syncretistic entanglements. . . . We need . . . to bear witness to that which is beyond every national and local culture, the story that is the real story of the human race in God's purpose.[28]

What we bear witness to is not our own religious truths but the life, death and resurrection of Jesus. As Christians, we have to admit that we do not possess the truth in and of ourselves. However, we do know to whom to look in order to find it. Therefore, says Newbigin, "we cannot keep silent about this, because it is the truth that concerns every human being. It is the truth about the human story. And so it must be told to every human being. That obligation remains till the end of time."[29]

And that brings us to the second reason that pluralism is not necessarily bad news for the church. Alister McGrath, in his book *Evangelicalism and the Future of Christianity*, says that rather than posing a threat to the mission of the church, in fact, it may actually bring the church closer "to the world of the New Testament itself."[30] McGrath quotes evangelist Michael Green:

> What's new? The variety of faiths in antiquity was even greater than it is today. And the early Christians, making as they did ultimate claims for Jesus, met the problem of other faiths head-on from the very outset. Their approach was interesting. They did not sit down and dialogue with other faiths very much, as far as we know. They did not denounce other faiths. They simply proclaimed Jesus with all the power and persuasiveness at their disposal. The Christian proclamation has always taken place in a pluralistic world.[31]

In Acts 17 we read of Paul's second missionary journey, which brought him to the cradle of Western civilization and the center of Greek culture, philosophy and education—the city of Athens. We are told that upon entering the city, Paul was deeply distressed at the idolatry present in the city. While he was preaching in the marketplace, some of the Greeks who heard him were intrigued and invited him to come to the Areopagus. The Areopagus, or Mars Hill—named after the god of war—had once served as a council meeting place and high court, but in Paul's day it served as a place of philosophical debate. Some of the best minds in Athens gathered there to exchange ideas and seek truth. To be invited to the Areopagus was an honor. Those who had invited Paul wanted to know more about this new religion he was teaching. They wanted to know who were "these foreign divinities" whom he proclaimed.

Looking down on the city, Paul begins not with condemnation but with flattery: "Athenians, I see how extremely religious you are in every way. For as I went through the city and looked carefully at the objects of your worship, I found among them an altar with the inscription, 'To an unknown god. What therefore you worship as unknown, this I proclaim to you" (Acts 17:22-23). This idol was dedicated to appease any god whose name they did not know and who might take offense at being forgotten and thus punish them. Paul uses this as a point of entry—to make known what is unknown, to name "the name which is above all names," to point them to the one who is "the Way, the Truth, and the Life." Paul's point here is not *religious relativism* ("after all, we all worship the same God") but *religious revelation* ("what therefore you worship as unknown, this I proclaim to you").

Paul pulls no punches in his presentation of the gospel. He says to the Athenians: "The God who made the world and everything in it, he who is Lord of heaven and earth, does not live in shrines made by human hands, nor is he served by human hands, as though he needed anything, since he himself gives to all mortals life and breath and all things" (Acts 17:24-25). The God whom we worship is not enshrined in culture but transcends culture. We worship the Creator, not the creation.

Paul then tells of God's providential blessing for all the nations: "From one ancestor he made all nations to inhabit the whole earth, and he allotted the times of their existence and the boundaries of the places where they would live, so that they would search for God and perhaps grope for him and find him—though indeed he is not far from each one of us" (Acts 17:26-27). Though God elected one nation as his servant, the salvation that comes from God is intended for all. The God in whom "we live, and move, and have our being" is not Middle Eastern or Greek, Jew or Gentile, but the God of all nations.

Paul concludes his sermon to the Athenians by confronting them with the universal implications of God's action in history: "While God has overlooked the times of human ignorance, now he commands all people everywhere to repent, because he has fixed a day on which he will have the world judged in righteousness by a man whom he has appointed, and of this he has given assurance to all by raising him from the dead" (Acts 17:30-31). Paul was not afraid to name the name, to make known what had been unknown. Paul was not ashamed of the gospel. Out of love for those who listened to him, he invited them to repentance and new life in Jesus Christ. The reviews were mixed: some scoffed, others wanted to know more, and some believed.

As Paul would later write in his letter to the congregation at Rome:
"Everyone who calls on the name of the Lord shall be saved." But how are they to call on one in whom they have not believed? And how are they to believe in one of whom they have never heard? And how are they to hear without someone to proclaim him? And how are they to proclaim him unless they are sent? As it is written, "How beautiful are the feet of those who bring good news!" (Rom 10:13-15)

Like Paul, Lesslie Newbigin spent a lifetime in the "beautiful feet" ministry, as a missionary bringing the good news of Jesus Christ to cultures around the world. At the end of this ministry, Newbigin's question is less about who will follow in his footsteps to carry the gospel abroad than about who will proclaim the gospel here:

Like others who have returned to the West after a lifetime as a foreign missionary, I am moved to ask, Who will be the missionaries to this culture? Who will confront this culture of ours with the claim of absolute truth, the claim that Jesus Christ is the truth? Who will be bold enough to say, not that the Christian message can be explained in terms of facts as we know them, but rather that *all* so-called knowledge must be tested against the supreme reality: God incarnate in Jesus Christ, present yesterday, today, until the end, in the power of the Spirit?[32]

To that question we now turn.

4
Be My Witnesses

••

PRINCIPLE: A multicultural church is empowered by the Holy Spirit.

"But you will receive power when the Holy Spirit has come upon you; and you will be my witnesses in Jerusalem, in all Judea and Samaria, and to the ends of the earth." When he had said this, as they were watching, he was lifted up, and a cloud took him out of their sight. While he was going and they were gazing up toward heaven, suddenly two men in white robes stood by them. They said, "Men of Galilee, why do you stand looking up toward heaven? This Jesus, who has been taken up from you into heaven, will come in the same way as you saw him go into heaven."
ACTS 1:8-11

*T*he miracle of the first Pentecost was not just that people could proclaim the good news of salvation in other tongues, but that in their diversity of languages, through the power of God's Spirit, they understood one another. In the same way the miracle of the growing number of multicultural congregations involves not so much cultural or linguistic diversity, but the willingness to seek understanding and unity through the language of faith. To make theological sense of the church in a multicultural world, one must view it through the eyes of Pentecost.

A missionary friend of mine, Rhett Thompson, tells what happened following a worship service in the church he was serving in Chirique, Panama, when a three-year-old boy came up to him and asked, "Rhett, are you a *gringo* or are you a people, a *gente?*"

Rhett wasn't quite sure how to answer his friend, because if he answered "gringo" then he wasn't a people, and if he answered "people" then he wasn't a gringo. After a couple of moments of thinking about it, he told the little boy that, in fact, he was a gringo.

The little boy looked confused. How could his pastor, his friend, not be a people like everyone else? So he asked, "Rhett, why? Why you a gringo and not a people?"

Rhett tried to explain that he was a gringo because he was born in the United States. Then he pointed out that the little boy was a Chiricano because he had been born in Chirique.

"Ah," said the boy, seeming to comprehend. Then in an act of acceptance and hospitality, he proclaimed, "Rhett, you Chirique-gringo."

Regardless of where Rhett had been born, in the little boy's eyes Rhett was "people" too.

The apostle Peter wrote:

Once you were not a people,
> but now you are God's people;
once you had not received mercy,
> but now you have received mercy. (1 Pet 2:10)

As a Pentecost church, we would do well to follow the example of Rhett's little friend in Chirique. Pentecost represents nothing less than the hospitality and acceptance of God. It is the manifestation of God's desire for the world. Pentecost is the clearest symbol of what God wants, expects and intends for God's people. Pentecost reminds us that we, who once were strangers to God, have now been welcomed and claimed by God. Whether we are gringos or Chiricanos, whether we were born in the U.S. or Panama (or anywhere else for that matter), we are now God's *gente*, God's people. In the kingdom of God there are no undocumented persons, for our passport is the blood of the Lamb.

The Great Co-mission

Ernest Campbell tells the story of a bishop who was asked to preach at a Christian conference on missions. For many weeks he did not respond to the invitation. Finally the person responsible for scheduling the conference wrote to him: "We must know if you are coming. We need to make our plans." The bishop wrote back that he was waiting for the guidance of the Holy Spirit on the matter and that he would let them know his decision in four weeks.

An exasperated secretary fired back this letter: "Bishop, please don't even bother. Cancel the invitation. We are not interested in having anyone speak at our conference who lives four weeks away from the Holy Spirit."[1]

The book of Acts opens with the disciples waiting and listening. This waiting for God to act and this listening for spiritual direction, however, must not be construed as passive. The disciples of Jesus were actively waiting in expectation and hope.

The basis for the disciples' hope lay in Jesus' last words to them. In Acts 1:8, just before his ascension into heaven to reign at the right hand of God, Jesus gives the church its mission statement: "But you will receive power when the Holy Spirit has come upon you; and you will be my witnesses in Jerusalem, in all Judea and Samaria, and to the ends of the earth." First, these disciples have the confidence to know they are not being left alone in the world to fend for themselves; as Jesus has promised, he will send another: "you will receive power *when* the Holy Spirit has come." Not *if*, but *when!* In the Gospel of John, Jesus makes the promise of the Holy Spirit more explicit when he says: "I will ask the Father, and he will give you another Advocate, to be with you forever. This is the Spirit of truth, whom the world cannot receive, because it neither sees him nor knows him. You know him, because he abides with you, and he will be in you. I will not leave you orphaned" (Jn 14:16-18).

Second, they have hope because they have a purpose. The last three years of their lives have not been for naught—it is only the beginning. Their work in Jesus' name has just started: "You *will* be my witnesses in Jerusalem, in all Judea and Samaria, and to the ends of the earth." They will witness and point to the truth of the risen Christ (1) at home (in Judea), (2) to their neighbors, even the ones they don't particularly care for (in Samaria), and (3) to all the nations, near and far (to the ends of the earth). This statement of the church's mission in Acts is evocative of Jesus' final words in the Gospel of Matthew, the Great Commission: "Go therefore and make disciples of all nations, baptizing them in the name of the Father and of the Son and of the Holy Spirit, and teaching them to obey everything that I have commanded you. And remember, I am with you always, to the end of the age" (Mt 28:19-20).

Presbyterian preacher John Killinger tells about a time he was traveling in the English Cotswolds and saw a faded sign on an old barn. It said "Bellow & Son, Ltd., Makers." It didn't say what Bellow and his son made—only that they were makers. Killinger thought about what a wonderful moment that must have been when this father and son joined into a partnership, sharing in the family business of making and creating—and "how proud both Mr. Bellow and his son must have been when that sign was painted there, announcing their new working relationship." Killinger goes on to say "how glorious it is for us to be called children of the Creator of the world," where our own heavenly parent has called us to join in the family business of making and remaking the world. "Just imagine," says Killinger, a sign on the front of the church that reads: "God and Son, Makers, or God and Daughter, Makers. It's a beautiful thought, isn't it?"[2]

Christians are coworkers, partners together with the Lord. But that is exactly what God is calling us to in the Great Co-mission—a joint partnership to remake the world in God's image and according to God's purposes: "*Go . . . make* disciples of *all* nations."

God indeed has a mission, and God has a missionary, the Holy Spirit, and as these verses testify, God's mission does, in fact, have a church, an "ecclesiastical partner and place with which to bring God's work to fulfillment."[3] These verses announce that God does not intend to fulfill God's purposes for creation apart from humanity, nor does God intend the church to accomplish this mission apart from an active relationship with God. God will fulfill this mission as a joint partnership between God and God's children.

Immediately following Jesus' ascension, Luke reports that angelic strangers appeared to the disciples who were gazing heavenward. They asked the disciples, "Men of Galilee, why do you stand looking up toward heaven?" (Acts 1:11). In other words, it is time to get to work. We can approach ministry with the confidence of the children of God that we have not been left alone in the world to fend for ourselves. We have the certain promise of the risen Christ that he is with us until the end of the age, and that he is also sending another, who will comfort us, be our advocate, and give us the power to be God's partners in blessing the nations.

They Understood Each Other

The first act of this activist church is to pray (Acts 1:12-14). The disciples waited for the coming of the Holy Spirit by actively listening to God. The temptation the church always faces is to take ministry into our own hands, to (as the Nike commercial says) "just do it!" The danger inherent in such action-oriented ministry is that what happens is based on *our* desires, efforts and agendas rather than on God's. The church of Acts first patiently waits for God to make good on God's promises. In word and deed, these first Christians witness that they believe God is who God says he is, and that God will do what God says he will do. So they wait prayerfully, fully expecting something to happen. And does it ever!

Scripture says that on the morning of Pentecost, when the disciples were all gathered together in an upper room praying, "suddenly from heaven there came a sound like the rush of a violent wind, and it filled the entire house where they were sitting. Divided tongues, as of fire, appeared among them, and a tongue rested on each of them" (Acts 2:2-3). This dramatic display of sound and fury is none other than the descent of the Holy Spirit upon the believers. Newly filled with the Holy Spirit, these believers received the ability to speak in other languages. Will Willimon says that the very first gift of the Holy Spirit to believers was "the gift of speech, [specifically] the gift of speech in different languages. So we are hearing a story about the irruption of the Spirit into the community and the first fruit of the Spirit [is] the gift of proclamation."[4]

Jerusalem, already an international city at the time, was even more so during the festival of Pentecost. Held fifty days after Passover to celebrate the harvest, it was one of three major feasts held each year. Jews from all over the world had gathered in the holy city to give thanks to God for his gifts. When the day was over, there was one more gift of God for which to be thankful—the gift of the Spirit.

At Pentecost these Jews "from every nation under heaven" heard the believers speaking in the language of their own country. The first miracle of Pentecost was one of understanding. "Amazed and astonished, they asked, 'Are not all these who are speaking Galileans? And how is it that we hear, each of us, in our own native language?" (Acts 2:7-8). Unlike the confusion of Babel, which was born out of fear, the temporary confusion of Pentecost was born out of amazement. They were listening to each other, and what's more, they were hearing each other.

When I first came to Culmore, one of the biggest problems we had to overcome in order to be one congregation was the barrier of understanding and being understood. Even though the church had been ethnically diverse for many years, there was still little communication among the members. Recent Filipino immigrants kept company with other Filipinos; the same was true with Latinos, Anglos and others.

One day I was having a conversation with an older Anglo member, who brought up this fact. I asked her why she thought this was the case. She said that she could speak only for herself: she was simply afraid of being embarrassed at not understanding what was being said to her. In speaking with several of the immigrant members of Culmore, she had found herself either asking for repetition or simply smiling and nodding her head in acknowledgment —without having the slightest idea what the person was saying.

Shortly thereafter, I had almost the exact same conversation with a first-generation immigrant for whom the southern dialect of English was considered a language unto itself. This fear of not understanding each other or of not being understood kept Christian brothers and sisters at arm's length from one another. But at Pentecost, the Holy Spirit drew the family of God together and broke down the walls of misunderstanding and confusion.

If the first miracle of Pentecost was the miracle of understanding, then the second miracle of Pentecost was the miracle of proclamation—"in our own languages we hear them speaking about God's deeds of power" (Acts 2:11). The baffled revelers wanted to know, "what does this mean?" Others accused the believers of simply being drunk. Into this uncertain crowd steps Peter, who proclaims a certain truth. Quoting from the prophet Joel, he says:

In the last days it will be, God declares,

that I will pour out my Spirit upon all flesh,

and your sons and your daughters shall prophesy,

and your young men shall see visions,

and your old men shall dream dreams. . .

Then everyone who calls on the name of the Lord shall be saved. (Acts 2:17, 21)

The response to Peter's sermon was immediate. Many in the crowd were "cut to the heart" and cried out: "Brothers, what should we do?" (Acts 2:37). Peter's response was simple and direct: "Repent, and be baptized every one of you in the name of Jesus Christ so that your sins may be forgiven; and you will receive the gift of the Holy Spirit" (v. 38). Acts ends this story of Pentecost by saying that "about three thousand persons were added" that day. Will Willimon, in his commentary on this passage, says: "For Luke the ability to repent and the possession of the Spirit are gifts of God. . . . The story of Pentecost day began with the gift of the Spirit to the assembled apostles. Now the day concludes with the gift of reconciliation for those who heretofore stood on the outside."[5]

Language as Passport

"It is only against the background of Babel . . . that we can understand the extraordinary event of Pentecost," writes Stanley Hauerwas. "The promised people themselves—who had been scattered among the tribes, learning their languages, were now reunited in common understanding. The wound of Babel began to be healed first among the very people God had called into the world as a pledge of God's presence."[6] What's more, writes Hauerwas, "at Pentecost God created a new language, but it was a language that is more than words. It is instead a community whose memory of its Savior creates the miracle of being a people whose very differences contribute to their unity. We call this new creation, church."[7]

In his book *The Nature of Doctrine*, George Lindbeck argues that theology does "not make scriptural contents into metaphors for extra scriptural realities, but the other way around . . . [not] that believers find their stories in the Bible, but rather that they make the story of the Bible their story."[8] When I speak of God, I am not describing an experience that is universally available. *God* is not a label to be attached to some natural knowledge of the divine that human beings possess inwardly. For example, if two people from different religious traditions speak of God, it cannot be assumed that they are expressing the same experience or truth. The religious experience of a Hindu is quite different from the religious experience of a Christian. Not only do their religious practices differ, but their assumptions about who God is and how God relates to creation also differ. The description of one's religious experience is less an intuitive expression of an inward reality than a confession of a revealed truth.

Hauerwas and Willimon, picking up on Lindbeck's image of doctrine as the language of faith, also argue that learning to be a Christian is a lot like learning to speak a language. "You do not teach someone a language . . . by first teaching that person rules of grammar. The way most of us learn to speak a language is by listening to others speak and then imitating them. . . . The rules of grammar come later, if at all, as a way of enabling you to nourish and sustain the art of speaking well."[9]

At Pentecost the newly created language was the language of faith. The church was born in the telling of the story of the life, death and resurrection of Jesus Christ. In the gifts of listening to and proclaiming the mighty acts of God in Jesus Christ, a new *polis* was created, an alternative community. As Hauerwas and Willimon put it: "Christianity is an invitation to be part of an alien people who make a difference because they see something that cannot otherwise be seen without Christ. Right living is more the challenge than right thinking. The challenge is not the intellectual one but the political one—the creation of a new people who have aligned themselves with the seismic shift that has occurred in the world since Christ."[10] As the letter to the Ephesians reminds us, "you are no longer strangers and aliens, but you are citizens with the saints and also members of the household of God" (Eph 2:19). And our passport to this new *polis* is the language of faith formed by the story of Jesus.

Bernard Adeney writes that "skill in a language acts like a *passport* to real friendship. Skill or fluency entails a deep understanding of the culture. Fluency is lacking as long as we translate *our* language into another. Fluency requires that we experience reality through the categories of the new language."[11] One Sunday before church, I was talking to Rich, a member of our church, who was sharing an epiphany he had experienced with another member of our church, Tomas. Tomas is from Nicaragua. Though he now works two manual-labor jobs—one full time and the other part time—he was a professor in Managua before emigrating. Rich and Tomas have come to know each other through the ESL classes—Rich as a teacher and Tomas as a student. Tomas's English is halting, and Rich's Spanish is nonexistent. Though their shared vocabulary was very small, they became friends.

Rich thought he was beginning to get to know Tomas fairly well, but he realized how little he really knew him when, one night, a bilingual Culmore member joined them in conversation. She was able to translate not only Tomas's words but also the depth of his feeling and character. Rich said that the Tomas who was revealed in that conversation was a deeply thoughtful and intellectual man with a poetic and compassionate soul. Until that moment, Rich said, he had caught only glimpses of who Tomas really was. With the aid of a translator, he was able to experience Tomas the professor instead of Tomas the student.

To really know God, to have friendship with God and friendship with each other as God's children, we must be immersed in the narrative of God's salvific history. We must indwell the gospel, letting it shape us into God's image.

The Power of Spirit

While the exact meaning of the name *Acts* remains somewhat uncertain, the protagonist of its narrative is very certain. The acts of the apostles are, in fact, the acts of the Holy Spirit.12 On that first Pentecost, though the believers had the assurance of Jesus' promise of a Comforter, they were alone, and they could not help but recall their act of betrayal. No one had remained faithful. As they awaited the Holy Spirit, they were broken people. Any illusion of self-sufficiency or bravery or courage had been shattered into a thousand pieces at the cross of Calvary. As they contemplated their spiritual lives, they must have seemed to them as dry as Ezekiel's valley of bones. "Mortal, can these bones live?" (Ezek 37:3). But God sent the Holy Spirit upon them, the spirit of life, to breathe into them new life.

God uses broken things. God uses broken people. Only what is broken can be made whole. Only what is empty can be filled. If it is already full, it has no need of filling. God's intention at Pentecost was to re-create his people in a way that can be compared only to calling them back from the dead.

The apostle Paul wrote, "If the Spirit of him who raised Jesus from the dead dwells in you, he who raised Christ from the dead will give life to your mortal bodies also through his Spirit that dwells in you" (Rom 8:11). God's gift of the Holy Spirit is the realization of that promise. The Holy Spirit is what makes the resurrection of Jesus real in the life of believers. The Holy Spirit is the one who enables us not only to know about Jesus but also to follow Jesus. The Holy Spirit is the one who makes it possible not only to be good but to be holy. It is the Spirit who conforms our will to the will of God. It is the Spirit who writes God's desires on our hearts. "I will put my law within them, and I will write it on their hearts; and I will be their God, and they shall be my people" (Jer 31:33).

To be perfectly frank, however, I have noticed in my time as a United Methodist pastor that believers (mainliners particularly but not exclusively) have often skirted the role of the Holy Spirit in the Christian life. Our trinitarian theology is just plain poor, to say the least. We pretend that the Spirit has but a minor role in God's great construction project of a new heaven and a new earth, when in fact the Spirit is the mover and the shaker. It is almost as if we are embarrassed by the Spirit.

But I really don't think it's embarrassment—I think it's fear. When the Bible speaks of the Spirit, it speaks of power and energy we cannot tame or master. The Spirit descended on God's people with fiery power. The first believers experience of the Spirit was as if "tongues of fire" had engulfed them. The Holy Spirit ignites those spiritual energies that God sowed within us before we were even born. When we experience the fire of God's Spirit, our souls explode with all kinds of spiritual possibilities that we had never used. This can be scary, which is one of the reasons we tend to shy away from the Spirit. But we do so to our own detriment.

Adeney says that the "fastest-growing segments of the church today are those that have elevated the Holy Spirit to a central place for the experience of life in Christ." He says that the mainline churches frequently criticize Pentecostals for an "overspiritualized message" and a lack of concern about social justice. But in his opinion that is simply not the case. The charismatic churches are most likely to minister in proximity to and with the poor. In recent years Pentecostal churches, particularly in the developing world, have developed sophisticated social programs to enable persons to rise above their poverty. Equally important, these churches are much more diverse in terms of both race and class than their mainline counterparts. And even more interesting, these conservative congregations are as likely to recognize women as leaders as they are men.[13]

Recent statistics estimate that Pentecostal churches are growing at the rate of 20 million new members each year, and that total membership is now more than 400 million. Citing data collected by David Barrett, an expert in religious statistics, Harvey Cox has observed that Pentecostalism is the largest grouping of Christians outside the Catholic Church, accounting for one out of every four Christians. Cox also says that it is the fastest-growing segment of the Christian church, growing even faster than Christian or Islamic fundamentalism.[14] It could very well be that when the history of the twentieth century is written, it will be known as "the Pentecostal century," with mainline and evangelical denominations receiving only a footnote.

For our purposes, what is interesting about the Pentecostal phenomenon lies in the origins of this movement. Cox has written a thought-provoking account of the unfolding of Pentecostalism in his book *Fire from Heaven*. Cox says that many Pentecostals believed that after the first Pentecost (when the Holy Spirit fell upon believers), "something went wrong." After the initial spiritual exuberance, Christians became preoccupied, self-absorbed and not a little bit lazy. They did not follow through in announcing good news to all the nations. But God did not give up on the church, waiting until the right time for the Spirit to descend once more.[15]

Pentecostals believe the fire from heaven began to fall again in 1906. A black southern preacher by the name of William Seymour launched a revival on Azusa Street in Los Angeles, a revival that was interracial in nature from its very beginning. According to Seymour: "The New Jerusalem was coming. Now the rich and the proud would get their just deserts. The destitute, the overlooked, and the forgotten would come into their own." Even more important, he believed that "God was now assembling a racially inclusive people to glorify his name and to save a Jim Crow nation lost in sin."[16] Cox says:

> In retrospect the interracial character of the growing congregation on Azusa Street was indeed a kind of miracle. It was, after all, 1906, a time of growing, not diminishing, racial separation everywhere else. But many visitors reported that in the Azusa Street revival blacks and whites and Asians and Mexicans sang and prayed together. Seymour was recognized as the pastor. But there were both black and white deacons, and both black and white women . . . were exhorters and healers. What seemed to impress—or disgust—visitors most, however, was not the interracial leadership but the fact that blacks and whites, men and women, embraced each other at the tiny altar as they wept and prayed. A southern white preacher later jotted in his diary that he was first offended and startled, then inspired, by the fact that, as he put it, "the color line was washed away by the blood."[17]

Pentecostalism is frequently identified with the gift of tongues, which Seymour emphasized as evidence of the baptism of the Holy Spirit. But toward the latter days of his ministry Seymour changed his mind. He grew disillusioned because some Christians could get caught up in the spiritual ecstasy of speaking in tongues and yet continue to despise their black brothers and sisters in Christ. As a result, Seymour came to believe that the truest sign of the presence of the Holy Spirit was not speaking in tongues but the demise of racial barriers between Christians. Only when this evidence is fully present, Seymour believed, will we know that the New Jerusalem is about to draw near.[18]

In the emerging Pentecostal congregations that are multiracial, multilingual and multiclass, the fire from heaven is falling again. And as in 1906, it is falling at a time when Americans as a nation are pulling apart, not pulling together. Today is a time when *separatism*, not *integration*, is the favored code word. So the Spirit descends again, falling on brothers and

sisters, Africans and Anglos, Asians and Latinos, documented and undocumented, rich and poor—God is once more breathing into us the Spirit of
life. Empowered by the Spirit's presence, we are called to bear witness to
the transnational, transcultural gospel of Jesus Christ.

Too often as the church of Jesus Christ, we confuse our own priorities with God's priorities, what we want for the church with what God
wants, our own definition of mission with God's definition. In this era
of our nation's history, we find ourselves polarized particularly around
the issues of race, ethnicity and immigration status. In the divisive
atmosphere in which we live, it would be easy to follow the trends of
our society rather than to obey the truths of the gospel. It would be
easy to rationalize our segregation as congregations along the ethnic
and linguistic fault lines of our culture, assuring ourselves that we are
only being "realistic." Particularly with many denominations facing
numerical decline in membership, voices will seductively argue that for
the church to survive and grow, we must reach out to those "who are
like us." They will argue that homogeneous ministry is really the only
way out of our decline—that transcultural or multilingual ministry is
a "wonderful concept" but certainly not practical. They will say that if
we are serious about church growth, we should emphasize churches
that are homogeneous, not heterogeneous. But clearly this is not what
the Bible says.

In my own denomination, the United Methodist Church, 95 percent of
members are non-Hispanic whites and only 12 percent of the laity are
under the age of thirty-five. Our very future as a denomination may well
depend on the ministries of multicultural congregations.

David D'Amico, in an article entitled "Evangelization Across Cultures:
What to Do When the World Comes to Us?" argues that the future impact
of multicultural congregations in the United States will be "overwhelming." "Ecclesiologically," he says, "it will revise church structures. Issues
such as training and empowerment of leadership, delineation of denominational structures based on geographic boundaries, and distribution of
human and financial resources, will be revolutionized by the year 2010."[19]

The world and our communities are rapidly changing around us. The
question before the church is whether our congregations are willing to
change and receive the gift that God is offering us through the Holy
Spirit—the ability to listen and proclaim the mighty works of God.

Once More Scattered

Emil Brunner once said, "The church lives by mission as a fire lives by burning."[20] The multicultural congregations of Pentecost are missionary congregations on fire with the Holy Spirit. As Charles Van Engen says in his book *God's Missionary People,*

> Missionary congregations are communities of those who live out the reign of God in their lives and society; they are uniquely suited to the anticipatory "first-fruits" of the kingdom in the world. The Church is not the kingdom in its fulness, but as an anticipatory sign Christians live in anxious waiting and suspenseful hope.[21]

Multicultural congregations bear witness, as Christ commanded us, to the reign of God and God's intentions for creation.

In the story of Babel, the advent of the multiplicity of languages was followed by scattering, so that humanity could fulfill God's command to "multiply, and fill the earth." In the story of Pentecost, the advent of the multiplicity of tongues and understanding is also followed by scattering, so that humanity could fulfill Christ's command to "be my witnesses . . . to the ends of the earth." One form of this scattering occurs when the Pentecost pilgrims "from every nation under heaven" who received the good news of salvation in Jesus Christ returned home. In Acts 13—14, we hear of the first missionary journey of Paul and Barnabas, who, by the power of the Holy Spirit, proclaimed the good news of salvation in Jesus Christ not only in Jerusalem, not only in Judea, but to Gentiles and to the ends of the earth! Together they boldly declared that the gospel is meant for all people of all ethnicities, speaking all languages, in all nations.

The other form of scattering occurs in Acts when the church, living out its mission, faces persecution from the world. The most vivid portrayal of this situation is in Stephen's bold sermon to the synagogue in Acts 7. Van Engen says that "in choosing Israel as a segment of all humanity, God never took his eye off the other nations." In addition, there was God's promise to Abraham that Israel would serve as "*pars pro toto,* a minority called to serve the majority."[22] Stephen's fiery sermon recalls this mandate from God. As Thom Hopler notes: "Stephen's explosive message made Judaism a universal faith. Anyone could come to God and be fully related to him without adopting an ethnocentric, Palestinian form of religion."[23]

The result, of course, was persecution and violence. In his commentary on Acts, Willimon notes what happened following Stephen's martyrdom:

> The community (except for the Twelve) is now hunted down and scattered into Judea and Samaria. Earlier, it had been predicted that the gospel would be taken by witnesses into "all Judea and Samaria" (1:8). Little did the followers know then that the impetus for this far-flung evangelism would be persecution! These refugees, scattered like seed, take root elsewhere and bear fruit. God is able to use even persecution of his own people to work his purposes.[24]

Of course, this was not true only of the Pentecost church of Acts; it is also true of the church today. The gospel continues to be spread, despite persecution, violence and the brokenness of the human family. As we have learned, God uses broken things.

When I think of my congregation, I think of the members who are here as the result of war and persecution. The list of nations represented at Culmore could easily be a state department list of sites of recent international conflicts: Angola, Cambodia, Cuba, El Salvador, Guatemala, Nicaragua, Nigeria and Sierra Leone, to name a few.

One day I was talking to Mills Jones, who is from Liberia. He said, "Ten years ago you would not have found many Liberians living abroad. But when the civil war erupted, so many left. Now you will find Liberians all over the world." Mills grieves for his homeland and looks forward to the return of peace and stability.

Although God is not responsible for the suffering of Liberia or any other nation, we still may have confidence that God can redeem even the bleakest of situations and lift hope from despair. I am grateful for the bold Christian witness of Mills and his family, which has strengthened this congregation's ability to fulfill Jesus' command to "be my witnesses."

Van Engen says that the church is "in many ways like a tree. . . . Around the world the Church as been planted small and weak and has grown to become a source of protection, of new life, and of increased health and nourishing spiritual food." As a result, says Van Engen,

> for the first time in the history of humanity we find the Church spanning the globe, sheltering one-and-one-half billion people who in one way or another confess allegiance to Jesus Christ and call themselves Christian. We are now at the beginning of a totally new era in the history of the world and of Christianity, a "global discipling era" characterized by "total global access to all peoples of the earth." For the first time the Church is large

and encompassing enough to be the missionary people of God. The opportunity exists for the one holy, universal, and apostolic community to witness to every tongue, tribe, and nation. And as local congregations are built up to reach out, they will emerge from their sapling stage to be their true nature, bearing fruit as missionary people."[25]

To return to Lesslie Newbigin's question raised at the end of chapter three: "Who will be the missionaries to this culture? Who will confront this culture of ours with the claim of absolute truth, the claim that Jesus Christ is the truth?" George Hunsberger, in his address to the Lausanne II Congress in Manila in 1989, approached this issue. He said that for too long the church in the United States has not considered itself "a field for mission" but "only a launching pad" for missions to other parts of the globe. Though, he says, there has been much talk about "reciprocal missions" or "missions in reverse," most churches still would not consider inviting an African or Asian pastor to be a founding pastor in a new church start. But that, he said, may be changing, if for no other reason than institutional decline.

D'Amico concludes from Hunsberger's comments that the "only hope of . . . survival for many of these congregations, especially in urban centers where their buildings stand unoccupied most Sundays, is to attempt to minister to Asian, Hispanic, or other ethnic groups."[26] Who will be our missionaries? It may very well be our international neighbors, Christians whom God has gathered "from every nation under heaven," who will serve as Jesus' witness to the American church.

The Fruit and the Seed

Ephesians 1 explains the missional theology of what God was doing through the church in Acts. Ephesians 1:4 says that God "*chose us* in Christ before the foundation of the world." The mystery of our salvation originated in the timeless mind of God long before we ever existed. Long before we created the distinctions of race, class and nation to divide us, God *chose* us. And not only has God chosen us, but God has "*destined* us for *adoption* as his children" (Eph 1:5). God marked us out beforehand. God picked us out of the crowd when we were orphaned and alone in this world and brought us into God's family and gave us a home. Ephesians 1:10 summarizes the whole of God's purpose in the promise that God has "a plan for the fullness of time, to gather up all things in him, things in heaven and things on earth" (Eph 1:10). The mystery of God's will was revealed in his

Son: to unite all people in all places for a purpose. God's purpose was that the redeemed and united creation, Jew and Gentile, male and female, slave and free, shall "praise God's glory" (Eph 1:12 TEV).

When I think of this passage, I cannot help but think of a small boy who, abandoned by his parents, ended up becoming a child of the streets in Chile. Alone, with no one to depend on but himself, he lived day to day, struggling to survive poverty and starvation. Then one day a couple noticed this homeless boy and saw potential within him for great things. Whereas others had seen him as simply another poor, homeless boy destined for an early grave, this couple saw a blessed child of God for whom God had a destiny and purpose. This couple chose this child, marked him out and claimed him as their own. They brought the boy into their home with their own family. It was a big, bustling household, full of joy and laughter.

The couple loved the boy as their own; they told him how special he was and how much God loved him and how God had a special purpose for his life. They sent him to school and educated him, and he grew in knowledge and grace. In time he claimed his chosenness in Christ and accepted God's destiny and purpose for his life He gave God his life for use in ministry; he went to seminary and was ordained. That little boy was named Juan Paredes, the adopted son of American Methodist missionaries Charles and Orpha Irle.

Together with his wife, Tita, Juan served eighteen appointments in Chile, mostly starting new congregations. Because of his work, there are congregations throughout Chile that would not have existed otherwise. God had a purpose for the boy living on the streets.

Juan and Tita thought that they had completed their work and retired from active ministry, but God had other intentions. To their surprise, God brought them to the homeland of Juan's adoptive parents. This adopted son of American missionaries completed the circle of grace by himself becoming a Chilean missionary to the United States, establishing the Latin American ministry in northern Virginia at Culmore and helping to further God's purpose for the church: that all people in all places may be united in order to "praise God's glory."

Juan Paredes and many of our other new immigrant neighbors are the fruit of the American missionary movement abroad. The offspring of this ministry have come home. And now, in this new homeland, they are becoming the seed for a new multicultural mission movement in our own land.

Americans are not accustomed to having missionaries sent to them. But then, I suspect, neither did the citizens of the Roman Empire know quite what to make of Paul and Barnabas, two Jews from one of the occupied territories, who had come to preach to them about one at whose name "every knee should bow . . . and every tongue confess that Jesus Christ is Lord" (Phil 2:10-11 NIV).

5
Choosing Life

•••

PRINCIPLE: A multicultural church accepts God's gift of being "born again."

I call heaven and earth to witness against you today that I have set before you life and death, blessings and curses. Choose life so that you and your descendants may live, loving the LORD your God, obeying him, and holding fast to him; for that means life to you and length of days, so that you may live in the land that the LORD swore to give to your ancestors, to Abraham, to Isaac, and to Jacob. DEUTERONOMY 30:19-20

When my bishop, Thomas Stockton, appointed me to Culmore seven years ago, it was a very different church from what it is today. I can still remember the first Sunday when I arrived at church with my family. We walked down halls lined with empty classrooms. Fewer than twenty people were in Sunday school, and almost all of them were adults. The congregation once boasted a membership of eight hundred, but when the time for worship came on my first Sunday, just over eighty people were gathered in the sanctuary. Prior to coming I had been informed about many of the difficulties the congregation faced. Nonetheless, I must admit that I wondered whether the bishop had sent me to Culmore to serve as a midwife assisting in a rebirth or simply to pronounce benediction and close the church.

The body of Christ at Culmore was very much on life support, and we weren't sure the patient would make it. We were losing members and struggling financially. We were a divided congregation. The Spirit seemed to have gone out of us. In short, we were dying. We had lost our way.

Today as I walk through the church, I hear the sounds of a nursery full of toddlers laughing and playing. I see the excitement of children rushing hand in hand, giggling and whispering as they go from Sunday school to choir practice. I hear the heavenly harmony of the All Nations Choir singing God's praise in many languages. I see young adults getting together for fellowship and band rehearsal, loudly practicing Christian "grunge" for Friday-night worship. I watch folk, young and old, rich and poor, gather before worship to pray for each other and for the future of the church. I look at the congregation reaching out to its community, the church's rooms filled in the afternoon with neighborhood kids in a gang-prevention ministry and at night with adults streaming in to learn English. And now Sunday after Sunday, I watch in anticipation as the sanctuary fills with God's people coming to worship because they hunger for the bread of life; they know they can find it in this place.

When I walk through our halls today, I know this church is alive! And I believe the church is alive for two reasons: (1) as Scripture teaches us, with God nothing is impossible—even dying churches have the opportunity to be born again; and (2) we chose to put aside our differences as a church and come together as Christ's body, intentionally claiming our identity as a multicultural congregation. We are alive, and, as a result, God has given us a future.

Of the multicultural congregations I visited during my sabbatical, including my own, most were resurrected congregations.[1] Each had faced decline, and, in many cases, probable closure. Their revitalization corresponded to their intentional decision to claim their diversity as a strength and not a liability. This difference in intentionality provided each one with an identity as a multicultural congregation. The intentionality also prevented them from simply being congregations in transition from one homogeneous ethnic group to another.

Choose This Day

In Deuteronomy 30 Moses challenges God's people to intentionally choose their future. They could choose life and prosperity on the one hand, or death and adversity on the other. Moses specified what choosing life meant: "loving the LORD your God, walking in his ways, and observing his commandments, decrees, and ordinances, then you shall live and become numerous, and the LORD your God will bless you in the land that you are entering to possess" (v. 16). But, Moses warned them, "if your heart turns away and you do not hear, but are led astray to bow down to other gods and serve them, I declare to you today that you shall perish; you shall not live long in the land that you are crossing the Jordan to enter and possess" (vv. 17-18).

Moses addressed a people who had been wandering in the wilderness for forty years. Many of them initially would have preferred the life of slavery they had known in Egypt rather than venturing forth into freedom in the Promised Land they did not know. And so it is with many congregations in decline. It is terribly tempting to choose the life we have known, because the past, for all its imperfections and inadequacies, is a known quantity, and its familiarity can be comforting. The unknown, however, is just that—unknown, and it can provoke within us fear and anxiety that may seem far worse than our present circumstances. Scripture reminds us that "all the Israelites complained against Moses and Aaron; the whole congregation said to them, 'Would that we had died in the land of Egypt! . . . Why is the LORD bringing us into this land to fall by the sword?" (Num 14:2-3).

In speaking to God's people, Moses urges them to choose life: "I call heaven and earth to witness against you today that I have set before you life and death, blessings and curses. Choose life so that you and your descendants may live" (Deut 30:19). The choice presented to the people is not necessarily an unbiased one. Moses makes it clear that one choice is better than the other. He doesn't say to Israel, "Well, I've brought you this far—now, it's up to you. So do whatever you think best. It really doesn't make any difference to me." Rather, Moses makes clear that there is a right choice—following God—as well as a wrong choice—following their own desires. With all his heart, Moses urges them to make the right choice—to choose life, to choose God—so that they and their descendants might live.

Biblical scholars suggest that the presentation of blessings and curses frequently occurred during a crisis or struggle within Israel. God asks his people to choose, to make a decision to accept or reject their identity as a covenant people. Scholars also suggest that the situation provoking this choice occurs at the time of a real or metaphorical crossing of a threshold. Moses addressed the Israelites as they stood on the banks of the Jordan, preparing to cross over into the Promised Land. Both literally and figuratively, the Israelites stood between their past and their future. It was time to choose.

Culmore Church, and congregations like it, have stood at the threshold between their past and their future. Our congregation easily could have chosen to stay with what we knew, with what was comfortable—and eventually died. But we did not. Instead, Culmore chose to trust God with the future. We chose to adapt ourselves in ministry. We chose to live.

The Valley of the Shadow of Death

The Lord took the prophet Ezekiel to a valley of dry and scattered bones. God asked Ezekiel, "Mortal, can these bones live?" He answered, "O Lord GOD, you know" (Ezek 37:3). Then God said to Ezekiel, "Prophesy to these bones, and say to them: O dry bones, hear the word of the LORD" (v. 4). And so Ezekiel prophesied to this valley of dry bones, and behold, there arose within the valley a vast multitude restored before his eyes. Then God said to Ezekiel, "Mortal, these bones are the whole house of Israel. They say, 'Our bones are dried up, and our hope is lost; we are cut off completely' " (v. 11).

In his book *Breaking the Patterns of Depression*, Michael Yapko argues that depression in individuals frequently comes from an inability to negotiate life's changes because these individuals may have never learned certain life skills that are necessary to manage the circumstances they currently face. What is more, these persons may not know they lack skills that could make their lives happier. As a result, they fall into self-defeating thoughts and behavior, only reinforcing the patterns of depression. Yapko's approach to depression focuses more on solutions than the problems that may have caused the depression. He argues that "you are not your depression."[2] One reason many people seek help, he says, is not so much to focus on the past, for that cannot be changed, but because they want to change their futures: "They want things to be different tomorrow, next week, next month, next year."[3] Although coming to terms with the past is important, people change their futures by learning new skills that help them manage the problems they face.

What Yapko's work teaches about breaking patterns of depression in individuals holds true for congregations. Is it not possible that declining churches are but fellowships of believers operating out of collective depression? Like Ezekiel's dry bones, they cry out, "Our bones are dried up, and our hope is lost; we are cut off completely." Facing changing circumstances both within the body and outside in their communities, these congregations lack the necessary skills or insights to successfully negotiate the problems they face. I believe that in choosing life, these congregations are saying they want to change their futures; they want things to be different "tomorrow, next week, next month, next year." They are saying they want to live, and they are willing to learn new ways of being God's people in ministry.

Is this not what justification and sanctification also signify in faith terms? We come to a crisis point in our lives when we must choose between our ways and God's ways. In choosing God's way of life and blessing, we also give ourselves over to the guidance of the Holy Spirit, who promises to restore within us the image of God, which has been previously corrupted by our sin. Justification may be a relatively brief experience in the life of a believer, but sanctification, the process of being perfected in God's image, may take a lifetime. And so it is with congregations. A congregation may choose to give itself over to God's purposes, but the process of learning holy and obedient living may take years.

Nick at Night

One of the many things I have learned over the past seven years is that change doesn't happen overnight. There are moments, however, when I forget this fact and I become impatient. One evening I met with our finance chair to plan our fall stewardship drive. I was bemoaning the fact that we should have been so much further along, financially and otherwise, than we were. He said that my expectations for congregational change were perhaps a bit premature. Instead of thinking in terms of five or seven years, he suggested that one must think in terms of a decade or more to effect lasting institutional change—if not longer!

One has only to turn to the paradigmatic passage on change in the Bible to see how this is true. John 3 tells us that in the middle of the night, under the cover of darkness so that no one will see him, a man by the name of Nicodemus pays a visit to Jesus. To his spiritual inquiry, Jesus tells him that those who would see the kingdom of God must be born anew. Nicodemus, of course, doesn't quite seem to get it.

What happens when conversion, spiritual change, is anything but dramatic or immediate? Does it mean that God isn't working in our lives, or that true renewal is not occurring? To all of us who are Nicodemuses at heart, Jesus says, "The wind blows where it chooses, and you hear the sound of it, but you do not know where it comes from or where it goes" (Jn 3:8), which was his way of saying that we do not have control over God's Spirit or our spiritual renewal. The Holy Spirit comes in God's own time, not ours. All that is needed is the openness and willingness to receive the gift when it comes. The last we hear from Nicodemus in this passage is yet another question: "How can these things be?" (Jn 3:9). Nicodemus still doesn't quite get it. And Jesus gently chides him, "Are you a teacher of Israel, and yet you do not understand these things?" (Jn 3:10). So might Jesus chide us: "Congregations, you instruct people on their relationship to God, and yet you do not believe that God can give you new life?"

And then with loving assurance, Jesus speaks to Nicodemus's heart some of the most hopeful words the world has ever heard: "For God so loved the world [indeed, the *whole* world] that he gave his only Son, so that everyone who believes in him may not perish but may have eternal life. Indeed, God did not send the Son into the world to condemn the world, but in order that the world might be saved through him" (Jn 3:16-17).

John does not report a dramatic conversion experience for Nicodemus. In fact, John doesn't report a specific conversion experience for Nicodemus at all. But the last time we hear of Nicodemus, in John 19, he joins Joseph of Arimathea in providing a burial site for Jesus' crucified body. One who had first come to Jesus under cover of night now comes in the brightness of day to honor the one who showed him the light.

Dr. Yapko says with regard to change: "Most often there are many small turning points in a person's life rather than one huge one."[4] The efficacy of rebirth cannot be judged in a short span of time; true change within the life of a congregation may not be measurable for years, or even until a generation has passed. This change does not come through one dramatic event, but through many small turnings that redirect the congregation's path.

The remainder of this chapter is dedicated to sharing those initial "small turning points" in our own congregation's life that enabled us to choose life. Although many, if not most, of these changes are less than complete (we still are very much a church "under construction"), I offer them as examples of the kinds of new skills and insights we had to learn in order to successfully and faithfully negotiate being God's people in ministry in a multicultural world.

Crossing the Jordan

Even with all the difficulties Culmore faced seven years ago, I wanted to serve as pastor. One of the reasons was that I had been told that of all the churches in the Virginia Conference (at that time), Culmore had the greatest chance of becoming a multicultural congregation—though it was by no means certain. Culmore had a history of at least twenty years of welcoming non-Anglos, especially international persons who came to live and work in the nation's capital.

One of the first non-Anglo families to arrive at Culmore and find a church home was a Cuban family. José and Concha were first-generation Cubans. José had fought with Castro in Batista's overthrow, but following the revolution, he broke with Castro, and secretly spirited his family to Miami. He arrived in Miami with little money or assets, but within a short time, he became an entrepreneur in computers and did very well for himself. He and Concha moved to Washington in the early 1970s and soon joined Culmore. They immersed themselves in the life of the congregation. José became the teacher of the main adult Sunday-school class. Concha worked with the women's mission group. One of her projects remains as a witness to the congregation each Sunday morning: the liturgical banners that now drape our walls on every side. One especially beautiful one incorporated an image of Culmore Church with a globe below it and strings reaching out to all nations. It reads at the top: "The World Is Our Parish." During their time at Culmore, though there was no specific congregational outreach to other nationalities, José and Concha began a Latin American fellowship. They helped the fellowship members with English, and also helped them find work, housing and so on. In addition, José and Concha held home Bible studies. Though it would be at least fifteen years before their outreach bore fruit in the congregation's overall ministry, they sowed the seed and taught the congregation the kinds of skills necessary to become an international fellowship.

An important pastoral presence during that time was Robert Casey. He arrived in the early seventies, as many of the internationals began to come to Culmore. Sam Itam, who still is a member of Culmore, remembers when he first arrived in northern Virginia from his home in Sierra Leone to begin working as an economist at the International Monetary Fund: "My wife and I moved within proximity to the church in 1976, and we soon began visiting Culmore. We were Methodists back home, and so it seemed fitting that we should visit the closest Methodist church. We were warmly greeted by Pastor Casey. After the first few weeks, he asked what the church might do to assist us. We told him that we were very interested in a Bible study, but something other than what was offered in Sunday school. So he arranged a special Bible study in the parsonage with some other members of the congregation. At that point there were only three or four non-Anglo families in the congregation, so most of those in the Bible study were Anglo. Since I did not drive until I came to the United States, I was afraid to drive at night. When I told Pastor Casey about this, he said that either he or another member of the church would pass by to pick us up. He showed a real concern for us, and also wanted to be sure that we were known by the others in the congregation. He would sit for hours and listen to us tell of life back home in Sierra Leone and Nigeria. His fascination with the world outside the U.S. led him to organize a congregational dinner in which he invited me and my wife to share our stories with others. He wanted the congregation to know of the world beyond its walls. His concern for us and his willingness to learn about who we were and where we came from was a strong motivation for why we joined Culmore and have stayed a part of this congregation."

Another important pastoral presence was Sam Espinoza, or "Brother Sam," as he came to be known at Culmore. Marie Williams, a long-time member of Culmore, says that with Sam, everybody was Brother or Sister "So-and-So." "He just made us feel like family," she says. Sam served the church during the early and mid-eighties. Sam is a first-generation Mexican who moved to the United States as a young adult and has served predominantly Anglo parishes in all his appointments. Sam's gift as a pastor was his strong commitment to evangelism. As a conservative evangelical, he could articulate a biblical rationale for why Culmore should reach out to its neighbors.

The 1980s was when immigration levels began to reach their highest levels ever. The Culmore community consists of many large apartment complexes. They were built in the late 1940s and early 1950s, when the postwar population boom of government workers necessitated housing near the city. In the 1980s these complexes became home to the large number of immigrants arriving in the metropolitan area. Because of the relatively low rent, these apartments soon became the first stop by first-generation immigrants on their way to the American dream. As these apartment dwellers became more ethnically diverse, Sam encouraged the congregation to evangelize the neighborhood. He encouraged Culmore to reach out to its neighbors and to begin to reflect the community surrounding it. Week after week, Sam organized visitation teams that went to the homes of those who visited the church on Sunday. Like Sam Itam, these new immigrants also came to Culmore not because it boasted a multiethnic ministry (it didn't have one at that time), but because of proximity. They could walk to church. Sam and his trained lay evangelists visited each home, prayed for the families, and invited them to church. If the family members had not accepted Christ, he encouraged them to do so.

Though different in approach, Sam Espinoza, like his predecessor Robert Casey, reached out in true concern and offered practical help to these new arrivals to America. Sam did not limit his visitation to church guests only. If he heard of new residents in the community or of a family of church members who had recently immigrated to the U.S., he visited them as well. By the time Sam left in 1987, roughly 30 to 40 percent of the congregation was non-Anglo. That was quite an accomplishment, because during his tenure there was no overt congregational conflict involving racial animosity.

When I arrived in the summer of 1991, however, Culmore was in a period of rapid decline. A few weeks before I was to arrive at Culmore, I had dinner with a long-time member, Les Gross, who was serving as a delegate to our annual conference. As we talked about the church and surveyed the seemingly overwhelming difficulties the congregation faced, I asked him what he thought was necessary for the church to recover. I vividly remember Les recalling the days he had spent with Brother Sam visiting from house to house. Les thought the church in recent years had lost its connection to the community, the connection that Sam had so strongly emphasized. Les felt that what was most important was that the church once again reach out in mission to its community, and that the congregation's composition should reflect the community around it. When I asked whether the congregation saw its ethnic diversity as a strength or a liability, he immediately responded that he believed it was Culmore's greatest strength. Les had joined Culmore when Robert Casey was pastor, and he had grown as a lay evangelist under Brother Sam. I was not entirely surprised, then, when I heard Les say, "We have to claim our identity as a diverse church. We *are* an international congregation. That's our future."

The first skill, or insight, that enabled Culmore to choose life was the ability to value its past without not being stuck in the past. Through the examples of pastors and lay leaders alike over the years, the congregation was able to catch glimpses of the future—and value it.

The Durable Saints
William Jennings Bryan III, better known as Bill Bryan,[5] was pastor of

Grace United Methodist Church when I visited him in east Dallas during my sabbatical in 1994. Grace had once been the church home to some of the most prominent Texans. There was a time in Grace's history when it would not have been unusual to see the governor, the mayor of Dallas, and many other Texas political or corporate leaders sitting in its pews. The neighborhood of east Dallas today is far different from its halcyon era. Bill showed me his parish, and we had lunch in a Cambodian restaurant (one of the many ethnic restaurants that occupy the shopping centers). As we drove around, I noticed that east Dallas looked a lot like Culmore's neighborhood, especially with its large population of Latinos and Asians.

Like Culmore, Grace Church had also faced a crisis, thirteen years before when Bill first arrived. And they, too, chose life. Today, Grace Church is a multicultural congregation, its gothic structure pulsing with the heart of mission. On Saturday mornings, the Agape Clinic, which is in the basement, opens its doors to the neighborhood. More than 5,000 people receive free medical treatment each year. In the church parlor, a Dallas judge, who is a member of the congregation, holds court, mediating justice for those who might otherwise find none. And an upstairs Sunday-school room, with its spiritual symmetry clearly evident, accommodates a Christian meditation center. Bill and I compared notes about our congregation's evolutions into multicultural churches, and one thing from that conversation especially has stayed with me. Bill was very clear that none of what the church is now doing would have been possible if the older adults of the congregation had not bought into the vision and committed themselves to it. They were not always comfortable with every development, and they did not completely value all the diversity in the congregation. Nonetheless they stayed, and they stayed not out of intransigence, but because they understood that the church needed to change and they wanted to be a part of that change. Bill called these folks the "durable saints" of Grace Church.

I suspect that each congregation that has chosen life as a multicultural church has its share of durable saints. Les Gross, who first claimed Culmore's identity as an international congregation, was certainly one of ours. As chair of our Administrative Council those first two years, Les worked hard to realize that vision. Carroll Hawkins, one of our retired ·members has since I arrived, spent thirty to forty hours a week volunteering around the church to fix broken light fixtures, wax the floors, repair broken windowpanes, and do other similar tasks. He doesn't do it because he has nothing better to do, but because he loves the church, and helping to maintain the facility is one concrete expression of that love. While Carroll looks after the building, Jim Yost dutifully cuts the grass week after week and takes care of the church grounds. Jim's wife, Jo, has worked behind the scenes with church dinners and new member receptions. The year I arrived, Jo organized a Thanksgiving dinner for all of our ESL students, feeding over 150 people. Then there is Burton French, who volunteers more than forty hours each week to keep the computer records and administrative files of the church complete. Wade and Adelle Gunn also work week after week, teaching Sunday school, organizing rides for people to get to doctors' appointments, and then leading a vespers service at a local nursing home. This list of our durable saints is far from complete, for I could name so many more.

Like Bill Bryan, I believe we could not have become the congregation we are now without the assent and cooperation of our congregation's older members. Of course, not all of our transitions have been free of discomfort, but these durable saints invested themselves not just in Culmore's past but in its future, and by their work they have helped make the change. These durable saints easily could have chosen to leave. Other churches nearby could have easily met their needs in a more homogeneous setting. Their calling, however, was to Culmore—not just as the church they had known but as a church being born anew. When Moses asked Israel to choose life, he also promised that their choice would bring blessing. For the durable saints of Culmore, one of the unexpected blessings has been in the younger, mostly immigrant adults who have come; how they have valued these older adults. Interacting with these youth from cultures in which older adults are revered and respected as elders, our older Anglos (whose children may live far away) are now finding a new sense of family in this congregation. What is more, instead of being displaced, they have found a new place of respect and honor.

Looking like Sunday Morning

Soon after I arrived in 1991, I met with Adelle Gunn, chair of the Staff-Parish Relations Committee. One of the concerns she expressed was the severe burnout the congregation was experiencing in its leadership. Because of its decline and membership loss, the church had compensated by asking a faithful few to take on more and more responsibility for making the church function. As a result, a few people in the congregation held a multitude of duties and titles. Something needed to change. "We need more people to take ownership and to help lead," said Adelle.

What was interesting about the leadership makeup of the congregation at the time was that even though the congregation was diverse ethnically, Anglos held all the key leadership posts. Though there was some ethnic diversity within the church committees, no chair of any committee was non-Anglo.

One of the positions that needed to be filled immediately was the chair of the Finance Committee. This vacancy was at a time of severe financial crisis in the church. We were running large monthly deficits, and no end was in sight. To make matters worse, the church boiler had broken down and needed to be replaced to the tune of twenty thousand dollars—a sum that we did not have, of course. I remember that on the second Sunday after I arrived, we held an Administrative Council meeting to discuss what had to be done. A cloud hung over the meeting as we considered the options. As the meeting was giving way to despair about whether we could raise the money, a man from the congregation stood up. His name was Jay Brown, a cheery Jamaican who just happened to work as an accountant. I soon discovered Jay's optimistic, can-do nature. He said, "Since I have been at Culmore, we have been able to do whatever we set our minds to. I believe that we should not get bogged down by this matter, but that we should approach it confidently. We simply need to let the congregation understand this need, and I am sure that they will come through." Needless to say, Jay was appointed to head up the fundraising efforts for the new boiler, and we did indeed raise the necessary money.

Once I saw Jay at work, I knew he was the person we needed to chair our Finance Committee. I spoke with Jay and asked him if he would be interested, and after some gentle arm-twisting, he agreed. I took his name to our committee on nominations, which was all Anglo, and they readily accepted Jay as finance chair. By the end of the year, there were no longer monthly deficits, and we found ourselves in a much healthier fiscal position.

A key factor in that first year of institutional change was the church's willingness to incorporate its non-Anglo members into key leadership positions. It was a practical necessity, of course, considering the high burnout rate, but this willingness also carried theological and ecclesiological integrity. After all, how could we really claim to be a multicultural congregation if all the power and decision-making belonged only to the Anglos of the congregation? Of all the changes that first year, this is the one that I believe had the most far-reaching impact on the spiritual health of the congregation. This decision said that we really were one congregation and that our leadership would come from all the membership, not just from a portion of it.

That fall our nominations committee adopted as operating policy several criteria for the selection of leadership. We said that leadership cannot be tokenism, but must be reflective of full partnership and trust. Without setting quotas per se, we committed ourselves to full inclusiveness within the total range of leadership positions. We also committed ourselves to promoting more young adults to key leadership positions. As in many churches and organizations, leadership at Culmore had been based more on longevity of membership and age. With the age of our immigrant membership far lower than the average age of our Anglo membership, however, we felt it was more important to incorporate younger adults right away than to make them wait to serve. We also reduced the number of positions and committees in order to streamline the decision-making process. We sought to find new ways of quickly assimilating new members and promoting them to leadership positions when deemed appropriate. More than anything else, we committed ourselves to a lay leadership that looked like Sunday-morning worship. We have followed these criteria every year, and they have led us to a truly inclusive leadership that is reflective of who the church really is.

Will There Be Others like Us?

One of the things I emphasized most my first year at Culmore was visitation. Though I did not incorporate lay members in the same way as Brother Sam, I committed myself to visit as many people in the congregation as possible, particularly the non-Anglo members. I also committed myself to visit as many first-time visitors in worship as possible. Though I felt that God had called me to Culmore for a reason, I also knew that only a small window of opportunity would determine whether the church would live or die. Attracting new members was a major concern. During the summer of 1991, worship attendance hovered around ninety to a hundred people. By the fall some members who had previously left returned, and we began to have new visitors as well. The average age of the worshiping congregation at that point was in the low sixties. Young Anglo adults were in short supply.

A young couple by the name of Mike and Diane Zevenbergen began visiting in the fall of 1991. After their third visit, I was able to make an appointment to visit them in their apartment. Mike was a recent graduate of Harvard Law School now working at the Department of Justice. Diane was a computer programmer. They were two very sharp and interesting people. I can remember how nervous I was visiting them. I wondered whether we had much to offer them as a church. We were still taking very small steps in our ministry at that point, still debating whether we had a future. As we talked about the church, I shared with them Culmore's history and the changes that were taking place. I asked them how they found us. It turns out that a pastor at a church just down the road had referred them to Culmore. That church was all Anglo and they told the pastor that they were seeking a church with more racial diversity. He told them that Culmore was the place to go, and so they did. They said that they enjoyed worship and the diversity of the membership. I asked them if they had any concerns or questions. Mike said that he did. Though the racial and cultural diversity was very important to him, he did wonder whether there would be others like themselves—other young adults who might share some of the same cultural, social or educational backgrounds. In other words, would they be the token young Anglo couple, or would there be others? I was not exactly prepared for that question. I thought for a minute and then, almost accidentally, I said, "There will be—if you come!"

Mike and Diane did join, and others also came. Mike and Diane quickly immersed themselves in the life of the church, teaching ESL classes, helping start a tutorial program and an immigration law clinic, serving on various committees. Mike and Diane easily could have gone to other churches, churches with numerous programs and ministries targeted especially to them. The reason they joined Culmore, however, was that they felt we needed them, that they could make a difference by joining.

As I have spoken to people who are considering joining the church, one of the determinative factors in their decision to join is that they feel they can make a difference. I believe our congregation has a special appeal—or calling, if you will—for individuals and families who want to belong to a congregation not simply because it meets their personal needs, but because the church needs them to make a difference.

At Culmore we have learned not to be shy in asking people to share themselves in ministry. This approach has a special appeal to the new immigrant who hears that this is a church where he or she is not only welcome, but wanted and needed. It also appeals to many of the young, Anglo professionals who are searching for authenticity in the church to which they belong. As a result, over the past seven years the average age of those attending worship has fallen by twenty years to the low 40s.

That's Not Very Christian

1991 marked the return not only of the young adults but of the lost sheep as well. As the church began to find renewal, many of those who had left earlier in the congregation's history began to return. One of these persons was Wayne Valis. Wayne grew up at Culmore. His mother was a charter member. They had lived just two streets from the church. Wayne still lives two streets from the church. But as Wayne became an adult, he, like so many, drifted away from Culmore and from going to church generally. Wayne became active politically and eventually served in the Nixon, Ford and Reagan administrations. Wayne currently works as a lobbyist in his own firm. Wayne began coming back to Culmore to worship on a periodic basis just after I arrived. The more I learned about Wayne, the more curious I became. Here was an influential, conservative Washington lobbyist, who had worked in three different Republican administrations, and where does he come to worship—Culmore! I have to admit that I just didn't get it. Why Culmore? There were so many other churches that, in my estimation, would have been a better fit. And yet here he was, sitting in a multicultural congregation, Sunday after Sunday, surrounded by recent immigrants. Culmore is by no means the prototypical congregation of the Washington elite. Finally as we got to know each other better, I decided to ask him why he came.

Wayne's initial response was like Sam Itam's: the church was in close proximity to his home and he felt welcome here. In addition, he had grown up in this church, and when he decided to go back to church it seemed appropriate that he should go back to Culmore. So he came back, and yes, the church was different—in fact, very different from the one he attended in the 1950s as a youth. Nonetheless, it was home. I decided to push a little more, so I asked what motivated him to come back to church after being away so many years. "Ah, that," he said, "is a whole other story. One day I went to the White House to work in a committee on a Republican response to a Democratic tax plan. The committee was chaired by Elizabeth Dole, a woman I admire and respect deeply. During the meeting I continually used words like *attack, demolish, pulverize* and *destroy* as ways we should respond to this tax plan. Finally, after I had become especially emphatic in my tone, Elizabeth turns to me and says, 'Wayne, that's not very Christian of you.' I was immediately taken aback. That single comment prompted me to reconsider what I was about spiritually. It caused me to ask myself what I was doing with my life and where I was headed. Elizabeth Dole had been a good friend before, but after that encounter I sought her out for spiritual guidance. Elizabeth is a deeply spiritual woman. She has since advised me in many ways. One of the things Elizabeth said that I should do is start attending church again, and so here I am."

Wayne, after a long period of spiritual seeking, committed his life to God on Christmas morning, 1996. Since then Wayne has chaired our Capital Funds Campaign and directed our Maundy Thursday dramas, among many other contributions.

One of the insights I gleaned from my experience with Wayne concerned my own bias in who I thought "fit" in a multicultural congregation and who might not. As Jesus said to Nicodemus: "The wind blows where it chooses" (Jn 3:8). God chooses who is and who is not called to be a part of each congregation. For that reason there can be no one correct profile of membership in a multicultural congregation. There will be no "Culmore Calvins" to join the "Saddleback Sams" or the "Willowbank Unchurched Harrys or Marys" of the church-growth methodology for profiling potential members. All that we can do is welcome each man and woman and help them follow God's calling in their lives.

Benoni's Friends

The story of the first Pentecost ends with the new converts devoting themselves to the apostles' teaching and sharing what they had in common. And to this Luke adds, "Day by day, as they spent much time together in the temple, . . . praising God and having the goodwill of all the people. And day by day the Lord added to their number those who were being saved" (Acts 2:46-47). Being a Pentecost people meant being alive in the

Lord and having something good to share!

My first Pentecost at Culmore just also happened to be Confirmation Sunday. Three of the youth to be confirmed and welcomed into full membership that day were from West African families, representing Ghana, Nigeria, and Sierra Leone. Just after worship the Sunday before, one of the parents had approached me. It was Benoni Johnson, whom I mentioned in chapter three. He had wanted to inform me that he was inviting a number of friends and family members to his daughter's confirmation. I responded, "Great, Ben. Invite as many people as you can."

As I looked out at the congregation on Pentecost Sunday, I thought we would have a good crowd, but certainly not an exceptional one. I wondered what had happened to Benoni's friends and family. After the service had started, visitors began to arrive, and more came throughout worship. As we did our greeting, visitors came in. As we took up the offering, more visitors came. As I finished my sermon, still more visitors entered the sanctuary. As we confirmed the youth, even more visitors arrived. As I pronounced the benediction, one or two more visitors walked in the door. By the end of worship, we had nearly three hundred people in the sanctuary, the highest attendance we have ever had. Of those present, nearly one-third were from Sierra Leone, Benoni's home country—and all because Benoni invited his friends.

One of the main ways we have grown as a congregation is by following Benoni's example. Because multicultural ministry is a relational ministry, personal invitation is one of the most effective ways to reach new people. And because of the familial nature of the immigrant community, those most likely to be reached have a great likelihood of being at least distantly related.

One specific trend within the immigrant community that may affect church growth is the nature of sponsorship under Immigration and Naturalization Service guidelines. Revisions in immigration law in the 1960s, which were more lenient in allowing persons to sponsor other family members, have resulted in growing populations in previously established immigrant communities. We have seen this situation reflected in our own congregation, particularly (but not exclusively) in the Filipino Fellowship. As members of Culmore sponsor families, it is probable that when they receive their visas they will join those who sponsored them. Of course that is not the only reason for newly arrived immigrants to join other family members. With much stronger extended family structures, family reunification might have been the result even without sponsorship. For evangelism in a multicultural church, it is important to use the already established familial and cultural networks to reach those who have no church home.

Thom Hopler put it this way:

Kinship is, in fact, one of the key funnels in the movement to the city. Most people do not go to a city in which they know no one and start looking for a house. Rather, they go to the city of a brother, a cousin or a distant uncle who can put them up for a while and help them find housing. . . . Every person is a doorway to a family, and every family is a gateway to a community.[6]

It has been said that "missions today should be defined in terms of people rather than geography."[7] Focusing on missions as something that happens outside and away from our local churches can create a problem. "The result of this neglect has been to create new groups of hidden peoples . . . immigrants . . . largely hidden from the ministry of the average church and the life and witness of most Christians. Sad to say . . . many peoples that were classified as 'reached in their homeland will become hidden after arriving in this country.'"[8]

Benoni's example taught us that missions means our doorstep; not only should the world be our parish, but the world should be *in* our parish. By personally inviting friends, family and new arrivals, many of whom were actively involved in church back home but have yet to find a church home here, we as a congregation have learned that evangelism means mission.

A Place to Call Home

Matthew 26 tells the story of the woman who anoints Jesus with expensive perfume, much to the chagrin of his disciples. They felt that she had foolishly wasted it, because she could have sold it and given the money to the poor. Jesus, however, admonished the twelve, saying that she had done "a beautiful thing." By anointing him with such a costly gift, she had, in fact, acknowledged the costly gift he was about to give to the whole world—his own life! Jesus told the disciples that wherever the good news is proclaimed, what she had done will be told "in memory of her" (Mt 26:13 NIV).

One Saturday morning I was at home when I heard a knock at the door. The woman standing at the door was relatively new to Culmore. I invited her in. As we sat in my office, she handed me an envelope and a small velvet box. I opened the envelope first and found a pledge card marked "a gift in kind." I opened the box and found within three small rings and two chains, all twenty-four-carat gold.

Seeing the surprise in my eyes, she began to explain. These pieces of jewelry were gifts to her on her wedding day and on the birth of her first child. They symbolized the two most precious moments of her life. She said that after much prayer, she felt called by God to give these gifts to Culmore as a thank offering for what God was doing in her life.

I responded by telling her that this jewelry was a beautiful gift, but I could not possibly accept it on behalf of the church. It was just too precious. Beyond monetary value, it symbolized the two most important things in her life—her relationship to her husband and her relationship to her firstborn. I told her I was not certain that God would want her to donate something so intimate to the Capital Funds Campaign.

Her response was swift and sure. She said, "Oh, but *I am certain* that God *does* want me to do this. Pastor Steve, I know this gift may make you feel uncomfortable, but this gift is about my relationship to God. God has given me so much, and I want to thank him. I especially want to thank God for Culmore. For the first time since arriving in this country, I finally feel at home. Culmore is responsible for this. I want to help this ministry grow so that others will also know the same kind of community that I have found here."

Like the woman who anointed Jesus, this woman also understood the meaning of God's giving and our response. God has given us eternal life and salvation through the most precious thing he had to offer—his own Son. In offering these rings and necklaces, this woman did "a beautiful thing"—offering the most precious things in her own life back to God.

This woman went on to say that she had been inspired to give this gift by a story she had heard about a pastor and a small group of laity who were given a vision by God of a church that they were called to build. They were few in number and without financial resources, so they drew upon the only thing available to them—prayer. Daily they gathered together and prayed that God would give them the strength and the resources to fulfill the vision. During one of their prayer meetings, they received another vision—this time of a vacant piece of land. They moved their daily prayer meeting to this vacant lot.

One day a beggar saw them praying out in the open in this lot. He went up to them and asked what they were doing. They shared the vision that God had given them of the church they were called to build. This beggar, who was not a Christian, gave them their first donation. He gave them the only things he had to give, the most precious things in his own life—the rice bowl and spoon he used each day to beg for food.

She went on to tell me that Yong-Ki Cho of Seoul, South Korea, now carries this bowl and spoon with him whenever he travels around the world to tell the story of how God used such "a beautiful thing" to begin his ministry. A church was indeed started. That congregation is now one of the largest in the world, with more than a half-million persons in worship each Sunday. She hoped we would use her gift similarly, to inspire others to fulfill God's calling for Culmore.

God uses "beautiful things." When we give to honor God, God uses those gifts to fulfill God's purpose for the world. This woman and others like her have taught us that we as a congregation must not only give ourselves away in ministry to others. Just as important, if not more so, we must be willing to graciously receive what our brothers and sisters in Christ from around the world have to offer us.

Ministry in any congregation, not just multicultural ones, must be a reciprocal movement. For ministry to have integrity, congregations cannot segregate people into givers and takers. Being a multicultural congregation means learning to receive the gifts, offerings, stories and talents that we may have not known we needed; by accepting these things, however, we may change the course of our life and ministry. Dr. Cho did not realize the importance of accepting that rice bowl or the impact it would have on his congregation. Who knows how God will use these rings and necklaces for Culmore's ministry, and how they will enable our congregation to be a home for other strangers in this strange land? But in whatever way God uses them, it is certain that when the good news is shared, "what she has done will be told in *remembrance of her.*"

The Church as *Avanzada*

The congregation of Grace Church in Dallas, mentioned earlier in this chapter, has an especially large segment that is composed of first-generation Christian Cambodians. When I asked the pastor, Bill Bryan, the reason for so many Cambodians in his congregation, he showed me a picture of his associate pastor, Pa Nous Pan, who is Cambodian. In this picture his associate is holding a picture of a Buddhist monk. When I asked Bill why, he answered that it was a picture of himself.

In Cambodia, Pa had been a Buddhist monk for many years. During the reign of terror of the Khmer Rouge, he escaped the killing fields, only to find himself confined to a refugee camp. There was so little food that most of the camp's population bordered on starvation. Most hoarded the small amounts of food they were given or else consumed it immediately. But one group of refugees shared their food with those whose physical condition was worse than their own. One day he went over to them and asked what motivated them to share their food when they themselves were malnourished. These refugees were Christians, and they told him of God's love through Jesus Christ, which motivated their sacrifice. He was so moved by their witness that he wanted to know more about their faith. Ultimately he professed faith in Jesus Christ and became a Christian.

After his arrival in the United States, he eventually became one of the first Cambodian pastors in the United Methodist Church. His work helped establish a growing, first-generation Christian Cambodian outreach, not as a separate church but as a part of Grace Church.

Bill marveled at opportunities this new ministry has presented him as a pastor and preacher. He said, "What I find so exciting is that when I tell the story of the prodigal son, many in my congregation may be hearing it for the first time! In other churches I served, everyone knew how the story ended, but not so at Grace. Many of the new Cambodian members are sitting on the edge of the pew. They want to know: does the son come back, and if he does, then what's the father's response? This first naiveté of reading of the Scriptures has helped me as a pastor hear and preach the gospel afresh."

Several years ago, when Lesslie Newbigin was at the Bangkok Conference on Salvation Today, he sat next to General Simatoupong, the general who commanded the military that forced the Dutch out of Indonesia. Newbigin said,

> We were discussing the global missionary situation, and Simatoupong had just made an intervention in the debate. As he returned to his seat beside me, I heard him say sotto voce, "Of course the number one question is: Can the West be converted?" I have often thought of that since. I am sure he was right. What we call the modern Western scientific worldview, the post-Enlightenment cultural world, is the most powerful and persuasive ideology in the world today . . . [yet the]

Christian gospel continues to find new victories among the non-Western, premodern cultures of the world, [while] in the face of this modern Western culture the Church is everywhere in retreat. Can there be a more challenging frontier for the Church than this?[9]

To be the church in a multicultural world means the church no longer views itself solely as a mission-sending entity. The church must also become a mission-receiving entity. One very significant change at Culmore is in the way it views itself as church. The days are long gone when we would have had a mental image of ourselves as the "church triumphant," loudly singing "a mighty fortress is our God." But then also gone are the days when we considered ourselves the "church tragic," mournfully singing, "Nobody knows the trouble I've seen." We are now the "church *avanzada*," confidently singing, "Here I am, Lord. . . . I will go, Lord, if you need me, for I hold your people in my heart."

In Latin America many downtown congregations begin mission churches in the poorer barrios. These mission churches are called *avanzadas*. The term is almost militaristic in nature, for it means an advance, a move forward, an attack. But the way it is used with regard to these missions congregations, it means to be out front, to be on the cutting edge. Avanzadas are missions churches that are out on the cutting edge of ministry.

Culmore is very much an avanzada, a mission church. We no longer just sponsor missionaries; we receive missionaries to advance the cause of Christ in our parish. One of the persons responsible for this reimaging of our ecclesiological identity, as well as being responsible for my being appointed as pastor to Culmore, was Bob McAden, superintendent of the Arlington District of the Virginia Conference. Bob had a vision for Culmore. Before becoming a superintendent, he had served as a missionary in Bolivia for eleven years, working with the Aymara Indians of that country. Bob is a lifetime missionary at heart. That means whatever he does, wherever he serves, he will approach his ministry with the passion and the perspective of a missionary. When he was appointed to the Arlington District, he noted the demographic changes that were rapidly changing the context for ministry in northern Virginia. Bob chose several churches in our district that he thought were in the right locations and were spiritually open to welcome their new neighbors and reach out in ministry to them. In short, he chose congregations to become avanzada churches. One of the churches he picked was Culmore.

Because of our proximity to a large Latin American community, in 1990, the year before I arrived, Bob appointed Juan Paredes, a retired Methodist pastor from Chile who had recently come to the United States with his children, to serve as a Spanish-language missionary in that community. Juan was given three tasks: to organize and start English classes for the adults in the neighborhood; to try to start a Bible study or small worship service to meet the spiritual needs of those who lived near Culmore and spoke only Spanish; and to reach out to the jails and hospitals nearby to minister to and translate for Hispanics.

The next thing Bob did was to meet with the Filipino members of Culmore, who made up the largest ethnic segment of the congregation at that time. Within this fellowship was a key family, meaning that of the Filipinos in the congregation, approximately two-thirds were related. A beloved uncle, Max Francisco, had recently arrived from Manila, where he had served thirty-five years as a church pastor in an independent evangelical congregation. Many of Culmore's Filipino members had previously been members of his church. He had come to America because he felt led by the Lord. Max was living with his family, waiting for the Lord to open the right door. Shortly before I arrived, Bob spoke with Max about the possibility of working to help organize the Filipinos in a language ministry, so that Culmore could reach the larger Filipino community in the metropolitan area.

When I arrived, Bob shared with me his vision for Culmore, and for the next year he coached me in the skills necessary to become a missionary pastor. Through his eyes and experience, he was able to shape my approach to Culmore as avanzada. He helped me grow a missionary's heart. He was also able to help both me and the congregation to avoid some of the pitfalls of conflict and crosscultural misunderstanding that might have occurred. Most important of all, Bob cultivated a vision for a collegial team approach to this multicultural ministry.

Though the church could not afford a staff-based ministry at that time, Bob helped find the funds to enable both Juan Paredes and Max Francisco to serve as part-time associate pastors of Culmore. One of the first things he encouraged me to do after they came aboard was to invite them to participate regularly in Sunday worship. Bob said that Culmore must come to see Juan and Max not just as pastors to Latin Americans and Filipinos but as pastors serving the whole congregation. Following this wise advice, I had them participate regularly.

A principle the church has adopted for our staff ministry is that we do not segregate or limit pastors or staff members to ministry within a particular ethnic or language ministry. It is both common and expected that all pastors and staff minister crossculturally in Culmore. While I have been writing this book, Max has graciously taken over congregational care visits, from ministering to bereaved families in the congregation to helping welcome newborns into the world. Seon-Young Kim, who is Korean, welcomes all first-time visitors to Culmore and leads those who are seeking a church home into membership. Ileana Rosas, our pastor for Latin American ministries, shares in pastoral counseling and crisis ministry. Won-Hee Kang, also Korean, leads a multiethnic choir each week and serves as program director for the Character Club, our after-school gang-prevention ministry, which primarily serves Latino children.

In his book *When Tolerance Is No Virtue*, S. D. Gaede writes:

It is terribly important that Christians today . . . develop a mental image of the church that corresponds to reality. When we think of the church we must conjure up a picture not of people like ourselves, but of people of all colors and shapes and ages, women and men speaking different tongues, following different customs, practicing different habits, but all worshiping the same Lord. Having such a concept is important because that is the church. It is important because that is the church that Jesus sees. And it's important because that is the church that Christ has called to represent his kingdom on earth. We do ourselves and Jesus a great disservice when we think otherwise. If our image of the church is wrong, we also set ourselves up for poor thinking about the issues of multiculturalism. For regardless of what we conclude about the pros and cons of that particular ideology, we ought to *feel* multicultural in our bones.[10]

The frontier of the West's conversion, I believe, is to be found in these multicultural avanzadas, such as Culmore, where missionaries from across the globe preach, teach and live the gospel of salvation. These are the places where the church is seeking a new image of what it means to be the church, an image that, as Gaede says, corresponds to reality. These are the places where the church is seeking to "feel multicultural in its bones." And when these churches feel multicultural in their bones, we know the answer to the question "Mortal, can these bones live?"

6
No Partiality

●●

PRINCIPLE: A multicultural church affirms cultural identity.

*Then Peter began to speak to them: "I truly understand that God shows no
partiality, but in every nation anyone who fears him and does what is right is
acceptable to him. You know the message he sent to the people of Israel, preaching
peace by Jesus Christ—he is Lord of all."* ACTS 10:34-36

What do you think of when you hear the word home? Do you think of a
country? a province? a state, city, town, neighborhood? Do you think of a
house? a church? family? When I think of home, I think of Kingsport,
Tennessee. I think of drinking the sweetest iced tea on the face of the earth,
an iced tea that only my Aunt Banty could make. I also think of sitting at
my parents' kitchen table, sipping strong, dark coffee and sopping up my
dad's homemade biscuits with gravy made from the remnants of fried
sausage. I think of the sweet smells of the lilac bush that my mother planted
in our back yard to remind her of her own home in southwest Virginia. I
think about Taft and Oleta Marshall, our next-door neighbors, who taught
me to love books and to enjoy working in the garden. These skills they
passed on have continued to remind me that happiness comes from
improving your mind and soul, but also from the world around you. And
when I think of home, I also recall the deep-green mountains that surround
our town in a warm embrace.

Home for me is certainly a sense of place, of belonging. Home is also
about community, about people to whom I'm related by blood or by heart.

But maybe more than any of this, home is who I am—it is my identity. Home is where I was born and given a name. Home is where I was first claimed by God and where I discovered that I belonged to an even larger family: the congregation of St. Matthew's United Methodist Church.

Home is where my roots are; it is my heritage, my cultural memory. Home reminds me that I am a Southerner, but even more important than that, I am an Appalachian. I belong to the mountains, because no matter how many years I wander in the concrete cities, I still long for their restful shade. When I think of home, I think of my mother constantly cautioning me to remember who I am and where I come from. The biggest sin you can commit in our family is the sin of pride, or as my mother would put it, "gettin' above your raising" or "too big for your britches."

But if home means only memory, only something in our past, then Thomas Wolfe is right: "You can't go home again." In the Gospel of John, chapter 14, Jesus is talking to his disciples, twelve men whom he asked to *leave* their homes and families. As he himself prepares to leave them, they are wondering what will become of them. What will they do? Where will they go? Where is home for them? Jesus then tells them: "In my Father's house there are many dwelling places. If it were not so, would I have told you that I go to prepare a place for you? . . . I will not leave you orphaned; I am coming to you" (vv. 2, 18). Then Jesus tells them: "Those who love me will keep my word, and my Father will love them, and we will come to them and make our home with them" (v. 23). Jesus promises not only to provide a home for them in the future but that God will come to them now and make God's home among them. They will not be alone. They will not forget to whom they belong.

I often think about the homes, families and cultures of my congregation. Our homes, our families, may look so different from each other's. Homes, families and cultures *are* peculiar things—they come in all shapes and sizes. Generic homes and one-size-fits-all cultures are nonexistent. They are all unique. To try to make homes all look alike would be to take away all that makes them what they are.

As Christians, we believe that water is thicker than blood; that our baptism, our connectedness in God, is far more important than the people to whom we are biologically related. Lesslie Newbigin puts it this way:

> The Christian community, the universal Church, embracing more and more fully all the cultural traditions of humankind, is called to be . . .

a particular community among human communities. It cannot pretend to be otherwise. But it has a universal mission, for it is the community chosen and sent by God for this purpose. This particularity, however scandalous it may seem to a certain kind of cosmopolitan mind, is inescapable.[1]

God values culture. As I argued in chapters two and three, the God revealed in Scripture *is* a God revealed in particularity, *but* for universal purposes. This scandal of particularity—that God chose one nation, Israel, to mediate and proclaim God's universal story to all nations—is also present in God's self-revelation through cultural specificity in the incarnation of Jesus Christ. When God revealed God's self to the world, it was in cultural and ethnic particularity—a first-century, Middle Eastern Jewish male. But God does not lift up just one culture as worthy of God's attention and grace; the scandal is that God says to each of us in our cultural particularity that God will be with us and for us. Who we are is God's gift to us, something of which we may be proud.

In fact, as the apostle Paul reveals in his first letter to the Corinthians, it is God who values our cultural and ethnic identity even more than the world itself does. Through the incarnation, life and death of Jesus Christ, God's purpose was to value and redeem each person and culture. Paul reminds the Corinthians that of those among them who had first received the good news of salvation in Jesus Christ, "not many . . . were wise by human standards, not many were powerful, not many were of noble birth. But God chose what is foolish in the world to shame the wise; God chose what is weak in the world to shame the strong; God chose what is low and despised in the world, things that are not, to reduce to nothing things that are" (1 Cor 1:26-28). In the face of the world's divisions, ethnocentrism, racism, classism and prejudice, Paul holds up Christ crucified as "the power of God and the wisdom of God" (1 Cor 1:24).

This chapter is about how the Bible affirms cultural heritage and identity, but it also explores some of the limits and the danger they pose in obedience to the gospel.

Our Father's House

Richard J. Mouw and Sander Griffioen in their book *Pluralisms and Horizons* write that "the Bible . . . takes cultural differences seriously without becoming fixated on those phenomena." For example, they point out "Paul is ready to become like a Jew to the Jews, but he does so to win the Jews (1 Cor 9:20), to bring them to the knowledge of the One in whom there is neither Jew nor Greek (Gal 3:28). Not that this 'incorporation would make Jews cease to be Jews. Rather, a new quality is introduced: henceforth one is a Jew within a body of which Greeks are also a part."[2] Christian identity, while transcending culture, will nonetheless incorporate and value human culture.

The Bible doesn't use the term *culture*, which is a relatively new term, as words go. But that does not mean the Bible has nothing to say about culture. In both the Old and New Testaments, the words that most specifically correspond to culture have their root etymologies in what we would call *home, house,* or *family*.

The Old Testament primarily uses four words, the first of those being *šēḇeṭ*, or *tribe*. The tribe was the basic organizational structure in Israel, deriving from the twelve tribes (sons) of Jacob. Within Israel the tribe was a subculture of one's identity. It denoted status, geography and history.

The second word used is *mišpāḥâh*, or *clan*. As scholars point out, the translation of this word into English is awkward, and frequently is rendered as *family*. Though it did denote a family relationship, a clan often was composed of groups of families and tended to reflect territorial identity.

The third word used is *bēṯ-'āḇ*, or *father's house*. This term denotes the most basic and intimate social structure within Israel, the immediate and extended family. Scholars say that this is the level "in which the individual Israelite felt the strongest sense of inclusion, identity, protection, and responsibility."[3]

The fourth word is significantly related to *bēṯ-'āḇ*; it is *bēṯ-'āh*. Much like the translation of *father's house,* this term speaks of Israel as the covenant people who reside in God's home.

In the New Testament, the two words used most often for what we might call culture are also closest in meaning to *bēṯ-'āḇ* and *bēṯ-'āh*. These words are *patria* and *oikos*. *Patria* reflects the more genealogical understanding of family, that is, one's lineage: who is related to whom, both biologically and spiritually. *Oikos* especially has much in common with the *bēṯ-'āḇ* connoting the intimacy of immediate or extended family and household. In Ephesians 2:19, Paul uses a form of this word when he describes the inclusion of non-Jews in God's loving purposes. He says: "So then you are no longer strangers and aliens, but you are citizens with the saints and also members of the *household* of God." Scholars say that it is not surprising that "early Christians also took over the metaphorical use of family as a picture of the whole Church. As Israel could be called *bȇt-Yahweh*, 'house/family of Yahweh, ... so the church ... could be called the *oikos* of God."[4] Thus our cultural identity as a covenant people is biblically communicated in terms of family, household and home.

What Is Culture?

Biblically speaking, we can affirm that God values our cultural identity and uniqueness. But if God values our human cultural identity, we are still left with a lack of clarity as to what is exactly meant by the word *culture*. Bernard Adeney has observed that "The word *culture*, like the word *religion*, is very difficult to define. In one sense every different person is from a different culture. We each have our own symbol system and ways of defining the meaning of our life."[5] A legitimate question to ask is whether all persons are multicultural persons, with many different symbol systems or cultural worldviews operative within each individual. That, however, may imply a more individualized and overtly subjective understanding of culture than is otherwise intended. To assist us in the quest for an adequate understanding of culture, let us turn to three different perspectives about what we mean by the term *culture*.

The first perspective I offer is that of Lesslie Newbigin. Newbigin suggests that "by the word *culture* we have to understand the sum total of ways of living developed by a group of human beings and handed on from generation to generation."[6] *Culture*, then, is an encompassing term concerned with the transmission of human knowledge, not just between individuals, but also between generations. Thus, argues Newbigin, "central to culture is language. The language of a people provides the means by which they express their way of perceiving things and of coping with them."[7] One cannot grasp culture without the means of the transmission of knowledge and perception: language. What kind of knowledge and perception needs to be conveyed, then, through the conduit of language from one generation to another? What is at the center of the transmission of culture? Newbigin says that "Around that one center one would have to group their visual and musical arts, their technologies, their law, and their social and political organization."[8] But cultural knowledge includes not only what we might label *immanent* knowledge; it is also concerned with knowledge of the transcendent: "any . . . set of beliefs, experiences, and practices that seek to grasp and express the ultimate nature of things, that which gives shape and meaning to life, that which claims final loyalty."[9]

A second attempt to define culture is represented by the work of the Willowbank Report of the Lausanne Committee. They defined culture as: "1) an integrated system of beliefs (about God, or reality, or ultimate meaning), 2) of values (about what is true, good, beautiful and normative), 3) of customs (how to behave, relate to others, talk, pray, dress, work, play, trade, farm, eat, etc.) and 4) of institutions which express these beliefs, values and customs (governments, laws, courts, temples or churches, family, school, hospitals, factories, shops, unions, clubs, etc.) which bind a society together and give it a sense of identity, dignity, and continuity."[10]

The Willowbank Report has several similarities with Newbigin's definition: the emphasis on transcendent beliefs and meaning; culture is an integrated (as opposed to a compartmentalized) experience that seeks to reflect the totality of our corporate knowledge and perception; culture reflects our learned behavior (customs), which helps us cope and behave correctly; and culture is represented most concretely in the form of human social and political organizations.

The last definition of culture I offer is presented by the work of Thom Hopler, which has commonalities with both Newbigin and the Willowbank Report. "First," says Hopler, "culture is *a mental road map*. It helps us get from morning to night without running into dead ends or roadblocks. . . . Our culture teaches us how to act in standard ways in normal situations. . . . Our culture has trained us. It has given us a series of shortcuts so we can function at a basic level every day."[11] Second, culture represents the *"sum total of our lived experience*. . . . You may not know how to play the violin, but it is part of your culture if you recognize and appreciate it when you hear it."[12] Third, "culture also provides us with *a system of values that directs our activities*. These are not absolute within each culture. Some people always insist on 'breaking the rules.' And cultures have slightly different values for different age groups, economic classes, localities or working groups."[13] And finally, "culture defines *the limits of possibility*. For many years the four-minute mile was a barrier that people said could not be broken. It was impossible."[14] That limit of possibility lasts, of course, only until it is broken.

What conclusions may be gleaned about culture from these three perspectives? I believe they suggest that (1) culture is collective and generational in nature; (2) culture expresses beliefs and practices determined to be of transcendent ultimate worth and concern; (3) culture teaches customs, traditions and values that shape our behavior toward what we have defined as having ultimate worth; (4) culture shapes collective behavior in how we organize ourselves to express our beliefs; and (5) culture constitutes a kind of knowledge about what is both known and knowable.

These definitions of culture tend to be value-neutral. But what happens when, biblically speaking, a given culture values the wrong things, gives us an incorrect "road map," organizes itself around the wrong concerns, shapes behavior that may only be described as sinful?

You see, I believe we would be naive, if not negligent, not to admit that we view our Christian identity through our own culturally biased worldviews. Culture and the incarnated church, the *oikos* of God, are in an inescapably symbiotic relationship. In fact, Newbigin says that "every statement of the gospel in words is conditioned by the culture of which those words are part, and every style of life that claims to embody the truth of the gospel is a culturally conditioned style of life. There can never be a culture-free gospel. Yet the gospel, which is from the beginning to the end embodied in culturally conditioned forms, calls into question all cultures, including the one in which it originally embodied."[15]

Get on the Bus: A Critique of Culture

Spike Lee has produced a film about the Million Man March called *Get on the Bus*. It follows a group of African-American men from very diverse backgrounds as they make an individual and collective pilgrimage of cultural introspection and affirmation to the 1995 march in Washington, D.C. The movie piqued my interest because a close friend of mine, Ted Smith, attended the march.

A few weeks before the march was held, Ted told me that he was planning to go. We got into a long conversation in which I voiced my concern about Louis Farrakhan's role and what that might mean for future race relations. I was confused. Why would Ted, a Christian pastor, a person who values inclusivity and whose own family is interracial, go to the

Million Man March? My concern was that the march excluded nonblacks and women and could (if successful) strengthen the once-marginal and antisemitic voice of Louis Farrakhan as a leader of the African-American community.

In response, Ted told me in no uncertain terms that he wasn't going because of Minister Farrakhan. In his opinion, the Million Man March was not about Farrakhan; it was about his identity as a black man. He wanted to join with other black men in celebrating who he was.

Ted, like so many others, came back from the march renewed and hopeful. Whether or not the march elevated Farrakhan to the mainstream is less important than the healing and pride that this gathering of black men represented.

As Lee's movie suggests, to discover pride in one's cultural heritage and identity is not to be equated with capitulating to groupthink. Each of the characters in his movie is different in personality and also has unique reasons for wanting to march. Although the movie does celebrate individual differences while in search of cultural identity, it should also be noted that the one character in the movie who is intentionally excluded is a black Republican. They literally stop and throw him off the bus because he doesn't fit in!

We would be less than honest if we did not acknowledge that in this age of increased emphasis on cultural and racial conformity to one's subculture, all of us feel some degree of pressure "to get on the bus." In other words, we feel pressure to conform in our own identity to the expectations of our ethnic and racial subculture. As noted in chapter one, this era, which Michael Lind calls "Multicultural America," places great value on the ideal of authenticity with regard to one's identity. What this authenticity may mean in actuality, however, is abject conformity. Now, instead of integrating the bus so that everyone can ride, we are calling each other to be sure we get on the *right* bus—the Euro-American bus, the African-American bus, the Latino-American bus or the Asian-American bus, for example—but get on the bus we must!

Newbigin uses a similar kind of bus metaphor to talk about culture, conformity and self-awareness. Newbigin argues that "trying to criticize one's own culture is like trying to push a bus while you're sitting in it."[16] He says, "The question of the relation between the gospel and the different human cultures is a very lively one in contemporary missiology."[17] At one end are those who say that "God accepts culture," who tend to "absolutize culture and to minimize the cultural changes which conversion ought to imply. People who accept the gospel, they affirm, ought to retain their traditional culture," but clearly, says Newbigin, they "are thinking here of such aspects of culture as music, art, dress, habits of eating and drinking, and—of course—language. They would not, certainly, agree that the gospel leaves unchallenged such elements of culture as cannibalism, the death penalty for petty offenses, or the ancient Indian custom of *sati*—the burning of a man's widow with his body on the funeral pyre."[18]

Newbigin says that no one is willing "to accept a total relativism about culture. All of us judge some elements of culture to be good and some bad."[19] In fact, Newbigin says, "We are to cherish human culture as an area in which we live under God's grace and are given daily new tokens of that grace. But we are called also to remember that we are part of that whole seamless texture of human culture which was shown on the day we call Good Friday to be in murderous rebellion against the grace of God. We have to say *both* 'God accepts human culture' *and also* 'God judges human culture.' "[20]

In a similar vein, Arthur Schlesinger writes in his critique of Afrocentricism: "All major races, cultures, nations have committed crimes, atrocities, horrors at one time or another. Every civilization has skeletons in its closet. Honest history calls for the unexpurgated record. How much would a full account of African despotism, massacre, and slavery increase the self-esteem of black students? Yet what kind of history do you have if you leave out all the bad things?"[21]

As long as we only get on our own cultural bus, focusing on our own particular identity, not only will we isolate ourselves from others who are different from us, but we also may forgo the invaluable crosscultural interaction that would enable us to view ourselves, our cultures and our worldviews in more critical and truthful ways.

As Bernard Adeney has said: "Christians believe that what is good is determined by the will of God, not by culture. [Our goal] is not cultural conformity but transformation into the likeness of Christ. All Christians in every culture are invited to have the mind of Christ, to humble themselves and be servants to others."[22]

Crosscultural interaction is not only the good, tolerant and open-minded thing to do as Christians, but it is also the means by which we may discover our full identity as the children of God. As the apostle Paul puts it: "For now we see in a mirror, dimly, but then we will see face to face. Now I know only in part; then I will know fully, even as I have been fully known" (1 Cor 13:12).

Money, Water and War

When I think of the crosscultural nature of multicultural ministry, I think of the friendship shared by Charlie Day and Isaac Tuazon. Isaac is a thirty-something Filipino who works as a certified public accountant. Given his occupation, it was not surprising that soon after arriving at Culmore he found himself in the position of church treasurer! Isaac represents the phenomenon of extended family migration and family reunification. Isaac's wife, Winnie, had relatives who were already members of our congregation. When they moved from the Philippines, it was only natural for them to join Winnie's family in northern Virginia.

When Isaac was asked to take on the job of church treasurer, he was still in his first year in America. Isaac was adjusting to many things. Because the workload of church treasurer proved to be more than he initially bargained for, he requested an assistant to help him. Specifically, he asked for Charlie.

Charlie was a seventy-six-year-old Anglo who had attended Culmore off and on for more than forty years but had never joined. His wife, however, had been a member since the mid-1950s. They had raised their children at Culmore. Though Charlie had fond childhood memories of going to church with his father each Sunday, he never felt strongly about the matter as an adult. Charlie characterized himself as a seeker. He knew there was a God, but he still wasn't quite sure about this thing called church.

Charlie agreed to become assistant treasurer for Isaac, in part because he felt he could share some of his own bookkeeping knowledge with Isaac. Isaac had a young family and a full-time job, and he had taken on the church finances, which were precarious at best. Charlie knew Isaac needed all the help he could get. The other reason Charlie wanted to help Isaac was that Isaac was Filipino. Charlie had served in the Philippines during the brutal fighting there in World War II, and he still carried physical and spiritual scars from the war. This shared connection of the Philippines provided Isaac and Charlie with common ground in which they cultivated the fruit of friendship.

One day Charlie came to me and said he was ready to join the church. When I asked what had happened to change his mind about making such a serious spiritual commitment, Charlie told me that Isaac had begun to share his faith with him. As a result, Charlie began to find spiritual healing and growth, eventually coming to the point of wanting to give his life to Christ.

Charlie had one reservation, however: at seventy-six, he was embarrassed about being baptized in front of the congregation. He was more than willing to stand before the congregation and profess his faith and take the vows of membership. But something in the act of baptism itself was so intimate for Charlie that he could not bring himself to do it in public.

Charlie and I struck a deal. He would take the vows of profession of faith in Sunday worship before the congregation, but he would be baptized in the chapel in a private ceremony. I asked Charlie if he wanted to invite anyone to his baptism besides his wife, Margaret. He said that he wanted Isaac and Winnie. Charlie said that he would not have committed his life to Christ if not for Isaacs friendship. So fifty years after Charlie had risked his life fighting for the freedom of the country where Isaac would be born, Isaac stood beside his friend and colleague as Charlie entered the baptismal waters of new life.

How Beautiful Are the Feet

To become aware of one's cultural roots, heritage and identity is only half the journey we must make. As Newbigin says: "The fulfillment of the mission of the Church thus requires that the Church itself be changed and learn new things. Very clearly the Church had to learn something new as a result of the conversion of Cornelius and his household. . . . So the Church is moved one step on the road toward becoming a home for people of all nations and a sign of the unity of all."[23]

In Acts 10 we hear the story of two very different people, not unlike Charlie and Isaac; one is a long-time believer, and the other is a seeker, who admires God from afar. This is the story of Peter and Cornelius, two people who were changed by God through their crosscultural encounter with one another.

Cornelius was a Roman and a Gentile. From Luke's description we can infer that he was a person of education, position and wealth. He was a centurion, thereby representative of those who executed Jesus. Yet Scripture says that "he was a devout man who feared God with all his household; he gave alms generously to the people and prayed constantly to God" (Acts 10:2). The other person in Acts 10 is Peter, an uneducated, Jewish fisherman from a small village next to the Sea of Galilee. Whereas Cornelius is portrayed as devoted to his family, Peter abandoned his family to follow Jesus. Peter was impulsive and brash, yet he is the one to whom Jesus said: "You are Peter, and on this rock I will build my church, and the gates of Hades will not prevail against it" (Mt 16:18). Peter did not behave much like a rock most of the time. Jesus chose people who were not perfect, but who could be changed by God's unconditional love.

These two unlikely people, Cornelius and Peter, are brought together by visions they received from God while in prayer. Cornelius's vision was of an angel of God, who told him that his prayers were pleasing to God and that he should send representatives to a man called Peter, who was staying in the city of Joppa. In Peter's vision, a sheet seemed to be lowered from heaven and on it were all kinds of animals. Three times Peter was invited to kill and eat one of the animals because he was hungry, yet he refused because they were considered ritually unclean. For Peter being a Christian also meant being a good Jew and observing all the laws, including the dietary ones. These laws were a tangible sign of his fidelity to God. In his commentary on this passage, Will Willimon says: "Only these laws stood in the way of the assimilation. . . . They identified, demarcated faithfulness in the midst of incredible pressure to forsake the faith, drop one's particularities and become a good citizen of the Empire. . . . The dietary laws are not a matter of etiquette or peculiar culinary habits. They are a matter of survival and identity for Jews."[24]

Even so, a voice spoke to Peter from heaven, admonishing him by saying, "What God has made clean, you must not call profane" (Acts 10:15). When this vision is over, Cornelius's representatives arrive and tell Peter of all that that has happened to Cornelius, including his vision. Peter immediately realizes that this vision must be God's invitation to carry the gospel to the Gentiles, so he goes with them.

When Peter and Cornelius finally meet, the powerful army officer Cornelius falls on his knees, clutching Peter. Peter asks him to stand. They meet eye to eye, face to face. Peter asks Cornelius why he sent for him. After recounting how God revealed God's self to him, Cornelius tells Peter that God has brought him to this house to share the gospel with him and his household.

Then Peter makes a humble acknowledgment: "I truly understand that God shows no partiality, but in every nation anyone who fears him and does what is right is acceptable to him" (Acts 10:34-35). For one whose faith was based on partiality, it is an incredible reversal to admit that "God . . . does not play favorites."[25] Although Peter was always open to the possibility of Gentiles becoming Christians, he always assumed that they would have to become good Jews first; that is, they would have to be circumcised, obey the dietary laws, and so on. In other words, the Gentiles would become like him. Yet here he is, face to face with Cornelius, a Gentile who loves God, who prays faithfully, gives alms to the poor, and now is ready to give his life to Christ. It becomes clear to Peter that God has something in mind for Cornelius other than becoming a good Jewish Christian: "I truly understand that God shows no partiality." Peter then says, "Can anyone withhold the water for baptizing these people?" (v. 47). Scripture tells us that Cornelius and his whole household received the Holy Spirit and were baptized in the name of Jesus Christ. In so doing Peter acknowledges that the love of God knows no bounds—that Jesus was not sent to be the Savior of any one denomination, or culture, or nation or race. Jesus Christ is Lord of all!

Willimon asks: "Is this a story about the conversion of a Gentile or the conversion of an apostle?" His answer, of course, is both—"Both Peter and Cornelius needed changing if God's mission is to go forward."[26] The Peters and the Corneliuses of today still need each other; we still need to be changed by God through our encounters with one another. Lest we be tempted to reduce this story to a morality tale of liberal open-mindedness, Willimon reminds us that the true hero of this tale of crosscultural conversion is neither Peter nor Cornelius; rather, "the real hero of the story . . . [is] the gracious and prodding One who makes bold promises and keeps them, who finds a way even in the midst of human distinctions and partiality between persons."[27]

Notice how God moved in this story. It is true that God prepared both Peter and Cornelius for their encounter through the work of the Holy Spirit in the dream-visions, but God also worked through the persons involved, in all their cultural particularity. God's mission to the world included the Gentiles only because Peter was willing to obey God, defying his own cultural understanding of what was possible, and proclaim the gospel to Cornelius and his family. Newbigin says that despite Cornelius's spiritual receptivity mentioned in Scripture, it would be "a complete misreading of the story to conclude from it that the going of the missionary is unnecessary. On the contrary, if Peter had not gone to Cornelius's house there would have been no conversion and no story. God prepared the heart of Cornelius before Peter came. But God also sent Peter, and Peter had to go and tell the story of Jesus. It was the telling of the story that provided the occasion for the radically new experience which made Cornelius a Christian, and which radically changed the Church's own understanding of its gospel."[28]

As the Scriptures say: "But how are they to call on one in whom they have not believed? And how are they to believe in one of whom they have never heard? And how are they to hear without someone to proclaim him? And how are they to proclaim him unless they are sent? As it is written, 'How beautiful are the feet of those who bring good news!' " (Rom 10:14-15).

Who Is Greater Than God!

Another of our members who taught our congregation a great deal about crosscultural witness—about being Christian and about being Nigerian, about living and about dying, was Onyekachi Itam. Onye (pronounced Oh-knee) was born in Port Harcourt, Nigeria. She was one of seven children born to Chief Henry and Mrs. Mary Offonry. Her family was of the Ibo tribe, and her father served as one of the "chiefs of the kingmakers" in Nkpa, of the Abia State of Nigeria. Her father had also served as an advisor and commissioner to the government following the Nigerian Civil War, helping in the formation of a constitutional government.

When Onye was a teenager, she went to London to finish secondary school. Following her graduation, she attended Queen Mary College at the University of London, where she studied for the Bachelor of Laws. Here, she met and fell in love with a budding economist from Sierra Leone, Sam Itam. After their marriage Onye joined Sam, who had already moved to the United States. In Sam's own words: "She became a part of him, and he a part of her." Together they shared this life of love and friendship with their two children, Paul and Uchenna.

Onye completed her law degree here in the U.S. After graduation from law school, she worked at Legal Aid, where for several years she represented and interceded for the poor. As an attorney, Onye took very seriously her role as an advocate for those who could not stand up for themselves. Her compassion for people motivated her to make the law work in favor of her clients. She also used her skills as a lawyer in Culmore's ministry, frequently providing guidance and counsel for those in need of help. Her sense of justice and concern for the poor sowed seeds in this congregation that are now bearing fruit in new outreach programs, such as the immigration law clinic and the health-care ministry. These ministries would not have been established without her vision and dedication.

In 1989 Onye began her battle with breast cancer. Through it all Onye refused to yield to her disease. Though often in incredible pain, she went to extraordinary measures to fight it. Throughout her treatment, even as she received reports that were not encouraging, she refused to concede to anger or bitterness. Rather, she chose to see God's presence in her life, not in spite of her illness but by using her disease to bring healing to others. She became a living example of what the apostle Paul meant when he wrote: "So we do not lose heart. Even though our outer nature is wasting away, our inner nature is being renewed day by day. For this slight momentary affliction is preparing us for an eternal weight of glory beyond all measure, because we look not at what can be seen but at what cannot be seen; for what can be seen is temporary, but what cannot be seen is eternal" (2 Cor 4:16-18).

Onye was a woman of deep faith. She was baptized as a Christian in the Nigerian Methodist Church, in which her father served as a lay preacher. From the very beginning of her life, faith in Jesus Christ formed the core of her identity. Her sister, Chioma, remembers how as a teenager in the youth fellowship Onye loved to participate in the singing, clapping and drumming of worship. As youth, they would go into nearby villages and preach the gospel in Ibo. Onye continued to preach the gospel, with her life itself becoming the sermon.

My fondest memories of Onye will be of the Friday-night praise services she attended, lifting us up with her testimony of God's goodness in her life. She would come worn down by radiation treatments but lifted up with the Holy Spirit. During testimony time, she would share bits and pieces of her life and culture and the tapestry of God's grace that she saw being woven with each day. One night Onye brought a tape of Christian tribal music sung in Ibo. As the music played, Onye swayed, translating these praises to God into English.

The night I will never forget was when she shared the meaning of her name. She told us: "Most of you know me as Onye, but that is only part of my name. My full name is Onyekachi. My father gave me that name when I was born, and it is a name with a meaning. In Ibo my name means 'Who Is Greater Than God.' Now my father did not intend my name to be a question but an affirmation, an exclamation point. My name is to be a conviction of faith, that there is no one 'who is greater than God!'"

Onye's struggle with disease, and ultimately death, was marked by this conviction of faith. The testament of family, friends and coworkers who gathered around her was that Onye's life meant courage. Onyekachi lived out in her faith the name she had been given.

Onye's favorite biblical passage was in John 14, where Jesus says to his anxious disciples concerning his departure: "Do not let your hearts be troubled. Believe in God, believe also in me. In my Father's house there are many dwelling places. If it were not so, would I have told you that I go to prepare a place for you? And if I go and prepare a place for you, I will come again and will take you to myself, so that where I am, there you may be also" (Jn 14:1-3).

God values human culture. God values our identity, our ethnicity, our heritage. Yet those things cannot wholly define us, nor can they save us. Rather, God invites us into his house, his home—*bêt-Yahweh*, the *oikos* of God. As Onye taught us at Culmore, although our culture may tell us where we've come from, our identity in the family of God tells us where we are going, where we belong: "You are a chosen race, a royal priesthood, a holy nation, God's own people, in order that you may proclaim the mighty acts of him who called you out of darkness into his marvelous light" (1 Pet 2:9).

7
The Alien Among You

••

PRINCIPLE: A multicultural church is a contrast community.

When an alien resides with you in your land, you shall not oppress the alien. The alien who resides with you shall be to you as the citizen among you; you shall love the alien as yourself, for you were aliens in the land of Egypt: I am the LORD your God. LEVITICUS 19:33-34

When we hear the word stranger, *most of us do not usually think of ourselves* as being one of them. Strangers are those people who are unfamiliar to us, persons whom we have not previously met. Whether we are aware of it or not, however, others frequently considered us the strangers. In his book *The Company of Strangers,* Parker Palmer writes:

> The stranger is . . . a central figure in biblical stories of faith, and for good reason. The religious quest, the spiritual pilgrimage, is always taking us into new lands where we are strange to others and they are strange to us. Faith is a venture into the unknown, into the realms of mystery, away from the safe and comfortable and secure. When we remain in the security of familiar surroundings, we have no need of faith. The very idea of faith suggests a movement away from our earthly securities into the distant, the unsettling, the strange.[1]

The biblical story of Ruth and Naomi is a story of two women who risked themselves in faith by becoming the strangers. The story begins with a famine in Israel forcing Naomi, her husband and two sons to journey from their home in Bethlehem, seeking refuge in the land of Moab. While there,

Naomi's husband dies, and her two sons marry Moabite women. Soon the sons also die, leaving Naomi dependent on her daughters-in-law. Because Naomi is both a foreigner and a widow with no male family to support her, she prepares to return to Bethlehem. When she tells her daughters-in-law to return to their own families, Ruth confesses her love for this Jewish woman and pledges to go with her, thus herself becoming a stranger in a strange land:

> Do not press me to leave you
>> or to turn back from following you!
> Where you go, I will go;
>> where you lodge, I will lodge;
> your people shall be my people,
>> and your God my God. (Ruth 1:16)

Ruth's declaration to Naomi is all the more amazing when we realize that nothing legally bound these two women. Ruth had been freed from any obligation to her mother-in-law. The pledge she makes is freely chosen. This covenant is her duty in the sense that it arises out of love. In his book *Clergy and Laity Burnout*, Will Willimon has written:

> Duty has become a dirty little word in modern parlance. *Duty* has a gray, dogged, ugly sound, cousin to similarly uninspiring words, such as *dullness, drudgery, discipline,* and *determination.* . . . *Duty* connotes blind obedience, mindless reaction, . . . behavior that is little more than habit rather than heroic choice or decision.[2]

But as Willimon goes on to say, duty in its best sense *is* heroic choice. To do one's duty is not to do something because you *have* to do it. Rather, to do one's duty means to choose to do something because you are free to do it. Duty arises out of grace, not out of law. Willimon puts it this way: "Duty *is a response,* not to whom we are or to whom most people ought to be but to whom the Master is. Duty arises not from self-interest or even from the kind of concern for the self-interests of others, but rather out of a relationship between servant and Master."[3] Put differently, we love others because God has loved us—we commit ourselves to others because God has committed God's self to us.

Ruth did her duty in committing herself to Naomi. She did so, however, not because she was legally or morally obligated to her, but because she was responding to the image of God she witnessed in Naomi's life. Ruth saw something in Naomi that changed her life—she saw an incarnation of

God's grace. Ruth's declaration is not merely an act of friendship with another woman; it is the proclamation of her conversion: "Your people shall be my people, and *your God, my God.*"

By embracing and being embraced by the stranger, we begin to see the presence of God who is wholly other in new and empowering ways. Palmer writes:

> The role of the stranger in our lives is vital in the context of Christian faith, for the God of faith is one who continually speaks truth afresh, who continually makes all things new. God persistently challenges conventional truth and regularly upsets the world's way of looking at things. It is no accident that this God is so often represented by the stranger, for the truth that God speaks in our lives is very strange indeed. Where the world sees impossibility, God sees potential.[4]

This is particularly true with Ruth.

The book of Ruth was written during the time of Nehemiah, which was a period of religious and national intolerance. This book carried a protest message: God's grace transcends and defies racial, religious and national exclusiveness. It serves to remind the people of Israel that if Ruth had been rejected because she was a Moabite, then there would have been no David or Solomon, for their lineage was traced directly to Ruth. In the book of Ruth, the foreigner, the stranger, is embraced and honored as an instrument of God's mercy.

Like the period in which the book of Ruth was written, the current time is marked by national intolerance toward the stranger and sojourner in the land. Both the passage of Proposition 187 in California and the work of the 104th Congress mark some of the most restrictive and punitive legislation in recent memory concerning immigrants.[5] Both legal and illegal aliens have been given an unambiguous message: "You are not welcome here, and if you choose to stay, we will make life as difficult and miserable for you as possible."

Am I overstating the case? Consider that the United States, whose current economic fortunes are in part dependent on the cheap labor provided by the immigrant population, now says to this same community that they are the reason for our national decline. It is scapegoating, pure and simple. Consider the practical consequences of the recent laws. Legal immigrants who have played by the rules but have fallen on hard times will no longer qualify for means-tested assistance, such as Medicare or

Medicaid, food stamps or Aid to Families with Dependent Children—*solely* because they are immigrants. Consider that in this country, where national political rhetoric has echoed the need for "family values," immigrant families are now targeted for separation under new deportation regulations—*solely* because they are immigrants.

Under the old laws, family unity was a high priority. Now, if immigrant parents are undocumented but their children are citizens by birth, the families face making the decision to (1) separate, leaving the children in the hands of friends or family so that they can have the benefits of living in the United States while the parents return to their home country, or (2) remain together but take their English-speaking, Americanized children who are U.S. citizens to their home countries, where, in many cases, few opportunities are available. Prior to the new regulations, illegal parents of children who are citizens had avenues available to them so that they could become legal. These avenues now are so severely restricted that many of these parents will be forced to make drastic decisions regarding the welfare of their children. Some parents now are even moving their children from one school to another frequently in hopes of protecting the parents' anonymity as undocumented.

Consider the plight of the undocumented worker, who is expected under the law to pay all U.S. taxes if he or she works yet is prevented from legally working under those same laws. The government is more than willing to receive tax revenue from undocumented workers, but compliance exposes the workers to the risk of deportation; in addition, they are unable to receive benefits from the taxes they pay. If they do not pay the taxes, they are criminalized further.

As of September 1997, undocumented immigrants who unlawfully remain in this country for more than 180 days are barred from returning to the United States for at least three years. If they are unlawfully present for more than a year, they are barred for ten years. Many Americans will say, "Good, that's what we should have been doing all along." The practical implication of the new laws, however, is that people have few avenues even to apply for green-card status. These laws are so onerous that they actually encourage people to disobey them.

What most people do not consider is that most of the people whom we are so willing to deport also support a large segment of our economy. A lawyer friend of mine put it this way:

Imagine that the INS could actually hire enough new employees to deport everyone who is in the United States illegally. This is, of course, a never-never-land scenario, but imagine that it happens. All of sudden, two or three million people who have been living in this country for a long period of time, who are paying mortgages, car loans, hospital bills—in the blink of an eye, they are all gone! What do you think will happen to the banks, the savings and loans, all the U.S. businesses that rely on them and the money they spend? Imagine the broken leases, the defaulted loans, the closed businesses, the abandoned properties which would result from the implementation of these laws. And furthermore, imagine all the families thrown into chaos because of the departure of nannies and domestics!

More than 800,000 documented foreigners are immigrating to the United States each year, and an additional 300,000 undocumented persons are immigrating or overstaying their visas. Such large numbers do promote anxiety and hostility in this country of immigrants. Historically speaking, every period of large immigration in America has been followed by anti-immigrant sentiment and restrictive legislation. With the last fifteen years constituting the largest foreign-born migration in the history of the United States, it should not be surprising that we now find ourselves in a period marked by xenophobia and nativism.

The question for the church is not whether a nation (any nation, for that matter, not just the United States) has a legal or moral right to protect its borders or to determine whom it wants or does not want to let in. Though that is an important question, it is not the question for the church. With more than four million undocumented aliens already residing in the United States and, despite legislation, more arriving each day, the real question for the church is, How shall we, as God's people, treat the foreigner, the alien, in this land? Under the new guidelines for immigration, it is more difficult than ever for churches to be advocates for undocumented persons to do the "right" thing legally, without putting the persons we minister to at risk of deportation.

In an article about immigrants in *Christianity Today,* Joe Maxwell reports,

A recent bout of raids on "illegal immigrants" had one Hispanic pastor's church members frustrated and worried. As the Latino believers—some in the United States illegally, most legally, yet all in search of a better life—gathered for a service, their pastor spoke reassuringly. . . . He said, paraphrasing the words of the biblical refugee Jacob, "This is not the office of immigration. It is the house of God and the door of heaven!"[6] If a church is in ministry with the undocumented, it is increasingly forced to choose between following the letter of the law and actively encouraging persons not to reveal their status and to remain here in a hidden capacity. Why not simply encourage them to go home? some ask. For many, political or economic factors eliminate going home as a viable alternative. Options for what was once the middle way—encouraging the undocumented to become documented—have all but disappeared. What is our Christian duty in this case? How should we respond?

When the Wedding Bells Refuse to Ring

One of the first times I became aware of the complicated nature of being pastor to undocumented immigrants in my community occurred when a couple who belonged to the church fell in love and asked me to marry them. I was especially honored to perform this wedding because of my relationship with the bride and groom. The woman I had met the first Sunday after I arrived at Culmore. She had been brought to the United States by an affluent Latin American family to serve as nanny to their children. Coming to the United States was a blessing for this woman at the time. Her home country was torn by civil war. Her father and her brother were both killed in the fighting.

The family that brought her to the United States did so on a false visa, a fact that, under INS regulations, would automatically exclude this woman from *ever* receiving legitimate documentation. Under the new regulations, as of April 1, 1997, if you enter without inspection, within the first two years you can be removed without a legal hearing. After two years you have a right to a hearing, but you are considered "not admitted," that is, a person not legally in the United States with due process. It is as though you had never entered the country at all. Under the old laws, it was actually better for an undocumented person to walk across the Texas border and be here illegally than to enter under false documentation. The person who walked across the border at least had the hope of one day getting a green card, whereas the person who flew into JFK Airport on a false visa did not. The only exceptions to this rule are if you are a son, daughter or spouse of a U.S. citizen or permanent resident, or in certain circumstances if you are seeking political asylum. Also, you must prove that your parent or spouse would suffer extreme hardship if you were denied a visa. Only then may you apply for a waiver of fraud or the misrepresentation ground of exclusion. This does not necessarily guarantee a visa, but it at least allows for the possibility.

This woman, because she had followed the instructions of her employers, had forfeited any chance of receiving permission to stay in the United States legally. The real tragedy of this tale is that when she was no longer useful to the couple, they let her go. With no family or friends in the country, she found herself among the "hidden ones." The neighborhood around our church is populated by these hidden ones: undocumented aliens who are mired in poverty and fear, who live in cramped, decaying apartments and who are dependent on day-work provided by the suburban *jefes* (boss men) who come by the 7-Eleven to pick up laborers.

Pastor Juan Paredes came upon this woman soon after he started a program of English classes at Culmore. At that time everything seemed to be going wrong in her life. Her seven-year-old son had just arrived from her home country. She had just given birth to another son, whose father had deserted them. She had no job. She was renting a bed (not a room, mind you) in an apartment that already housed two other families. Although it is not unusual in our neighborhood for three or four families to rent an apartment together, it was an act of charity by the other families to give this single mother with two children a place to stay while she recovered from giving birth.

Pastor Juan invited her to the church and the English classes. She soon came, and in her words, "I found the family I left in my home country." She became a Christian and a member of the church, and asked to have her newborn son baptized. I was caught off guard, however, when she asked if I would also be the boy's godfather. Juan explained to me that unlike here in America, this was no mere formality but constituted a pledge to be a *real* father to this boy and look after him as my own, especially since his own father had abandoned him. Thus began one of the most meaningful and formative relationships I have had at Culmore. My friendship with this woman and my two new "sons" (how could I serve as godfather to one and not the other?) profoundly changed them and me.

So when the woman walked into my office and told me that she had fallen in love with a Latin American man in our congregation, I was elated.

I thought they were very lucky to have found each other. We began making preparations for the ceremony.

The first hint of trouble came when they arrived in my office after visiting the county registrar. They had been turned down for a marriage license. I was stunned. I had never heard of anyone being turned down for a marriage license. I asked them what happened. They had been asked for identification, which they both had, but they were told by the registrar that the documents they gave were not sufficient. She wanted to see a social security card, a visa, a driver's license or some similar form of identification, which, of course, they did not have. Dejected, they left and came back to my office.

Immediately I called a fellow pastor to see if he had ever had a couple turned down before. He had not, nor had he ever known a couple to be questioned about identification. Of course, he noted, most of the couples he married were Anglo, not Hispanic. He wondered whether their ethnicity had triggered the question about identification.

My next call was to Tom Elliot, an immigration attorney who assisted many persons from our congregation. First I asked him whether undocumented persons are prevented by law from marrying. His answer was, in short, no. After I related their story, he suggested that the key to solving this problem was proper documentation—that is, they needed some sort of legal certification that they were in fact who they said they were. Since the woman had a recently expired passport from her home country, he suggested using this; only one of the persons actually needed identification.

Passport in hand, they returned to the registrar to get their license. Soon, however, they returned with no license. Once more I called Tom. He was surprised to hear that the office would not accept the passport. His next suggestion was that they take a notarized letter from him acting as their lawyer, stating their identities. A few days later, after receiving the letter, they tried once more and were turned down once more. The reason this time was that they needed photo identification.

My frustration and anger growing by the minute, I called Tom again. He then suggested that the easiest way to get a photo identification would be to go to the nearest department of motor vehicles (DMV) branch and get a Walker ID—a photo ID that looks like a driver's license but is not. The letter the couple already had from him should be sufficient, he said.

Off they went once more, and quickly they returned. The DMV people told them that they had to have a social security number in order to get a Walker ID, which was not legally true. Nonetheless, we were back to square one. If they had a social security number, they would not need a Walker ID. Franz Kafka could not have come up with a more convoluted tale of bureaucratic intrigue.

I then accompanied the woman to the DMV myself. For more than two hours we were passed from one clerk to another, each telling us that someone else could help us. Finally I demanded to see the manager. After she came, I painstakingly recounted everything that this poor woman had been through—how she had provided everything asked of her within her power and still she was being denied the simple request of a photo ID. I begged, I implored, I entreated, I beseeched, I pleaded with the manager to grant this simple request so that this woman could get married.

Taking it all in, she motioned for us to go over to the cameras, where—finally—the woman's picture was taken and she was issued an ID. And yes, the wedding bells finally did ring!

Since this episode occurred, the Virginia State Assembly has formally required that all Walker IDs be issued only to citizens or legal residents. I still marry people who are undocumented. Getting a marriage license depends on which clerks are on duty in the county registrar's office and how busy they are. Some people are asked for ID, others are not. It's now the luck of the draw as to whether a license is issued. If you are turned down, you try another day or another clerk.

The church's ministry to the undocumented is as simple, and as complicated, as getting a marriage license. What is the church to do when Caesar refuses to give permission for two Christians to marry? To whom should my primary allegiance be as a Christian pastor—the nation-state that gives me the legal authorization to marry persons, or our sovereign God, who calls a man and a woman to be married?

The irony of this story is that throughout my career as a pastor, one of the moral issues I have struggled with is how to minister to unmarried couples who are living together. How do I walk the fine line of encouraging them to get married without alienating them from the church because they see absolutely nothing morally wrong with living together before marriage? Yet here I had a young couple who desperately wanted to get married in the eyes of God *and* in the eyes of the state, but local and national laws hindered it at every step. What is the church's duty in this situation? How should we respond?

Taking Time to Be Holy

In the nineteenth chapter of Leviticus, the law explicitly says: "When an alien resides with you in your land, you shall not oppress the alien. The alien who resides with you shall be to you as the citizen among you; you shall love the alien as yourself, for you were aliens in the land of Egypt: I am the LORD your God" (vv. 33-34). This chapter is one of the great biblical passages on holiness as a defining character trait of God's people. From virtually every area of life, God's people are called to be holy in their relationship with each other because "I the LORD your God am holy" (Lev 19:2). Holiness, like duty, is not about who we are but about who the Master is. We are to be holy not because we are good or righteous in and of ourselves, but solely because the God we worship is holy.

Specifically, the holiness to which we are called as a people of God in Leviticus 19 is marked by the honoring of parents, reverence for God, keeping the sabbath, refraining from stealing, telling the truth—things American Protestants have typically considered qualities of holiness. But this code of holiness goes a step further. Being holy as God is holy also requires harvesting fields so that food is left for the hungry to glean, treating the handicapped with mercy, acting with justice toward the poor, not favoring the rich or powerful over the weak, treating older adults with respect, and treating the alien, the immigrant, as we would treat a citizen of our country.

As a pastor in the Wesleyan holiness tradition, I am familiar with this emphasis on piety, which is expressed in both personal and social obligations. But the sense of holiness expressed in Leviticus is different from what I learned in my own church. Since the Social Gospel movement of the early twentieth century, this dual nature of "evangelical wholeness," I believe, has received a lopsided misinterpretation. We have come to see personal holiness as just that—personal—and thus not subject to social conformity or correction. Social holiness has been seen as the primary focus of the church: our job as Christians is social reform. In many instances this has led to the imposition of our own spiritual, theological or ethical agendas onto social institutions, without necessarily our adopting them for ourselves first.

In her provocative essay, "John Wesley and 'Social Ethics,' " Sondra

Wheeler, ethicist at Wesley Seminary, argues that it is a misreading of Wesley to speak of him as having "social ethics." She says, "Because both of the distinctions implied in that term—the distinction between social and personal ethics . . . are alien to Wesley's thought and life."[7] What's more, says Wheeler,

> Enlightenment philosophers, desperate to avoid the bitter religious and ideological conflicts of the preceding two centuries, sought to relegate religion to the realm of the private and personal. But Wesley thought that this kind of compartmentalization, however well-intentioned, was fatal, and it was something he protested against throughout his life.[8]

Wheeler argues that

> Wesley knew nothing of our modern distinction between evangelism and social action because the only gospel he had to preach was the good news that in Jesus Christ the kingdom of God has come near to us. . . . This is the context [of] Wesley's constant work with the poor and the despised of the earth, and his involvement in the societal problems and controversies of his day.[9]

Leviticus 19 thus challenges our modern, liberal Protestant assumptions of the nature of holiness: that personal and social holiness can be differentiated and compartmentalized from one another. As scholars of this passage have pointed out:

> Holiness cannot be regarded as an optional luxury of a believer's life-style. If Lev. 19:2 sets the mark high at "be holy because I, the Lord your God, am holy," . . . the standard is not abstract or philosophical but personal and concrete; it represents the very character and nature of the Lord. . . . The people of God are called to be holy, not because holiness is an arbitrary religion game that God wants played, but because God is holy. Because God is holy, God's people are to be holy by being like God in the world. . . . To be holy is to roll up one's sleeves and to join in with whatever God is doing in the world. That is why, in this great chapter on moral holiness, the emphasis falls on social justice. . . . In Leviticus, if you want to be holy, don't pass out a tract; love your neighbor, show hospitality to the stranger, and be a person of justice.[10]

In their essay "Facing the Postmodern Scalpel," J. Richard Middleton and Brian Walsh point out that because of this foundation of holiness, Israel's standard for justice as a nation served as a "beacon in the ancient Near East." Because of Israel's divine election, their call to be a holy nation meant bearing God's standard of justice to all the nations, something best done by practicing this standard of justice at home first.[11]

It is not accidental or an afterthought that the Lord God commanded Israel to treat the alien, the foreigner, as a fellow citizen. In fact, God does not call for mere fairness for the immigrant, God calls for love: "You shall love the alien as yourself." Why does God call for the Israelites to love the immigrant in their land? Because, as God reminds them, "you were [once] aliens in the land of Egypt." There we have it! Israel was once the stranger and sojourner in a land not their own. In Egypt, Israel's freedom, their identity as God's people, their heritage were taken from them, and they were subjugated and oppressed under unjust laws. When Israel became free, the people reclaimed their unique calling as a sacramental nation, their heritage was restored, they began living in the land promised to Abraham and his descendants. Their fidelity to God would now be judged by how they treat others who sojourn among them. Their holiness would be judged by their hospitality.[12]

Leviticus 19, of course, is not the only biblical injunction to treat the immigrant with mercy. Exodus,[13] Jeremiah[14] and Ezekiel[15] contain admonitions to "do no wrong to the alien." Scholars estimate that Israel is warned about this matter more than thirty-six times in the Old Testament.[16] Frequently this admonition is coupled with a warning about how Israel should treat the widow and the orphan, for "like the widow and the orphan, the sojourner is in a distinct social class, part of a group which requires special care and protection."[17]

Strangers and Sojourners
The theme of holiness was so influential in the early Christian church that the writer of Hebrews admonishes the church to "pursue peace with everyone, and the *holiness* without which no one will see the Lord" (Heb 12:14). Many scholars see Leviticus 19 as the basis of the book of James passages concerning the moral life of believers.[18] But the passage in the New Testament that I most often think of with reference to Leviticus 19 is in Paul's letter to the Ephesians: "So then you are no longer strangers and aliens, but you are citizens with the saints and also members of the household of God" (Eph 2:19). Once again holiness is linked with hospitality. Our fidelity to God will be judged by how we treat the stranger. We who once were strangers to God's grace have been welcomed into the

household of faith. We who once sojourned in a land not our own have been made citizens of God's kingdom. And now we who are recipients of God's hospitality are called to share with others what we ourselves have received.

This is why the most important virtue any church can embody is the virtue of hospitality. Because God has welcomed us, we are called to welcome others—and not because it is the nice and polite thing to do, but because it is the holy and just thing to do. Scripture warns that our unwillingness to be hospitable may cause us to miss out on God's grace altogether. As the letter to the Hebrews advises: "Do not neglect to show hospitality to strangers, for by doing that some have entertained angels without knowing it" (Heb 13:2). Simply put, we have to welcome and be gracious to everybody, because we can't be sure who the angels are.

Think about Abraham and Sarah. Three strangers appeared at their tent in the desert. Now Abraham and Sarah easily could have been suspicious and fearful—and probably were. After all, strangers can be enemies just as well as friends. But Abraham and Sarah welcomed these strangers into their tent and gave them food and rest. And as you know, these three turned out to be angels of the Lord who came with a blessing, a promise that Sarah would give birth to a son, Isaac. This was the beginning of the covenant with Abraham that his descendants would inherit the earth and bless the nations. Think what would have happened if Abraham and Sarah had given in to their fears and refused to be hospitable!

Remember the story of the two disciples who were traveling on the road to Emmaus? These two disciples, who were distraught because their Lord had been put to death, encounter a stranger, and they invite him to join them on their journey. It was only at the end of the day, when they were tired and hungry, that they extended hospitality to this stranger by inviting him to sit down and rest and share supper with them. And in the breaking of the bread they recognized that this stranger is the Lord risen from the dead. Think what would have happened, though, if these two disciples had refused to walk with this stranger or to invite him to supper!

And remember Jesus' teaching about the Last Judgment, when he said that our faithfulness will be measured by whether we have fed the hungry, given water to the thirsty, welcomed the stranger: "Truly . . . as you did it to one of the least of these who are members of my family, you did it to me" (Mt 25:40).

You see, Jesus identified with the stranger. He knew what a lack of hospitality feels like. He knew how it feels for people to be suspicious and afraid. He knew what it means to be rejected. And that's why his whole ministry was spent identifying with those most of us spend our lives trying to avoid. Jesus knew that the stranger, the outcast, is not just the one who needs us; we also need the stranger. If we are willing to open our lives to the "least of these," then there is some hope that we may open our lives to God.

Hospitality, when you get right down to it, is unnatural. It is difficult to place others first, because our inclination is to take care of ourselves first. Hospitality takes courage. It takes a willingness to risk. But as our Lord reminds us, if we only love those who we are sure will love us and welcome those who will welcome us, then we have done little to share the love of God, for as Jesus says, even the heathens do that.

You see, most of us know what true hospitality feels like. It means being received openly, warmly, freely, without any need to prove ourselves. Hospitality makes us feel worthy, because our host assumes we are worthy. This is the kind of hospitality that we have experienced from God, and all that God asks is that we go and do likewise, particularly to "the alien among us."

The Colony of Heaven

Hospitality and holiness mean doing our Christian duty, and doing it because of "who the Master is." The dilemma of how we as God's people should treat the stranger and sojourner brings us to the cusp of what it means to be a postmodern people. We cannot serve two masters. We cannot serve the nation-state and our sovereign God, especially when we receive such drastically different messages about the "alien among us."

As noted in chapter two, Stanley Hauerwas has said that the church must recognize that its first task is to be itself. He argues that for the church

> to adopt social strategies in the name of securing justice . . . is only to compound the problem. . . . At the very least [the] church's first political task is to be the kind of community that recognizes the necessity that all societies, church and political alike, require authority. But for Christians our authority is neither in society itself nor in the individual; it is in God.[19]

The church is called to be the church. In other words, we are to be a community of God's people who are constantly forming and being formed into God's image. We are called not only to be good, but holy. We are the "contrast community" by which the world realizes that it is indeed the world. We are the "city set upon a hill," whose very brilliance reminds the world that it still lives in darkness. We are the alternative. Like Israel, we are a particular people, who through our call to holiness, witness to God's justice by how we ourselves treat the stranger and sojourner.

Paul calls us nothing less than a colony of heaven (Phil 3:20). We are the outpost, the beachhead, of God's coming into this world. Hauerwas puts it this way:

> We are a people who have become part of a peaceable kingdom that has been made possible by the life and death of Jesus Christ. It is not our task to make the "world" the kingdom; but it is our task to be a people who can witness to the world what it means to be confident of the Lord of this world that we wish for no more than our daily bread. . . . Thus, within a world of violence and injustice, Christians can take the risk of being forgiven and forgiving.[20]

In *Resident Aliens*, Hauerwas and Willimon argue that "Christianity is more than a matter of new understanding. Christianity is an invitation to be part of an alien people who make a difference because they see something that cannot otherwise be seen without Christ. Right living is more the challenge than right thinking."[21]

Needless to say, many have interpreted this "sectarian" understanding of the church's mission as a tribalistic withdrawal from active engagement with the world, but Hauerwas and Willimon maintain that this is an offensive rather than a defensive posture for the church: "Jesus Christ is the supreme act of divine intrusion into the world's settled arrangements. In Christ, God refuses to 'stay in his place.' The message that sustains the colony is not for itself but for the whole world."[22] Like Israel, the church is called by God as one people from many, a particular people for God's universal mission. This is no withdrawal into tribalism, Hauerwas and Willimon argue. If any institution can be described as tribalistic, they say, it is the nation-state:

> The church is the one political entity in our culture that is global, transnational, transcultural. Tribalism is not the church determined to serve God rather than Caesar. Tribalism is the United States of America, which sets up artificial boundaries and defends them with murderous

intensity. And the tribalism of nations occurs most viciously in the absence of a church able to say and to show, in its life together, that God, not the nations, rules the world.[23]

Imitate Us?

Sometimes when my daughter, Hannah, and I are together, I look into her face and see myself. It may be a smile, a certain expression, a gesture, but there I am. This realization is both wonderful and terrifying, because it reminds me just how much our lives intersect and influence one another. As Christians, we should have a greater sense of responsibility in how we live, knowing that others are watching us and taking their cues about life and values from us.

When the apostle Paul wrote his letter to the Philippians, he was in prison, suffering because he lived as a resident alien in a hostile culture. But even from his jail cell he is able to say with confidence: "I regard everything as loss because of the surpassing value of knowing Christ Jesus my Lord. For his sake I have suffered the loss of all things, and I regard them as rubbish, in order that I may gain Christ" (Phil 3:8). Paul, who has been forced to leave behind family, friends, his Jewish heritage and identity, and finds himself languishing in a Roman jail awaiting death, is still able to say that it has been worthwhile. Paul thus shares his confidence in God's reign to encourage his friends in the Philippian church. He is aware that they have faced opposition not only from the Roman culture surrounding them but even from within the church itself.

In this context Paul urges the Philippians: "Brothers and sisters, join in imitating me, and observe those who live according to the example you have in us" (Phil 3:17). Although it certainly sounds like it, Paul is not being egotistical, for he was the first to admit that his relationship to Christ was still far from perfect. But he realized that his leadership in the church placed him in a position of responsibility. In the first century, converts had no New Testament to read for guidance, and few pastors were around to nurture and teach the congregations. So Paul offered himself as their teacher, even while he was still learning the faith.

Paul's point is as valid for us as it was for the Philippians: just as we learn by example, we teach by example. We learn how to live as Christians so that we, in turn, might teach others how to live as Christians.

Though our country is increasingly building walls to keep the alien, the sojourner, out, we, as Christians, must remember what Ephesians states so eloquently, we

> were [once] without Christ, being aliens from the commonwealth of Israel, and strangers to the covenants of promise, having no hope and without God in the world. But now in Christ Jesus you who once were far off have been brought near by the blood of Christ. For he is our peace; in his flesh he has made both groups into one and has *broken down the dividing wall*, that is, the hostility between us. (Eph 2:12-14)

Christ has knocked down the barriers, the border gates, the razor-barbed fences and all the walls that separate us from our relationships to God and to each other. As a result, no longer can we divide ourselves into strangers and friends, residents and aliens. We, as God's people—documented and undocumented—are together "*citizens* with the saints and also members of the household of God" (Eph 2:19).

8
Someone to Guide Me

●●●

PRINCIPLE: A multicultural church emphasizes evangelical wholeness.

Then the Spirit said to Philip, "Go over to this chariot and join it." So Philip ran up to it and heard him reading the prophet Isaiah. He asked, "Do you understand what you are reading?" He replied, "How can I, unless someone guides me?" And he invited Philip to get in and sit beside him. ACTS 8:29-31

Mark Lykins, *pastor of Good Shepherd United Methodist Church, a* multicultural congregation in Durham, North Carolina, tells of an unusual opportunity for Christian witness that presented itself shortly after his church started ESL classes. Good Shepherd is an exceptional congregation in many respects. Of all the churches I visited on my sabbatical, this was the only one to have begun as a multicultural congregation. It was also one of the most diverse. This diversity was not necessarily intentional, however. When plans were made to begin Good Shepherd, church leaders in North Carolina carefully examined the greater Durham area for the location to begin a new, fast-growing, homogeneous, suburban congregation. When the site on the southern fringe of Durham was selected, Mark and his wife, Pat, a diaconal minister, were appointed to lead this new ministry. What church leaders had not counted on, however, was the work of the Holy Spirit. Now, of course, they hoped the Spirit would be at work, but working to fulfill the plans they had made for Good Shepherd. While working through Mark and Pat, however, the Holy Spirit brought new meaning to the words of the psalmist: "The LORD brings the

counsel of the nations to nothing; he *frustrates* the plans of the peoples"
(Ps 33:10). Perhaps the words of Jeremiah are even more appropriate:
"For surely I know the plans I have for you, says the LORD, plans for
your welfare and not for harm, to give you *a future with hope*" (Jer
29:11).

Mark and Pat were meeting one night for Bible study with a small group
of laypeople who had committed themselves to help start Good Shepherd.
This Bible study occurred even before they had ever held their first worship
service. The text they were studying that night came from Acts, and it
described the crosscultural witness of Philip to an Ethiopian eunuch. As
they explored the text, they began to ask each other, "Does this Scripture
describe the kind of church God is calling us to be?"

At this point in their journey together, all the participants in this new
church start were white. The one-night study lasted for three more weeks,
and they continued to ask, "Is this the kind of church God is calling us to
be?" They soon found out that it was!

When I visited Good Shepherd in Durham in 1994, I initially thought
it had an unusual location for a multicultural congregation. The church
was not in a major city, and this area did not have a history as a center for
immigration. I still viewed Durham as a part of the traditional old South—
more progressive than the surrounding rural countryside of North Caro
lina, yet certainly no hotbed of multiculturalism. As I talked with Mark,
however, I understood why a significant immigrant community existed
there. Several reasons accounted for the immigrant population: (1) the
nearby universities draw many international students, many of whom
decide to stay and work in the area; (2) the African News Service is located
there, making the Durham area an important center for the African
immigrant community in the United States; and (3) most important of all
is the presence of Research Triangle Park (RTP), an international conglom-
eration of businesses intentionally cultivated by the state of North Carolina. RTP has drawn many scientists, researchers and businesspeople from
around the world.

Mark tells the story of how, after beginning their first English class, he
received a phone call from a Chinese official. One of Mark's members had
taken ESL fliers to RTP. This Chinese supervisor took notice of the class.
She explained to Mark that she was supervising four Chinese factory
managers assigned to RTP as part of a business-exchange program. They

were in the United States for only one year, and they had run into a problem: the Chinese were finding it difficult to communicate. The official wanted to know if the managers could come to Good Shepherd's English class. Mark immediately said yes, they were more than welcome to come. Then she asked if any religious requirement was involved, since the class was held in a church. She explained that they were atheists and their government discouraged them from religious activities. Mark told her there were no requirements; the church did host a devotional following the classes, but it was completely optional.

The four Chinese factory managers and their supervisor showed up for class the next week. After checking it out, the supervisor left the managers there and did not return again. Mark had agreed to pick up the managers and also return them to their apartments after class. As expected, the four did not attend the devotional that first night. But week by week, slowly they began to inch their way from the hallway . . . to the door . . . to the back pew. After about six weeks, they finally landed in the front row, clapping, singing and becoming full participants in the devotional. Devotionals consisted of teaching simple songs, a short spoken meditation (Christianity 101, as it were) and a time of prayer. Then Mark concluded by inviting any of the students who wished to become Christians to stay and talk to him.

This routine went on for a number of weeks, with the Chinese managers singing, praying and sharing their lives with the other students. Then came the time for them to return to China. Their last night at the English classes was filled with tears as the students bade them farewell.

As he had for several months, Mark drove them back to their apartments. To make this last trip memorable, he took them in his restored black, four-door 1954 Chevy. As they rode down winding country roads with the windows rolled down, the factory managers began to speak to each other in Chinese. Then Mark heard one say in English, "You ask him," to which another responded, "No, you ask him."

Finally, the man who was sitting next to Mark in the front seat said to him, "We want you teach us *sin*."

"What?" shouted Mark, wondering what kind of sin they specifically wanted him to teach them.

Then the woman in the back seat, who was more fluent in English, said, "No, no, no. We want you teach us *sing!*"

The car erupted in laughter when they realized the faux pas in pronunciation. Mark asked them which song they wanted to learn. The woman said, "Jesu love me," which Mark had taught them in devotionals.

Mark began to recite the words, but the woman in back said, "No, no." Then the man next to Mark said, "No, we *sing* Jesu!"

So on this May evening, with a warm breeze blowing through the car, the four Chinese managers rode singing at the top of their lungs: "Jesu love me, this I know, for the Bible tell me so. Yes, Jesu love me . . ."

They finally arrived at the apartment complex, and everyone got out and said their goodbys. The woman who spoke English well shooed the others on inside while she stayed to speak to Mark. In hushed tones, she said to him, "This Jesu, I know him," and she pointed to her heart. "And I go back China, I tell all my friends about Jesu."

Now, somewhere in communist China, several factory managers are whispering of Jesus' love.

Scripture as a Second Language
Multicultural congregations understand that the ministries of evangelism and social justice go hand in hand. Reclaiming the twin Wesleyan emphases of "spreading scriptural holiness" and "reforming the nation," multicultural churches understand that doing faithful ministry includes both piety and mercy. They remember Jesus' words: "I was hungry and you gave me food, I was thirsty and you gave me something to drink, I was a stranger and you welcomed me" (Mt 25:35). To this our own congregation would add, "I did not know English and you taught me, I was undocumented and you became my advocate, I was recruited by the gang and you helped me escape."

In the first chapter of Acts, just before he ascends to God the Father, Jesus gives the church its statement of mission: "You will receive power when the Holy Spirit has come upon you; and you will be my witnesses in Jerusalem, in all Judea and Samaria, and to the ends of the earth" (1:8). As noted earlier, the book of Acts is not so much about the actions of the apostles as it is about the acts of the Holy Spirit through the apostles. Luke is very clear that every initiative of the apostles to fulfill the mission of the church is by the prodding and leading of the Holy Spirit. God directs this mission movement, not us.

Acts 8 is a prime example of evangelical wholeness witnessed through

Philip as he helps fulfill the church's mission. He participates in this mission by helping the Ethiopian eunuch, who has come from the ends of the earth, come to know Christ. Beginning in verse 26, we are told that an angel of the Lord directs Philip to a deserted stretch of highway between Jerusalem and Gaza. Philip goes where the angel directs him, and comes upon an Ethiopian eunuch, who is sitting by the side of the road in his chariot, reading, of all things, the Scriptures, specifically the book of Isaiah.

This person is not just any Ethiopian, and not just any eunuch. Luke tells us that he is a chamberlain in the court of Candace, the queen of Ethiopia. Moreover, he is a member of the queen's cabinet, her secretary of the treasury. Philip has come upon a very important and powerful person, a high official in a foreign government. And here he is, sitting by the road reading the Hebrew Scriptures. Luke does tell us that he had "come to Jerusalem to worship." Although it is not clear whether he is a Jewish proselyte or simply a respecter of the Jewish faith, what is clear is that he is seeking something—seeking Someone!

Philip may have wondered why in the world God dragged him out to the middle of the desert, but when he saw this Ethiopian, he knew exactly why. You see, as Luke reports earlier, in Acts 8, Philip had just finished an evangelistic mission to Samaria, in which many people were baptized. Now Philip meets this Ethiopian reading Scripture. Immediately following, in Acts 9, Saul, "breathing threats and murder against the disciples" (v. 1), meets the Lord on another stretch of lonely road and becomes Paul the apostle. Immediately after that, Acts 10 chronicles the baptism of the first Gentile, Cornelius, as a Christian. God's movement is clear: the gospel should be carried from "Jerusalem, in all Judea and Samaria, and to the ends of the earth." We are to witness God's saving love at home, in our neighborhoods, to the people we despise most and to the farthest reaches of the planet. The doors of God's church are now open to everyone. The mandate is clear and without exception: "be my witnesses" to *all people*, says the Lord.

Philip immediately goes to the chariot. As he listens to this man read from Isaiah, his first question to him is "Do you understand what you are reading?" (Acts 8:30). The Ethiopian responds, "How can I, *unless someone guides me?*" (v. 31).

Philip becomes a teacher of SSL—"Scripture as a second language"— and reveals to this Ethiopian the Christian interpretation of the Scripture he is reading. The eunuch is reading what seems to be an odd passage from Isaiah:

> Like a sheep he was led to the slaughter,
>> and like a lamb silent before its shearer,
>> so he does not open his mouth.
> In his humiliation justice was denied him.
>> Who can describe his generation?
>> For his life is taken away from the earth. (Acts 8:32-33)

The Ethiopian asks Philip about whom the Scripture is speaking. Is it the prophet Isaiah himself, or is it someone else? Fred Craddock, professor of homiletics at Candler School of Theology, asks, "Why is this man so interested in this obscure, though beautiful passage from Isaiah?" to which he provides his own answer:

> I'll tell you why he is interested. He is a eunuch. A castrated male in government service—a person now of questionable sexuality—a maimed and wounded soul whose sexual identity has been removed from him—a man without generation, who did not have the possibility of descendants, family. The Scripture says quite plainly . . . "No one whose testicles are crushed or whose penis is cut off shall be admitted to the assembly of the LORD" (Deuteronomy 23:1).[1]

He reads the Bible, he searches the Scriptures to find out if he has any hope. Is there any good news for a eunuch? As he searches the Word, trying to find out where he fits in God's family, what his part is in God's story, all he hears is exclusion, not inclusion—judgment, not grace. Over and over again he hears God's people say to him, "You are not a part of us—you have no place in the family of God." He is a eunuch, a sexless person, who is cut off from the covenant people: what is the word of the Lord for him?

In Isaiah, though, he reads about someone very much like him, who also was *cut off* from the land of the living—who also had lost his posterity, had suffered in humiliation and was denied justice. "Who is this man," asks the eunuch, *"who is so like me?"* Philip begins to tell him of the one whom Isaiah described. He shares with him the good news of Jesus Christ, who fulfilled the prophecies of Isaiah, who brought about a new covenant and through whom God's blessings will be bestowed on all people, even eunuchs and Gentiles.

The prophet Isaiah also wrote in chapter 56 about the day of the Lord, when this new covenant is established:

Do not let the foreigner joined to the LORD say,
    "The LORD will surely separate me from his people";
and do not let the eunuch say,
    "I am just a dry tree."
For thus says the LORD:
To the eunuchs who keep my sabbaths,
    who choose the things that please me
    and hold fast my covenant,
I will give, in my house and within my walls,
    a monument and a name better than sons and daughters;
I will give them an everlasting name
    that shall not be cut off. (Is 56:3-5)

And foreigners who bind themselves to the LORD . .
who keep the Sabbath . .
    and who hold fast to my covenant—
these I will bring to my holy mountain
    and give them joy in my house of prayer.
Their burnt offerings and sacrifices
    will be accepted on my altar;
for my house [says the Lord] will be called
    a house of prayer for all nations. (Is 56:6-7 NIV)

And because Philip obeyed the angel of the Lord and went where he was sent, because he was willing to witness his faith, Philip was in the right place at the right time. He was there to guide our Ethiopian friend in finding his place in God's Scriptures, to help him find his name in God's Word. Philip helped the eunuch see where he fit in God's family, to find his part in God's story. The eunuch heard a word of inclusion, not exclusion—grace, not judgment.

The Scriptures tell us that upon hearing that the promises of God through Jesus Christ were for him too, the eunuch immediately saw a pool of water and said to Philip, "Look, here is water! What is to prevent me from being baptized?" (Acts 8:37). Philip baptized him, and then Luke tells us that the Spirit of the Lord then whisked Philip away. The Ethiopian didn't see Philip anymore, but the eunuch continued on his journey rejoicing! Eusebius, the church historian, says the Ethiopian returned home and became an evangelist, continuing to spread the good news of Jesus Christ to the ends of the earth.[2]

How many people are like this eunuch, searching for their names in the book of life, wanting to find their place in the family of God? Who will guide them to rejoicing in knowledge of the Lord? The Lord said, "Be my witnesses in Jerusalem, in all Judea and Samaria, and to the ends of the earth."

Living Within a Biblical Rationality

Alister McGrath has written that "the unique authority of Scripture rests on the activity of the revealing God, both in relation to the biblical material itself and in the subsequent process of interpretation and inward appropriation by the reader."[3] Considering Acts 8, then, one might say that God initially revealed God's self through the writings of the prophet Isaiah, and then to subsequent generations through their incorporation into the Hebrew canon. God, however, did not stop there. God also revealed God's self through the interpretive work of Philip to the Ethiopian. The Ethiopian, in turn, appropriated God's Word and self-revelation for his life with dramatic consequences. Quoting John Wesley, McGrath concludes that "The Spirit of God not only once inspired those who wrote the Bible but continually inspires those who read it with earnest prayer."[4] As Christians who take the Bible seriously, we cannot help but locate our own personal stories within the context of the biblical story. By doing so, we ourselves are reinterpreted by the promises and realities of scriptural truth.

In their critical assessment of narrative theology, Stanley Grenz and Roger Olson argue that the "genius of a life story lies in its potential for revision."[5] The narrative of each person's life is intended, they say, to lead us to self-examination, spiritually speaking. The reason is that we cannot be consumers of just our own spiritual stories. We live in a complex world of narratives that intersect, overlap and collide. Encountering other persons' stories, or the stories of other cultures, or the grand narratives that attempt to define humanity's raison d'être forces us to reexamine the tale of our own existence in light of what we learn from these other perspectives.

Grenz and Olson, referring to the work of George W. Stroup, say that when a person is confronted with another narrative that calls into question how he or she has previously understood his or her own personal story, the ensuing challenge to interpretation and meaning results in what Stroup terms a "collision of narratives." Grenz and Olson argue that as the new narrative causes the individual to sense "disorientation," to sense that the world as he or she has known it is coming apart, the process of faith begins. Because one's identity has been called into question by the new story, the person must reinterpret the personal story in accordance with the categories of the new narrative.[6]

They note that Stroup uses a much more traditional word for this "collision of narratives"; he calls it "conversion."

In other words, when we locate ourselves within God's story of creation, fall, redemption and consummation, we are invited to live under a new rationality, a biblical rationality, if you will. This new way of thinking and interpreting our existence calls into question all that we have been about. We ourselves are thus reinterpreted in light of the story of God's saving love made known to us in Jesus Christ.

Living under a biblical rationality does not necessarily end the collision of narratives. In fact, we may become all the more aware of the narrative entanglements of our lives, that is, how many different stories lay claim to our individual stories. Rather than lessening the tension of narratives, living in a biblical rationality may actually heighten it. Lesslie Newbigin speaks of that dilemma this way:

As a Christian I seek so to live within the biblical tradition, using its language as my language, its models as the model through which I make sense of experience, its story as the clue to my story, that I help to strengthen and carry forward this tradition of rationality. But as a member of contemporary British society I am all the time living in, or at least sharing my life with, those who live in the other tradition. What they call self-evident truths are not self-evident to me, and vice versa. When they speak of reason they mean what is reasonable within their plausibility structure. I do not live in that plausibility, but I know what it feels like to live in it. Within my own mind there is a continuing dialogue between the two. Insofar as my own participation in the Christian tradition is healthy and vigorous, both in thought and in practice, I shall be equipped for the external dialogue with the other tradition.[7]

The fact that living under a biblical rationality includes internal as well as external conflict is not necessarily bad news. As Grenz and Olson point out, this dialogue of rationalities—the competition of defining narratives—forces us to be self-critical. We examine our lives, our allegiances and our lords.

Hauerwas says that "what we require is . . . a true story. Such a story is one that provides a pilgrimage with appropriate exercises and disciplines of self-examination." Christians believe the Bible offers such a story: "The story of God does not offer a resolution of life's difficulties, but it offers us something better—an adventure and struggle, for we are possessors of the happy news that God has called people together to live faithful to the reality that he is the Lord of this world."[8] What's more, says Hauerwas, "by making the story of such a Lord central to [our] lives, Christians are enabled to see the world accurately and without illusion. . . . [We] have the confidence that Jesus' cross and resurrection are the final words concerning God's rule."[9]

Aunt Alma, Mr. Scofield's Notes and Revival

The Bible's witness to the beginning of faith is that it is always a corporate affair. The radical individualism of modern Protestant Christianity misleads us if we think we can come to know the story of God's saving grace by ourselves. Like the Ethiopian eunuch, we need someone to guide us. We need a biblical interpreter, a "Scripture as a second language" teacher, to translate God's story for us. Better yet, we need someone to help us translate our own personal narratives into scriptural categories.

My own spiritual guide was my Aunt Alma, a premillennial, fundamentalist, independent Missionary Baptist from east Tennessee. Although I had grown up attending the United Methodist church where my parents were married, Aunt Alma took it upon herself to make sure that I received a "proper" Christian education. After school I often found myself traveling the familiar path to her doorstep. As I sat in her kitchen, eating hot biscuits and half-runners—topped off with a glass of cold milk and a piece of fried apple pie—she would open up her King James Scofield Reference Bible to reveal God's story of salvation and its application for my life. Though I often got lost in her expositions of the rapture, the war between the angels, the archangels and the antichrist (not to mention the thousand years of tribulation and the mark of the beast), I must admit that Aunt Alma helped me to find my story within God's story. More than anything else, Aunt Alma helped me to understand that God's Word laid claim to my life. I understood that the Bible's message for me was that God loved me and God had a purpose for my life.

Aunt Alma spent a considerable amount of time worrying about my earthly destiny, not to mention my eternal one. She was, to put it mildly, skeptical that I was receiving proper spiritual guidance from my home church. One day she said to me, "Child, I do not understand why God sees fit to leave you in the Methodist Church. It is just beyond me, but his will be done!" Since she had left my denominational affiliation to the Lord, she decided it was up to her to be sure that if I was going to be a Christian in the Methodist Church, at least I would be a biblical Methodist.

You see, Aunt Alma was the first person to recognize my call. I knew that I felt God tugging at me, but I had no idea what God's purpose was. She took it upon herself to make sure that the call was authentic, that I recognized it and that I was spiritually prepared to answer it.

In addition to our kitchen-table Bible studies, Aunt Alma and her husband, Uncle Bob, supplemented my education by taking me to events at their church. One Sunday morning I went to Sunday school with them and attended the women's class, which Aunt Alma taught. That particular Sunday she had invited another woman to give a lecture on the rapture. I was both mesmerized and terrified. After church that day I asked her, "Do you really believe that stuff?"

Calmly Aunt Alma said, "Oh, absolutely, son." She pulled out Mr. Scofield's reference notes (which were not to be considered as authoritative as Scripture, she pointed out) to show me why she believed it.

I remember one warm, late-summer evening when she and Uncle Bob picked me up for a revival. I had been going through a bumpy time of teenage angst—questioning myself, the direction of my life and my relationship with God. It was a paradoxical time: I felt strongly called to serve God, but at the same time the least worthy to do so. We sat through the service that warm night, cooling ourselves with cardboard fans provided by the local funeral home. We sang song after song. We heard many testimonies of those who had given their lives to Christ. And the guest preacher, Pastor Bill Stafford, lifted up the Word on the subject of God's salvation and our assurance. He ended the service by inviting those present who had not accepted Jesus Christ as their Lord and Savior to do so. He also invited anyone who had a special spiritual need or prayer request to come to the altar and receive prayer.

As the congregation sang "Just As I Am," I looked at Aunt Alma, asking (not unlike the Ethiopian), "What is to prevent me?" So that night I made my pilgrimage down the aisle, knelt at the altar and renewed my commitment to Jesus Christ as my Savior.

As Pastor Stafford counseled me, I shared with him my sense that God wanted me to serve him, maybe even as a minister. I asked him what I should do about it. His answer was simple and to the point: "Son, when God calls, just be available."

God did call, and I was available, thanks to Aunt Alma, who helped me and guided me to find my place, my identity, in the story of God's saving work.

The "Bad News" Missionaries

Bernard Adeney, drawing on the work of William Dyrness, argues that Scripture is, in and of itself, transcultural. He says that the manner in which the Bible is interpreted or the priority certain parts of its message are given may be determined by a particular culture. The entire "canon of the Bible, on the other hand, is constitutive of what it means to be a Christian in every time and place."[10] Scripture is itself a bridge between cultures, and it can and does speak to persons in all their particularity. Scripture offers the bridge between a southern Anglo pastor and four Chinese factory managers, between a Jewish disciple of Jesus and an Ethiopian eunuch from the court of Candace, between a seventy-year-old Baptist Sunday-school teacher and a young, redheaded teenager full of mischief. Scripture is God's bridge: it transcends our cultural differences and enables us to discern our place together in the narrative of salvation.

It is by no means certain that God's narrative will be the story that interprets our lives. As stated earlier, we live in a world of intersecting, overlapping and competing narratives. Other stories also seek to locate us within their narratives and define us for their own purposes.

In the neighborhood surrounding our church, the majority of the children come from El Salvador, Guatemala, Vietnam and Cambodia. They are the offspring of their nations' wars. Dislocated by violence in their homelands, they are once again placed in harm's way by the ethnic youth gangs that comb the neighborhood, recruiting young warriors.

Although many of the youth gangs of northern Virginia are homegrown (local, as opposed to national), this situation has begun to change, as emissaries are sent from gangs in Los Angeles, Chicago, New York and Houston. One particularly sinister and violent gang that has moved into our neighborhood is Mara Salvatruca (MS), a Salvadoran gang from

California known for remorseless drive-by shootings. The history of MS can be traced back directly to the civil war in El Salvador. Since arriving in the United States, MS has sprung up in predominantly Salvadoran communities. Considered a transnational gang because of its members' ability to move easily between countries in drug trafficking, MS has developed a reputation as an extremely violent gang of urban guerrillas. Though relatively small in numbers, in recent years MS has sought to expand its membership and geographical base in order to become a major national gang, not unlike the Crips and the Bloods.

Mara Salvatruca arrived in northern Virginia in 1994. Approximately twelve emissaries from the Los Angeles gang were sent to take over the existing gang structure in Culmore and to organize them into *clicas*, or subgroups of the larger gang. Ironically, these emissaries are called "missionaries," but make no mistake, they are missionaries of very *bad news* for the children and youth of our community.

One day I was talking to the principal of a local elementary school, and she told me that the older gang members were dropping by after school and walking fourth- and fifth-graders home. This is one of the ways the gang recruits new members. These "bad news" missionaries were actually more in touch with the needs of our children than were we, the "good news" missionaries. The gang knew that many of the kids didn't like to walk home alone, for fear of being picked on or beaten up. The gang members were there not only to provide safety but to offer prestige to these children of single mothers as they were walked home by a macho, young-adult male.

Such protection has a cost for our children: gang affiliation. Mara Salvatruca gives its elementary-school "wannabes" black business cards. A senior probation officer for our area, Gerry Jackson, calls this the "card of death." The card's color signifies both the secrecy of the gang and the finality of membership—"til death do us part!"

Mara Salvatruca and the other gangs of our community have a narrative. They want to share their story with others. They are intentional in their missionary efforts to translate the personal stories of our community's children and youth through their own narrative framework. They know what they believe. They have a purpose. And they are more than willing to recruit others into their gang family.

When the children of the neighborhood ask, "Who will guide me?" the gang is already there, lying in wait. "We will guide you," they say. "We will tell you who you are. We know what you should be about, we know the purpose of your life. Come with us. Let us show you *the way* of the clica, *the truth* of the gang, *the life* of the homie."

While the gangs represent one other competing narrative, we can be sure that it is one among many. A pluralistic world contains many challenges to the gospel. We cannot assume that people know the story of Jesus or understand its importance for their lives. We no longer live in a Christian culture (if ever we did), and the church can no longer afford to be passive or reluctant in sharing the saving gospel of Jesus Christ.

Christians have a story to tell, and we must be every bit as intentional as the gangs. They also have a story, but it is one of despair. They have a purpose, but it is violence and self-destruction. They have direction, but it is the way of death. Our story, on the other hand, is one of life. Our purpose is one of love and redemption. Our direction is the way to God.

As God's people, we must always be prepared to share the good news of salvation, so that when someone asks, "Who will guide me?" we are ready to answer: "We will guide you. We can tell you who you are. We can tell you to whom you belong. We can show you the purpose of your life. Come with us. Let us introduce you to the One who *really* is the Way, the Truth, and the Life."

Miss Susan and Her Homeboys

The apostle Paul writes in 2 Corinthians: "Your very lives are a letter that anyone can read by just looking at you. Christ himself wrote it—not with ink, but with God's living Spirit" (3:3 *The Message*). Not only are we Christians to be translators of the gospel, but we are also called, says Paul, to be the living word of God to others. The good news is not only something we have to tell; just as important, it is something we must live if we want to be spiritual guides.

Last year a woman in our congregation, Miss Susan, as she is affectionately known, unexpectedly became an O.G.[11] (an O.G. for Jesus, to be exact) to a group of four "homies" in our community. Susan is a self-described "Spirit-filled, Bible-believing, committed Christian." A retired government service worker, Susan came to active faith later in life, making up for lost time by her passion and zeal for the Lord. Three years ago Susan fulfilled a dream: to go to Bible college to study for a year so that she could serve in full-time ministry as a layperson.

Near the end of her studies, she was asked to write a final paper describing what she understood as God's call for her ministry after she left school and how she was going to follow through with it. Susan prayed intensely about what it was that God wanted her to do. It finally seemed to become clear to her—God wanted her to return to northern Virginia and begin an urban ministry with young, at-risk girls.

Susan clearly has a heart for young people, and since she's single and never had children, it made sense to her that the ministry should be to girls. But as God continues to remind all of us: "For my thoughts are not your thoughts, nor are your ways my ways" (Is 55:8). Susan did get the urban youth ministry part right; just the gender was wrong!

After Susan returned to Culmore, she continued to pray for God's guidance in her ministry. One night Susan had free tickets to see *Romeo and Juliet* at a theater in Washington. Since she had more than she could use, she decided to invite some friends. It occurred to her also to invite four adolescent boys, who were coming to church at that time. These boys, who were between twelve and thirteen years old, lived in the neighborhood. They came from humble families and fit the profile of kids who are most at risk for recruitment by gangs. Susan was fairly certain that they had never seen a live play, so she asked the boys if they would like to go. She did not have to ask twice. The five of them, plus a couple of Susan's friends, went, and the boys had the time of their lives.

Susan enjoyed the outing but thought no more about it. What was really on her mind was how and where she would find those young girls to whom she felt called to minister. About a week later, Susan was on her knees in the church chapel praying, asking for God's guidance in starting her ministry. If God would just give her a little direction, she was ready to begin.

Her prayer time was interrupted when Pablo, one of the boys who had gone to the play with her, came into the chapel. Pablo said, "Miss Susan, I need to talk to you. Do you have time for me?"

"Of course, she answered.

"Do you think you could spend some time with me? You know, like hang out or somethin'? If you could, I'd like to do it every Tuesday."

Susan sat there dumbfounded. What had she just prayed for? What did this young boy just say? Could it be that God had just answered her prayer?

She found herself thinking, "Lord, I thought you said girls. I don't have any experience with boys, Lord. Are you sure about this? I think you've made a mistake, Lord."

But here he was, sitting right in front of her—a handsome, charismatic, teenage Latino *boy!* What could she say? After all, how often does a streetwise thirteen-year-old kid ask a seventy-year-old woman to hang out?

Susan looked at him and said, "Well, of course, Pablo, I would be happy to hang out *or something.*" They decided that they would meet once a week at church after school to have a Bible study.

After Susan and Pablo had their first Bible study, he asked if he could bring his best friend the next time. Susan said yes, so Theo, an African-American teen, joined them. Week after week they met, and the short Bible study came to include basketball and Baskin-Robbins. They were soon spending the whole afternoon together.

Pablo and Theo asked if they could ask another friend, Juan, to join them. With Juan came José, his brother. Now the four boys Susan originally took to the play were meeting not just one afternoon a week but two and sometimes three, not to mention on Saturdays. Miss Susan and her homeboys could also be seen sitting together many Sundays during church. For the next eight months the five of them went swimming, rode bumper cars and hung out at Susan's apartment. In Pablo's words: "We be just chillin' out at Miss Susan's all the time."

Susan spent time with these four boys, who very much needed someone to guide them, love them, value them and teach them what it means to be God's children. On Pentecost Sunday 1996, Pablo, Theo, Juan and José knelt before the altar of the church and received Christ into their lives. On that Sunday these four homeboys did join a gang, but it was God's gang, Jesus' posse, the Holy Spirit's homeboys.

And Now . . . the Rest of the Story

In many ways I wish I could say that this was the end of Pablo's story and that he lived "happily ever after." But alas, the story of our sojourn with God is not conducive to fairy-tale endings. Christian regeneration is not a linear process; a roller coaster is a more apt image. Our sin is so entrenched that our spiritual transformation takes a lifetime of God's work in us to complete. Until that day when we meet God face to face, there can be no neat and tidy endings. So in the tradition of that master radio storyteller, Paul Harvey, let me share with you the rest of the story.

Five months after Pablo knelt before the altar, I received a phone call. Pablo was in trouble—serious trouble. He had been arrested. Within a very brief period, Pablo was arraigned on four charges: three felony counts and one misdemeanor. Over the next few days, what began to emerge was another part of Pablo's life which had not been visible to either his mother or his church family. During the preceding summer months, Pablo had secretly joined a local gang.

Because of Pablo's natural charisma and innate leadership talents, several gangs had been wooing him for some time. Because of his relationship to the church, and especially his relationship with Susan, he had been able to resist their overtures. His resistance began to weaken, however, with the onset of normal adolescent rebellion and an emerging competitive, conflictual relationship with his new stepfather. As Pablo grew more disenchanted and unhappy at home, he sought solace in the homeboys of the neighborhood. Very quickly, the gang leaders seized upon his dissatisfaction with his family and pledged themselves as his new family. Before he realized fully what had happened, Pablo was initiated into the gang. This new sense of acceptance encouraged Pablo to please his new family. In fairly short order Pablo was transformed from gang inductee to gang recruiter, from confirmand to criminal.

At the church, we were absolutely stunned by these developments in Pablo's life. We asked ourselves how this could have happened without our noticing the changes. Did we not pick up any warning signals that Pablo had departed on another path? How could he have become so immersed in gang life while looking like such an angel sitting in Sunday-morning worship? And how could we reconcile such vastly different portraits of this young man? Which one was the real Pablo?

The truth, as it turns out, is that both Pablos—the angelic young confirmand and the devilish gang member—are part and parcel of who he is. For all Christians, identities are complex things. Most of us are better able to keep our sinful and more corrupt side hidden than was Pablo.

Because of the charges against him, Pablo was kept in juvenile detention from September until his trial in January. This was his first time to be in trouble with the police, but the legal consequences of his actions could not have been more severe. Because of new immigration laws, if Pablo were convicted of any of the felony charges, this young boy in all probability would be deported to his home country for incarceration in an adult prison. At thirteen years of age, his life, in effect, would be over.

I felt very strongly that he was salvageable—that God still had great plans for Pablo's life. Having watched him grow up, I had witnessed many of the complicating factors of his life. I knew many of the circumstances that had brought him to this moment. I decided to do everything within my power to see that he had a second chance. That fall I was in court on six different occasions. I visited the juvenile detention facility over twenty-five times.

Susan also went to work, regularly visiting Pablo to talk, to pray and to have Bible study. Soon others within the congregation and also the community were marshaling forces in an effort to help Pablo. We sought legal assistance for him from Chris Todd, an attorney in our congregation and a former federal prosecutor, who agreed to serve as cocounsel in an advisory capacity. But we still needed to secure another attorney with expertise in both juvenile criminal law and immigration law. In what can only be described as a providential twist, Pablo's probation officer recommended just such an attorney, who was also a Christian and the son of a minister. The legal defense was being readied, but Pablo's cooperation in his own defense remained an issue.

The months in juvenile detention had hardened Pablo. This sweet, formerly optimistic and outgoing teenager soon became a tough, street-smart and cynical detainee. Pablo's incarceration seemed to instill within him a sense of inevitable hopelessness. The reality of his limited options as an undocumented immigrant informed his despair. Pablo began to give up on himself. It became apparent to those of us ministering to Pablo that if he were unable to imagine a different future for himself, then even if we avoided the worst consequences of the current charges, he would only get in trouble again.

Susan and Pablo began to deepen their relationship in ways neither could have foreseen. She spoke truth to his hardened despair and embraced his broken spirit with her compassion. Their visits in juvenile detention were essential to reinstilling hope within Pablo. At the same time, it was becoming apparent that if Pablo was released from detention, he would need to go somewhere other than his own home. Susan offered to keep Pablo with her if and when he was released.

Thus a strategy began to fall into place. We told Pablo that we would work as hard as possible to defend him on the condition that he believe in himself, his own future and God's capacity to help him make a new beginning in his life. Second, we would try to solve his inability to return home by providing an alternative—Susan's home—with the permission and blessing of Pablo's mother. Third, we would begin to work on his immigration status so that he could envision a future with hope—that one day he even could go to college (a possibility not open to him as an undocumented alien).

In the end, a true miracle occured. Against all odds and words of caution from the attorneys not to get our hopes up, Pablo was convicted of only two misdemeanor offenses and was given probation. The two officers who arrested him even testified on his behalf. He was spared both further jail time and, more important, the possibility of deportation. In an agreement worked out with the presiding judge, Pablo received funding to attend a special academy for youth in order to get his life back together. In short, Pablo was given back his life. As the Scriptures say, "This son of mine was dead and is alive again; he was lost and is found!" (Lk 15:24).

One year later, Pablo's life began to turn around. In December, Susan legally adopted him. We tease Susan that of course it had to happen in December. She was our Elizabeth, becoming a mother only after she qualified for social security. With a new beginning in a new family, this child, who had had an uncertain (if not bleak) future twelve months earlier, now had a bright and promising future ahead of him.

I came away from the trial feeling that this episode summed up well why I went into the ministry—to be an advocate, to make a difference, to be a bearer of good news. I felt that maybe, just maybe, it was for this event alone that Susan and I had been brought together in mutual ministry at Culmore—to be present in this particular boy's life at this precise moment.

Jesus said:

The Spirit of the Lord is upon me,
   because he has anointed me
      to bring good news to the poor.
He has sent me to proclaim release to the captives
   and recovery of sight to the blind,
      to let the oppressed go free. (Lk 4:18)

9
Ambassadors for Christ

●●

PRINCIPLE: A multicultural church is both conflictual and conciliatory.

So we are ambassadors for Christ, since God is making his appeal through us; we entreat you on behalf of Christ, be reconciled to God. 2 CORINTHIANS 5:20

I received a phone call about 6:00 a.m. one Good Friday, and since no one ever calls that early, my first thought was that something terrible had happened. I was rather surprised to hear the breathless and fear-filled voice of Monte Campbell, the director of our English as a second language program. What surprised me was not that she was calling from the church at 6:00 a.m. Monte is a special education teacher who, in her free time over the past five years, has started nineteen different ESL programs in northern Virginia churches. She squeezes in more ministry before she actually goes to her job than most people do in a typical day. What really surprised me about the call was not the hour but the tone of her voice.

"Steve, I'm at the church photocopying materials for the English classes," Monte said. "Several minutes ago I began to hear thumping sounds coming from the sanctuary upstairs. And then I began to hear what I can only describe as weeping and wailing. Steve, I think that some homeless man must be destroying the sanctuary. I've taken the liberty of calling the police. They are on their way now. I'm just calling to inform you of what is happening."

As Monte reeled off this information, I was thinking, *Is there any other explanation for what she is hearing? Who else would be in the church this early?* I asked, "Monte, have you actually gone upstairs to get a look at who is in the sanctuary?"

"Well, no," she said. "When I heard the wailing and thumping, I decided not to go up. Why do you ask?"

"There is another possibility," I suggested. "I believe there are some Korean men who come to the church early in the morning to pray, and after all, this *is* Good Friday."

All Monte could say was "Oh my Lord . . . I'll call you right back." She promptly hung up.

I did not wait for Monte's return call but quickly got dressed and went to the church. I saw two police cars as soon I pulled into the parking lot. Monte was standing outside talking to the officers. When I walked up, Monte, with a bright red face, said, "Steve, I'm so sorry about this. I made a terrible mistake. I went upstairs after I hung up the phone and peeped in the rear of the sanctuary, only to find two Korean gentlemen in business suits kneeling in prayer. It was their prayers I heard. Their bowing must have been the thumping sounds. So as quickly as I could, I came out here and stopped these kind officers."

As she was explaining what had happened, who should exit the church but the two men, who had completed their morning prayers. Monte, the officers and I chatted and laughed with these parishioners: "Oh, just another early workday. Why else would we be here in the parking lot so early in the morning!" And then the men walked on to their car, not realizing what had almost happened.

Good Friday is a day full of penitence—truly a day to weep and mourn for one's sins, to bow before the Lord God Almighty and ask forgiveness. Where else should a Christian begin this day but at the church in prayer? Monte and I stood there uttering our own prayers to heaven, thanking God for divine mercy and intervention. The newspaper headlines surely would have read "Church Has Parishioners Arrested for Praying Too Loudly on Good Friday."

This story had a happy ending, but many times in multicultural ministry, crosscultural misunderstandings such as this one end in tragic confusion and conflict. God has blessed each one of us with our own cultural uniqueness, but when we interact with other persons in their own cultural particularity, we may forget that the very differences that distinguish us can also be a blessing from God. In crosscultural interaction we sometimes approach one another with fear—fear of difference, fear of what we do not understand, fear of what we do not want to understand. The challenge of Christian unity is the challenge of overcoming our fear of differences and adopting the humble posture of one who has something to learn.

The Bible invites us to transcend the myopia of cultural particularity so that we may remember the true source of our unity:

> For by the grace given to me I say to everyone among you not to think of yourself more highly than you ought to think, but to think with sober judgment, each according to the measure of faith that God has assigned. For as in one body we have many members, and not all the members have the same function, so we, who are many, are one body in Christ, and individually we are members one of another. (Rom 12:3-5)

God has given each one of us special spiritual gifts. Christian unity, then, presupposes spiritual diversity. But as Paul said to the Corinthian congregation, "To each is given the manifestation of the Spirit for the *common* good" (1 Cor 12:7). Spiritual diversity is not intended for personal edification or to differentiate the body of Christ; rather, spiritual diversity is intended to complete the whole, to ensure the common good, to build community.

The Folly of Christian Unity

In the story of Babel, we are told how the people, instead of relying on God's gifts to build community, decided that they would build a tower by their own efforts. The people of the earth said to one another, "Come, let us build ourselves a city, and a tower with its top in the heavens, and let us make a name for ourselves" (Gen 11:4). Whether it's in our own family, nation, ethnic group, race or cultural heritage, confusion and misunderstanding begin the moment we begin to say to each other, "Come, let us make a name for ourselves."

Such was the case in Paul's letters to the Corinthians, when he addressed a divided and quarreling congregation. Each faction in the Corinthian congregation was trying to make a name for itself, trying to prove that it was right and everyone else wrong. They used their spiritual diversity to tear down the community rather than rely on these gifts to build up the community.

The congregation at Corinth was an adolescent congregation, not so much in age but in spiritual maturity. Though they had been a congregation long enough not to be considered "babes in Christ," they had not been at it long enough to be considered wise. They were in between, struggling with their identity as Christians. In addition, the Corinthian church was about as multicultural as the Bible presents—both Jewish and Gentile Christians, poor and wealthy, slave and free, educated and uneducated. In all this diversity lay the potential for great misunderstanding, which was exactly what happened.

The division in the Corinthian church was less about theology than it was about politics—who had control, who held the power, who received the glory. Recent scholars have noted that the language Paul uses in this passage is essentially political. Paul asks the Corinthians, "Has the body of Christ been divided into pieces?" That sentence can be translated literally: "Has the body of Christ been split into parties?" Of course it had.

Corinth had four major factions. The Paul group stressed Christian freedom. The Apollos group loved philosophy and eloquence—they were the educated elite. The Peter group mostly consisted of Jewish Christians who emphasized tradition, authority and the need for organization. Finally, the Christ group believed themselves to be above the division, because they believed they had a unique spirituality and a direct line to God.

In a sense each group was right in its own way. The problem was that each had only part of the truth of the gospel, and none saw the whole truth. They needed each other in order to be the complete body of Christ, to *embody* the whole truth of the gospel. And yet here they were, dividing up the body of Christ, more concerned about getting their share of the bread than about whether everyone was fed! And all because they wanted to make a name for themselves.

The sin of the Corinthian congregation was pride. It was not pride in the sense that they were proud of their congregation and believed that they had something to offer others. God calls us to be proud in that way, for it is the pride of love and confidence in the gospel. The pride in Corinth was born out of insecurity and anxiety. It was the fear of being nobody. Pride, after all, always reveals our deepest insecurities. Pride and insecurity are two sides of the same coin. Consequently they clung to each other in groups and cliques, hoping that the persons with whom they associated proved to others how good and righteous they were.

Paul called on the Corinthian Christians to remember what made them good and righteous in the first place. He asked them to remember the cross of Jesus Christ, which he calls "a stumbling block to Jews and foolishness to Gentiles" (1 Cor 1:23). Paul reminded them that only something as scandalous as the cross of Calvary could ever bring them together in all their diversity. The Corinthians, however, were responding as embarrassed adolescents to God's totally uncool public display of acceptance and love in Jesus Christ. They tried to push the cross into the background, relying only on themselves, their own reputations, their own names, instead of relying on the name of Jesus Christ.

As long as Christians continue to divide themselves into groups in order "to make a name," the body of Christ will never be united. As long as we separate ourselves into categories—liberals versus conservatives, evangelicals versus social activists, charismatics versus traditionalists, middle class versus poor, educated versus uneducated, men versus women, white versus nonwhite, American-born versus immigrant—as long as we continue to say, "See how different we are?" we will never be able to accept the radical nature of God's love, which the prophet Joel says God has poured out "on *all flesh*" (Joel 2:28).

Amid our diversity of race, culture, class, gender, language and education, we must realize what we have in common. The only thing that can unite us and make us whole is our salvation in Jesus Christ, God's folly of love revealed in the cross.

As Paul says:

The message about the cross is foolishness [folly] to those who are perishing, but to us who are being saved it is the power of God. . . . For God's foolishness is wiser than human wisdom, and God's weakness is stronger than human strength. . . . But God chose what is foolish in the world to shame the wise; God chose what is weak in the world to shame the strong. (1 Cor 1:18, 25, 27)

Us and Them

Approximately four years ago, Culmore was going through a difficult period of turmoil, not unlike the congregation at Corinth. This time was still early in our transformation into an intentionally multicultural church. We were going through a transition in which we were trying to sort out our identity as a congregation. There was competition and jealousy between the language ministries. The fear was that one group would emerge as the largest and that Culmore eventually would become a homogeneous congregation of that ethnicity. Because many new members had not been personally integrated, and also because the model of an inclusive congregation was still new to us (we often made it up as we went along), trust and security were in short supply.

For several months I had been dealing with one conflict after another. Though my style of mediation had been interpersonal, it seemed a good idea now to address the congregation as a whole about how we should resolve our differences as the body of Christ. The following is an excerpt from that sermon.

Sisters and brothers of Culmore, we, like the congregation in Corinth, are a very diverse congregation: in ethnicity, in language, in age, in economic status, in theology, in the ways we worship—you name it, we've got it! You would be hard-pressed to find another congregation with as much diversity. But there are times when this diversity often feels like a barrier, an obstacle which keeps us from getting to know one another instead of bringing us together. There are times when it feels like we are three or more congregations instead of one. And some may well ask, wouldn't it be easier if we were separate congregations instead of trying to bring everyone together? It might be easier, but it would not necessarily be faithful. My grandmother had a saying: "Birds of a feather flock together." That's true in the natural world, but God has not called us to live in the natural world. As Christians, God has called us to live in the *supranatural* world, that is, to live *above* our natures—to live above our divisions, our prejudices, our fears. Here at Culmore we may not all have the same feathers, but we are all birds of the same flock.

Now I am here to tell you this morning that if it seems more difficult to follow Jesus at Culmore, that's because it is! You have to work harder at it. We do not and will not make it easy or comfortable. There are other churches where everyone is alike: where everyone is of the same race, speaks the same language, has a comparable income, the same educational level, or a similar theological bent. In those churches you can go in and with relative ease find someone who is like you. But at Culmore if you are not willing to go out of your way to intentionally get to know your neighbor, then chances are you won't.

I cannot tell you how many times I have heard different groups in the church say: Why don't *they* come to *our* activities? Why don't *they* invite *us* to theirs? Why don't *they* want to get to know *us*? I have heard this from Anglos and Africans, Filipinos and Latinos. Virtually every group in the congregation has said this at one time or another. What I hear in these comments is the pain of folk feeling like outsiders, waiting for someone else to invite them in. But what I have come to realize is that in a congregation like ours there are few, if any, true insiders to welcome the rest of us in. This, of course, means that it is the responsibility of each one of us to welcome, include and get to know each other. We cannot wait for someone else to do it for us.

One of our homebound members, Bonnie Lynn, tells the story of how when she was a newcomer to Culmore many years ago, she took the initiative and went and greeted each person whom she did not recognize. One Sunday she went up to a woman whom she had never seen in worship, assuming of course that this woman was a visitor. Bonnie Lynn greeted her, told her how glad she was that she had visited, and invited her to come back another Sunday.

Bonnie immediately saw that this woman had taken offense. She told Bonnie, "I'll have you know that I have been a member here for twenty years," to which Bonnie feistily responded, "Well, I am so glad to make your acquaintance, but you know, it sure would help us newcomers if you old-timers would come more often so we could get to know you!" Friends, what I want you to do today is to follow Bonnie Lynn's example.

I have been in most of your homes; I have gotten to know you and your families. We have laughed together, wept together, and prayed together. My greatest hope is that all of you will get to know each other as I have gotten to know you, and maybe a whole lot better. As your pastor, I have tried to build as many bridges between you as I can. But you must take responsibility for building true Christian community here at Culmore. I can't do it for you, and even if I could do it for you, I would not. You must *want* to get to know each other. You must be willing to overcome your fears, prejudices, discomforts. That doesn't mean you are going to be best friends with everybody, or that you are even going to like everybody. It doesn't even mean that everyone is going to respond to your hospitality the way you want them to. But it does mean that you must long for and work for common ground—and that common ground can only be found in our salvation through Jesus Christ! There is nothing else that will hold us together.

Of Creeds and Clapping: What Separates Us

At Culmore we have encountered several dynamics at play within our congregation, which frequently serve as sources of friction or misunderstanding. These dynamics are not necessarily problems to be solved, but more like factors to be recognized as we seek unity and harmony in the body.

How to say hello. During my first year at Culmore, one of the most perplexing issues I faced was how to greet my parishioners properly. Should I shake hands, should I bow, or should I give them a big ol' east Tennessee hug? How close should I stand? Should I look someone directly in the eyes, or should I avert my eyes? Although I was concerned with not violating any parishioner's cultural etiquette, my parishioners were very forgiving of any faux pas I may have committed. They deeply appreciated the small gestures by which I tried to communicate my willingness to learn.

I remember one Sunday morning early on. As I stood at the rear of the sanctuary, waiting for the folks to exit, one older woman from North Carolina came to the narthex with her arms open wide. I reciprocated her greeting with great warmth. Next came Pastor Max, our Filipino minister, and I also greeted him with a hug. Pastor Max, who is one of the warmest and friendliest people in the congregation, seemed taken aback. I could feel him physically stiffen as I embraced him. Unsure of what I had done wrong, I decided to err on the side of caution with the next person in line. It turned out to be a very expressive man from Bolivia. This time I thrust my hand forward, only to be grabbed by the torso and physically lifted off the floor!

After we had gotten to know each other better, I asked Pastor Max about what he considered a proper Filipino greeting. He shared with me that between male peers, a handshake is usually most appropriate. He said that it is important to preserve an appropriate distance between each other. Men generally do not hug, unless it is a time of crisis and comforting is needed. Men and women may embrace, but only if they are close friends. He told me not to be surprised if some of the younger Filipinos took my hand and touched it to their foreheads. This is called *mano po,* and it is intended as a sign of respect. Since that time, however, Pastor Max and I have become very close, and it is not unusual for us to embrace. We are both learning.

I also asked Pastor Juan Paredes what he considered a proper greeting in Latin American cultures. He replied, "Steve, we Hispanics are not so cold as the Anglo-Saxons. Our natures are very warm. So when we have Christian confidence in each other, we frequently greet each other with *ósculo,* or as Saint Paul puts it, the "holy kiss." Particularly between Christian brothers and sisters, it is appropriate to kiss each other on the cheek. Also, hugs are important. They are a sign of warmth and affection." I asked him how he would feel if someone he was close to did not greet him with an embrace. He responded, "I would probably take offense. I would take it as a sign that something was not right in our relationship and wonder what I had done wrong."

I posed the same question to Kwang-Ho Lee, a Korean seminarian in our congregation. He said that bowing is a noble way to greet one another, especially if there is an age difference. It is a sign of honor and respect that originated in the Confucian heritage. Between friends, however, shaking hands is usually acceptable. Men and women, however, generally do not touch, because it assumes a familiarity that is awkward and embarrassing.

One other thing I have learned from many Asian cultures is the tendency to avert the eyes when addressing each other. As Pastor Max explained it to me, looking someone directly in the eye when speaking to him or her could be interpreted as intrusive or even as an aggressive gesture. I then shared with Max how in my own culture averting one's eyes is a sign of dishonesty. One's character and integrity are judged by one's ability to "look someone in the eyes." We laughed at how radically differently a single gesture of body language can be interpreted.

One afternoon I visited a young African nurse who was relatively new to our congregation but had stopped coming to worship. As we talked, it became clear that something had happened to hurt her. I asked her what had occurred. She told me about an incident that took place one Sunday during greeting time in worship. Greeting time at Culmore is not a simple "passing the peace," in which you turn to the people seated immediately around you and then sit down. From the beginning we encouraged the family of God to greet each other as brothers and sisters in Christ. So midway through the service each Sunday, the members of the congregation get up and for five to ten minutes roam around the sanctuary, noisily hugging, kissing and greeting one another. It has become a distinctive mark of worship at Culmore.

On this particular Sunday, as the African nurse was greeting others in the congregation, she stretched out her hand to a man who was seated near her. At first he did not seem to want to take her hand, but then he did, although he was clearly uncomfortable. He too was an immigrant member, but she could not identify what ethnicity. She interpreted his discomfort as prejudice, that he did not want to shake hands with her because she was a black African. She told me of numerous experiences of racism she had had in the United States.

It would have been easy to see this incident as yet another rejection of her because of the color of her skin. On the other hand, maybe the man's own cultural background made him uncomfortable shaking hands with her, possibly because he was a man and she was a woman. I was never able to discover who the man was, and she moved to another part of the state shortly thereafter. We will never know whether it was a cultural difference or racism. The one thing I do know is that in a multicultural church, not even saying hello is an easy matter.

What Did You Say?

Another source of miscommunication, beyond body language, is the very words we use. As I mentioned in an earlier chapter, when I first came to Culmore, even the act of talking to a person of another ethnicity was cause for anxiety for many in the congregation. When English is the second language to a majority of the congregation, there is more than ample room for questioning the accuracy of pronunciation, not to mention the meaning of the words chosen.

Won-Hee Kang, our choir director, recently told me a joke that pointed out how much responsibility this places on the nonnative English speaker. Won-Hee asked me, "Steve, what do you call someone who speaks three languages?"

"Trilingual?" I ventured.

"Yes," she responded. "What do you call someone who speaks two languages?"

"Bilingual," I said more confidently.

"Right," she said. "Now what do you call someone who speaks only one language?"

I thought for a minute and finally said, "Monolingual?"

"No," said Won-Hee. "You call him an American!"

When a congregation uses a second or third language as its means for communication, misunderstandings are going to arise. One congregation I visited on my sabbatical had recently gone through a period of turmoil. The controversy arose from a misunderstanding in the choir. (Charlie Day, an Anglo in my congregation, likes to say, "You know, Steve, the devil always comes in through the choir.") The choir in this congregation was multiethnic. The choir director was Anglo. He was renowned for the classical pieces his choir performed. In many ways this director ran the choir as if it were composed of professional musicians rather than volunteers, and he always encouraged them to excel.

One night during practice, while the director was working the members particularly hard, he said something that offended three of them. These three women were Asian. They turned to each other, and one asked, "What did he say?"

"I think he just called us stupid," said another.

Immediately all three left the rehearsal, mad as wet hens, as we say in the South.

This matter was soon brought before the church, and an investigation ensued. Had the choir director in fact called three of his members stupid? As it happened, because of the director's fastidiousness, he routinely taped the rehearsals. Thus a tape of the rehearsal existed. Those who investigated the incident listened to the tape and discovered that what the director had actually said was *stufe*, a German musical term for degree. By the time this misunderstanding was discovered, however, the damage had been done. The director soon left for a new position, and the three women quit the choir.

Passing Me By

An issue that in my opinion is more divisive than race in the multicultural church is class. Class, of course, is by no means the sole property of the multicultural church. Where I grew up in east Tennessee, class (such as it was!) determined everything: where you lived, where you went to school, who your friends were, and of course, where you went to church. When I went to college, I thought education allowed you to transcend class designation. Little did I know.

While in college I went to Nashville to hear Hans Küng lecture at Vanderbilt University. I also decided to attend a revival being held at a large, affluent downtown church. The Reverend Lord Donald Soaper, an evangelical Methodist from England, was the guest preacher. Why this conservative, upper-class congregation invited Lord Soaper, a socialist street preacher and pastor to the poor, to preach a revival I will never quite understand. It was fascinating to watch him preach from the pulpit as if he were at Speaker's Corner in Hyde Park, asking—even demanding—those in the congregation to stand up and debate him as he spoke. Those who accepted his invitation never stood a chance. I had never before heard anyone speak so passionately about the church's obligation to be in ministry with the poor. I was absolutely enchanted by this white-maned British prophet.

The first night I attended the revival, I entered the large, neo-Gothic sanctuary and nervously made my way down toward the front pews. I had never been in a church this large, and I found it more than a bit intimidating. As I sat down, a man seated in the pew directly in front of me turned around and struck up a conversation. He noticed my twangy Appalachian accent and immediately asked, "Son, do you know where you are?"

Well, I thought I knew, but then maybe I didn't. Maybe I had mistakenly entered the wrong church. Did I look lost? Did I look like I didn't know where I was supposed to be? Finally I said to him that I thought I knew where I was.

He then proceeded to tell me how large and influential the congregation was, that it was the "mother church of Methodism in middle Tennessee." He concluded by telling me that his church was well known throughout the region, because, he said, "Son, we make bishops here!"

Then he turned around and our conversation ended. I suddenly felt very uncomfortable, wondering whether I was in the right place. Maybe I had entered the wrong church after all. I thought about his last statement and found myself wondering, *Do you make Christians here too?*

Nothing quite offends my own Appalachian populism as much as cultural elitism ("come, let us make a name for ourselves"). And yet this is part and parcel of many of the cultures represented in ethnically diverse congregations. Many societies highly value elitism and gentility. In such societies braggadocio and machismo are seen as signs of personal strength and dignity. They are an outward presentation to the world, in effect saying, "I am somebody and you will take notice." Elitism thus becomes a means of achieving individual respect. Although I have always assumed that we

Americans have cornered the market on pride, self-promotion and our can-do philosophy, I must admit that some of my Latin American brothers in particular can put me to shame in terms of machismo. The downside of this strong sense of pride, however, lies in the human need to identify and separate the elite from the common—those who merit respect from those who do not.

Class distinctions I have noticed in our congregation have been based on factors such as where one comes from (the city or the countryside), how much education one has had, whether one is a professional or a manual laborer, the shade of one's skin color, one's regional accent, one's family's connections back home, and how well one knows English—to name just a few. Most often these distinctions have tended to manifest themselves *within* ethnic groups at Culmore rather than between groups. Thus much of the conflict resolution I have been involved in has been ethnocentric. It is not uncommon for a member of one group to feel slighted by another member of that same group. The phrase "passed me by" is often used, as in "so-and-so passed me by and did not take notice of me or greet me." In American street slang, one might say "I was dissed." It is a way of saying that refusing to recognize someone as a person is signaling that one has no respect for that person, that the person is not worth one's time or attention. In cultures in which time itself is viewed relationally (that is, time is quantified not by what is accomplished but by how it is spent with others), there could be no greater offense.

When Yes Means Yes

Another common issue in multicultural congregations is what Duane Elmer calls the "relational yes."[1] In many cultures pleasing a person is more important than being completely candid: yes may mean yes, but yes can also mean no. This issue tends to accentuate the Western versus non-Western perspective more than most. Whereas the majority of Americans prefer a direct answer of yes or no, most other cultures value personal honor over such directness. To have to say no to someone, especially someone you naturally want to please, in a sense brings shame on that person, because you have caused disappointment to him or her. It may be far more preferable for non-Americans to say yes, even when the request is not possible to fulfill, than to openly disappoint and place the relationship at risk. Elmer puts it this way:

Westerners prefer direct forms of communication and are not good at reading between the lines. Yet in most cultures the people are masters at indirect speech, and one must become accustomed to it if one is to survive and prosper in the Two-Thirds World. Although at first it seems mystifying and frustrating to be constantly decoding people's speech, it soon becomes second nature, and eventually one finds enjoyment in practicing the new skill.[2]

I agree with Elmer on the "mystifying and frustrating" part, but I am not yet convinced about its becoming second nature. I have yet to really understand the relational yes. I still find myself disappointed when, for example, we are having a cleanup day at church and I have spent several hours making calls to secure enough volunteers for the day, but not many people show up. Although I get many yes responses over the phone, I am never really sure just how many people will actually come. Too often it seems that picnics were already planned, a person was previously scheduled to work that day, family members are coming in from out of town—and all of this is known when we talk on the phone. It is more important to my parishioners, however, for me to be assured that they will come and for me to be pleased by their answer than whether they actually show up on that day.

Kimchi in the Kitchen

While visiting congregations during my sabbatical, one conflict that emerged over and over again is what I call "kimchi in the kitchen." *Kimchi* is a traditional Korean dish of cabbage, garlic, chili, shrimp sauce and green onions, among other ingredients—a mélange that is marinated in saltwater for five or six hours. Some Koreans like to let kimchi ferment for long periods of time to make it especially spicy and hot. In many ways kimchi is the Korean equivalent of the American pickle. Kimchi is eaten every day in most Korean homes, and with virtually every meal. For many persons kimchi is not only the favorite part of the meal but the most important.

When Korean fellowships meet in churches to share a meal, one can be sure that kimchi will be present in large quantities. Many non-Koreans perceive kimchi as having an aroma that is strong and pungent—and not altogether pleasant. But then most cabbage dishes are not known for their pleasant fragrance. Take sauerkraut, a dish from German immigrants of another era; it too is known to leave a lingering odor in the kitchen. When

I was growing up, my mother frequently cooked sauerkraut with hot dogs mixed in. Though I did not particularly like its smell, I did like the way it tasted!

The kimchi issue in multicultural churches, or Anglo churches sharing their facilities with Korean congregations, is neither about kimchi itself nor about its smell. It is about territorial control and identity. For many congregations the smell of an exotic food, the sound of strange and different music or, as demonstrated at the beginning of the chapter, a different type of prayer are things that may precipitate a problem. Such factors force congregations to confront the cultural differences that are present, as well as the changes they bring.

I have found that in most congregations, change is accepted until that change forces concessions from the majority culture. The moment that members of the "old guard" (referring not to age but to length of time in the congregation) are asked to modify their behavior, to adapt their ritual or to acclimate their customs, conflict ensues. It is precisely at this point that the issue of assimilation enters the congregational dialogue: "Why can't *they* eat the same kind of food *we* do? . . . Why should *we* learn *their* songs? This *is* America. If *they* are going to participate in *our* worship, *they* should learn English. . . . Don't *they* know that this is *our* Sunday-school room? *We* have been meeting in here for thirty years. Let *them* use some other room for *their* English classes." One can imagine the effect these kinds of words have on people who thought they were being welcomed into the congregation as full participants. Instead they discover they are perceived less as partners in ministry and more as tenants—to the majority culture's role as landlord.

Pastor as *Patrón*

In my first three years at Culmore, decision-making became more and more hierarchical as we became more diverse. As pastor, I suddenly found myself in a position of more authority and administrative control than I would have ever been allowed in an Anglo United Methodist congregation. At the same time, the committee structure, which is standard in our denomination and notorious for its bureaucratic methodology (we are, after all, *Method*-ists), just did not seem to work. Now, to any pastor who has chafed under the constraints of most congregations and has longed for the opportunity to play benevolent dictator, let me say one thing: it's not what it's cracked up to be! I have actually come to long for the security and accountability that traditional American church structure provides. Yet in this congregation, culture and circumstance have coincided to create a pastoral model present in most multicultural and immigrant churches but little talked about: pastor as *patrón*, which is Spanish for "boss man," that is, the overseer who organizes the workers.

As I explained in chapter five, one of the first transitions we went through as a multicultural church was to include younger adults and non-Anglo members, in order to reflect who we were becoming as a church and to infuse the leadership with new blood. But with these changes, we did not foresee the extent to which the new leaders would desire a different way of organizing the church. When I asked young Anglos to serve in particular positions in the church, they would often agree to do so only if the church explicitly limited their administrative responsibilities. On more than one occasion a young Anglo has said, "Steve, I don't want to come to meetings to *plan* ministry, I just want to *do* ministry." It was often easier to recruit persons for "hands-on" ministry, such as teaching English, than to get them to come to a planning meeting for English classes. One factor in this preference is generational: baby boomers and Generation Xers are not interested in activities perceived to be a part of institutional support and maintenance. They are more interested in ministries they think will meet a need and make a difference. Consequently as our congregation rapidly became younger, fewer and fewer persons came to meetings and made decisions.

A second factor in this leadership equation was the regional lifestyle of metropolitan Washington, D.C. As in most major cities, the lifestyle pace here is hectic: long commutes, traffic jams, and workdays that last until 8:00 or 9:00 p.m., not to mention the second or third job if you are an immigrant. With factors such as these, it was no wonder that many in our congregation wanted to maximize their participation in the life of the church by cutting to the chase and getting right to ministry.

A third factor in the leadership equation was the unfamiliarity of volunteerism among many of the first-generation immigrants. For many of them, churches back home tend to be smaller and more family- and community-oriented. There may not be much need for extensive organizational structures. The way one is expected to participate in church is to go to worship and Bible studies, attend early-morning prayer, sing in the choir and so on. Only a select few laity, often called elders or deacons, are chosen to work with the pastor to make major decisions for the church, decisions that the congregation is expected to abide by.

One of the ways we dealt with the issue of time availability was to reduce the number of committees in the congregation and to develop more of a staff-based approach to ministry. The underlying concept was that if our laity did not have the time to plan ministry, our staff would take the responsibility so that we might encourage people to be active in the life of the church. The flaw in this approach was also its logic. Ministry was indeed well planned, but the transition of ownership to the new membership base was not properly cultivated. The more staff-oriented the decision-making became (or, to tell the truth, pastor-oriented), the less responsibility the congregation assumed.

Miami Urban Ministries, in a seminar entitled "Cross-Cultural Leadership and Participation in the Local Church," found that among many immigrant populations (in their case, particularly Caribbean and Latin American), national and political history has been shaped by a succession of all-powerful leaders. The legacy of the conquistadors in Latin America, for example, continues to have an influence that permeates and determines the social values of leadership, emphasizing (1) power and control over inclusion, (2) hierarchy over equality and (3) status over humility.[3]

As a result, a divergence between our church's stated organizational structure and our true operating system often develops. Many of our folks, for example, come from nondemocratic backgrounds, both culturally and religiously, which makes it difficult for them to adapt readily to the more egalitarian and democratic decision-making structure of the U.S. church. Pastors in multicultural churches are thus caught between two radically different leadership paradigms. Although it might seem like a good thing for pastors to have more power, the downside is that true congregational ownership may not occur in the ministry of the church. In addition, native-born Americans who are accustomed to democratic decision-making feel frustration and resentment in such a system.

Recently we were debating an issue in our church council. One of the members, Mary, who is Filipino, asked my opinion on the topic. I said that I preferred not to share my opinion but to let the council decide. On previous occasions Mary has expressed frustration with the way we make decisions at the church, always encouraging me to take a much stronger role in leadership. After I refused in the meeting to share my own opinion, she admonished the council to "follow the pastor" on this matter, saying that the pastor's opinion should determine our decision.

An American friend who was sitting next to her said, "Well, you know, Mary, that's not the way it works here—this is a democracy."

She responded, "I come from the Third World, and I also come from a democracy, but in our country the president has a lot of say. You don't bypass the president. You listen to what he says. If you don't trust the president, then why did you elect him? It's the same way with our pastor. The Lord has put him here. Don't you think we ought to listen to what God is saying through him?"

Worship Wars

An issue that is almost as divisive as class in the multicultural church is worship. Not only do our members speak many languages, come from different countries and represent different ethnicities, but they also manifest myriad ecclesiological worship styles. Of the new members who have joined Culmore from Christian congregations in their home countries, the two largest church backgrounds represented are the Catholic Church and Pentecostal churches. A significant number also come from independent Bible churches. Only a relatively small portion of our new members reflect transfers from within our denomination. As a result, the worship preferences of our congregation run the gamut: from mainline Protestant to charismatic, liturgical to revivalistic, stoic to emotive, sedate to enthusiastic, passive to fully participatory. And as one might expect, the inclusion of one element in worship that may please some always poses the threat to offend another.

The inclusion of the Apostles' Creed has been a particularly sensitive issue. For many traditionalists in our congregation, a worship service is not complete without the recitation of the Apostles' Creed; they assume it has a place in the service. I, on the other hand, am at least part rooted in the revivalist tradition. I can remember going to my home church some Sunday mornings and feeling both lost and bored by liturgical orthodoxy. I was far more moved, spiritually speaking, by Aunt Alma's independent-fundamentalist church revivals than I was by my own church's Sunday-morning worship. As a pastor, therefore, I tend to be biased more toward worship that moves people spiritually than toward liturgical correctness—

not that they are always incompatible, of course. I can sympathize with the youth and young adults who sometimes complain about being bored and lost in my services, and I have tried to accommodate them as I am able.

Early on in my ministry at Culmore we did not use the Apostles' Creed frequently. It wasn't long before I heard from some of the durable saints on this issue. They were very concerned that it be reinstated in the service. I promised that I would try to include it frequently, but not necessarily every Sunday.

A few Sundays after I had begun including the creed in worship, some of our newer members came to me and asked why I was using a "Catholic" ritual in a Protestant church. When I asked what Catholic ritual they meant, they pointed to the creed. I then asked why they considered it Catholic. Did they not use this creed in their home churches? As it turns out, among many *evangélicos,* or native Protestants, in predominantly Catholic countries, their status as a small minority led them to distinguish themselves from the dominant religious culture by eliminating liturgical practices that seemed even nominally Catholic. I learned that not only was the Apostles' Creed unfamiliar to many, but so were formal or written prayers, responsive readings and the like. Often the reason for this radical differentiation was persecution. As a Protestant minority, they were frequently the target of the majority culture. Pastor Juan Paredes has shared with me many times his difficulty in being a Protestant pastor in Chile: the overt persecution, the threats and the prejudice he and his parishioners faced. When these new members complained of the inclusion of "Catholic" liturgy, they were speaking out of their bias, yes, but also out of their pain.

Another significant worship issue in our congregation is how much congregational participation is too much. Many of our parishioners—Catholic, independent and Pentecostal alike—came from churches in which the congregation participated fully by clapping hands, shouting "Amen" and lifting up hands to praise the Lord. Needless to say, some of this expressive behavior has been shocking to our durable saints, who came of age in the churched-culture renaissance of the 1950s, when services were predictable, participation was passive, communication was one-way (from the pastor to the people), singing was formal, everyone stayed seated, and if a baby cried, the ushers quickly helped the mother find the nursery. And most important of all, everyone got out exactly at noon, in order to beat the Baptists to the diner.

On most Sundays at Culmore, we have a synthesis between the extremes. People continue to come into worship at half past the hour. Children and adults may walk in and out of worship as needed. On some Sundays we do say the Apostles' Creed, prefaced by a statement that the word *creed* means "I believe." When we recite the creed, therefore, we are witnessing the basics of the Christian faith. We sing a blend of traditional hymns, *coritos* and contemporary praise choruses. Most parishioners are quiet through the sermon, but the occasional "Amen!" or "Praise the Lord!" rises from the congregation. We don't quite finish at noon, but we don't go until one o'clock either.

I have concluded that although I wish we could be all things to all people, that is not realistic. On most Sundays the majority of the people get most of their spiritual needs met, but never all. That may be enough for such a diverse congregation.

Our Ministry of Reconciliation

If there are so many potential land mines in multicultural ministry, you may be asking, "Is there any hope?" As Rodney King once remarked, "Can't we all just get along?" Although it is true that the multicultural church is conflictual, the gospel tells us that it is also conciliatory. By facing the tensions of such diversity, we may in fact discover what it means to be ambassadors for Christ.

For conflict resolution in multicultural ministry, a key passage to consider is Acts 15. In this chapter the first-century church is struggling through the implications of its growing multicultural identity. Immediately following the successful mission to the Gentiles, the question is no longer "Can Gentiles be Christians?" but "What are the requirements for Gentiles to be Christians?" A conference was called in Jerusalem to debate this issue. Some people within the early church believed that for Gentiles to be "good Christians" they would have to be "good Jews" first, particularly regarding the requirement of circumcision. On the other side of the debate were Paul and Barnabas, who adamantly argued that circumcision now had no place in the discussion of salvation.

James, Jesus' brother, cited both Amos and Isaiah in reminding the others that God had always intended to include the Gentiles in the covenant. James then proposed a compromise, using the scriptural requirements of the aliens in Israel and applying them to Gentile Christians.

It has been suggested that the Jerusalem conference is a model for how the church should deal with controversy. All factions were invited to the table to discuss their opinions. All the participants acknowledged the seriousness of the controversy and worked together with civility to find a solution. Each faction presented its case and the scriptural antecedents for its position, as well as what the faction felt to be God's leading. When James proposed the compromise position, it was affirmed that it was the leading of the Spirit. Finally, everyone equally shared in the responsibility of the decision and put the decision in writing to be shared with others.

Will Willimon, in his commentary on this passage, says that this is how the church should argue: not by avoiding controversy or the diversity of opinion but by facing it prayerfully. "For one thing," says Willimon, "the church listens to its leaders . . . [and not just as] mere managers or bureaucratic functionaries. The church needs people of bold vision who know what is at stake in our arguments and who argue with clarity and courage."[4] Also notable are the standards used for making decisions: "New *revelation* along with confirmation by *experience* and with testing by *Scripture* are the proper measurements of the church. A church without these three standards," says Willimon, "is unable to have a good argument. All differences must be suppressed, and we dare not admit them for fear the church be destroyed by our debate."[5]

When we speak of diversity in the church, whether theological, ethnic or something else, we often use benign and feel-good metaphors. As I mentioned in the introduction, however, the metaphor that I believe best fits such diversity is a pot of marbles: our diversity can either grind us down or shine us up, depending on how we handle our genuine differences.

Diversity overload is a frequent companion to this ministry: diversity of socioeconomic levels, of culture and race, of theology, of worship styles, to name just a few. All these differences are potential sources of conflict for the church of Jesus Christ. The fact is that misunderstandings and outright clashes are inevitable. But the Bible teaches us that congregations are in a position to mediate and constructively resolve these differences. The conflict-resolution style modeled by the Jerusalem conference reminds us that we can be skilled negotiators and diplomats in these "international conflicts" of race and culture and theology, adding a new dimension to our calling to be ambassadors for Christ. But too often we deny our conflict and therein hamper the work of God's Spirit—and denying our differences does not mean our differences go away.

Leonard Sweet has observed that

one hundred or even just 50 years ago, congregational singing sounded much different than it does today. While we would recognize many of the tunes and titles . . . the *sound* of these songs was quite different. Every congregation—no matter how large or how small—sang in four-part harmony. Soprano, alto, tenor, and bass . . . blended together to create a rich, layered sound in each hymn. . . . Today almost every piece of congregational music is belted out according to a single melody line. . . . What happened? . . . When hymnbooks were precious and in short supply, children and newcomers learned the hymns by standing close by and listening to their neighbor. . . . [But] when everyone got his or her own hymnbook, the harmony began to flatten out. With the words printed on the page right in front of them, and the new piano or organ banging out the melody, people no longer had to listen to their neighbors. Ironically, as everyone increasingly listened only to themselves, they all began to sound alike.[6]

And so it is with multicultural congregations. If we listen only to our own opinions, thoughts and viewpoints, the beautiful melody of the gospel of Jesus Christ becomes bland, if not downright discordant.

Won-Hee and Pamela Atkins, our children's choir director, were explaining the concept of harmony to the children one Sunday. They described harmony as being like two or more colors that aren't alike but do go together. Just as a rainbow is made up of many different colors, so too is music made up of many different sounds.

Archbishop Desmond Tutu, preaching in Norway, said a similar thing about the church of Jesus Christ:

At home in South Africa I have sometimes said in big meetings where you have blacks and whites together: "Raise your hands!" Then I've said, "Move your hands," and I've said, "Look at your hands—different colors representing different people. You are the rainbow people of God." And you remember the rainbow in the Bible is the sign of peace. The rainbow is the sign of prosperity. We want peace, prosperity and justice and we can have it when all the people of God, the rainbow people of God, work together."[7]

We are God's rainbow church, a church of holy harmony that reveals the fullness of God's glory and grace. We succeed not by trying to make each other alike, but by celebrating each person's uniqueness and particularity—our callings, our gifts, our heritages, our languages—and by affirming that through this wonderful diversity God is weaving a multicolored tapestry of unity in Jesus Christ. Like Joseph putting on his coat of many colors, when we as God's people put on Christ, we see the brilliant rainbow of God's eternal hope.

10
By the Rivers of Babylon

••

PRINCIPLE: A multicultural church is a community of perseverance.

By the rivers of Babylon—
there we sat down and there we wept
when we remembered Zion.
On the willows there
we hung up our harps.
For there our captors
asked us for songs,
and our tormentors asked for mirth, saying,
"Sing us one of the songs of Zion!"

How could we sing the LORD's song
in a foreign land?
PSALM 137:1-4

*T*he first time I met Zenobia Mensah, I found her sitting in my office with her three children: Kingsley, Jeffrey and Melissa. She said, "You do not know me, but I am a member of your church." As it turned out, Zenobia was among the first African families who joined in the mid-1970s, and she helped to begin our journey toward a truly international fellowship. She told me that she had not been back in several years, due in part to the transient nature of her family. They had moved several times during recent years, and with each move they found it more difficult to return to Culmore.

Zenobia had come this day because she needed a pastor. She explained that she and her husband, Stephen, wanted to get married. Seeing the look of confusion on my face, Zenobia explained further. She and Stephen had been married in a ceremony many years before at the Ghanian embassy. She was not certain, however, whether that ceremony was legally recognized. What made her situation urgent was that Stephen was dying. He was in the hospital where she worked as a nurse. Apart from the legal necessities of validating their marriage, Zenobia wanted to renew her vows with Stephen. Even in his sickness and imminent death, she wanted him to know how much he meant to her. I told her I would be more than happy to marry them.

I met Zenobia at the hospital the next day, and she walked me to Stephen's room. The room was filled with friends and relatives from Ghana. Several men from National Airport—taxi drivers like Stephen—also came. Many of the nurses at the hospital who were friends and coworkers of Zenobia also joined us.

Stephen was indeed very ill. We visited for a few moments. I explained to him what Zenobia had asked me to do, and then I asked him if he also wanted this wedding. He answered, "More than anything in the world."

He and Zenobia joined hands, and I asked each in turn, "Do you take this person, to have and to hold from this day forward, for better, for worse, for richer, for poorer, in sickness and in health, to love and to cherish, until you are parted by death?" They both answered, "I do."

Stephen died two days later, and once again the room filled with family, friends and coworkers. This time, however, tears of grief replaced tears of joy. Stephen's funeral was held in his home church in Washington, D.C. Though Zenobia was a Methodist, Stephen had remained a lifelong Presbyterian. The sanctuary was filled to overflowing, and more than six hundred people attended the service. The Ghanian community had turned out to honor one of its leaders. Stephen had been president of the Kwahu Community Association, a Ghanian tribal fellowship in the metro area. The service lasted for more than three hours, as hymns were sung, testimonials offered, prayers lifted up and eulogies preached. When the formal service finally ended, the family was ushered to yet another service, a more traditional Ghanian service held in a social hall nearby. This service lasted into the early hours of the morning. A few days later Zenobia and her children took Stephen's body home to Ghana to rest in the land of his ancestors.

It has been several years since Stephen's passing, but Zenobia and her children still feel his absence. Zenobia returned to Ghana at the end of the first year after his death for a brief visit, officially ending her period of mourning—but the tears still flow. Supporting her family alone as a single parent is difficult for her. She works as a nurse in two or three different hospitals each week, and although she would rather be home with her children, that is just not possible.

The psalmist recognized the difficulty of facing life's challenges in a land that is not one's own:

> By the rivers of Babylon—
>> there we sat down and there we wept
>> when we remembered Zion.
> On the willows there
>> we hung up our harps.
> For there our captors
>> asked us for songs,
> and our tormentors asked for mirth, saying,
>> "Sing us one of the songs of Zion!"
>
> How could we sing the LORD's song
>> in a foreign land?
> If I forget you, O Jerusalem,
>> let my right hand wither!
> Let my tongue cling to the roof of my mouth,
>> if I do not remember you,
> if I do not set Jerusalem
>> above my highest joy. (Ps 137:1-6)

Though the psalmist presents the perspective of captives forcibly taken to another land, this passage nevertheless speaks to the deep anguish of trying to "sing the Lord's song" in a foreign land. How can one sing Zion's joyful songs amidst the trials and struggles of living as a stranger in a strange land?

The psalmist pledges not to forget home. The psalmist takes hope in the fact that the Lord is still sovereign, and God's lordship extends to them, even in Babylon. The psalmist ends with a prayer, asking that the Lord remember them—that as God's people, they will try to remain faithful by never forgetting Jerusalem. They also pray that the Lord will remain faithful to them by never forgetting them or the circumstances they face.

Afflicted but Not Crushed

The life of first-generation immigrants is marked by change, adaptation and struggle. Moving from one place to another is never an easy experience. Add to the normal stresses of a move the many other stresses: learning a new language, leaving family and friends behind, trying to figure out what behavior is culturally appropriate. Soon one is having an experience that can be described, at best, as overwhelming. Those who navigate the shoals of immigration and acclimation must possess the virtue of perseverance, keeping at it even when everything seems to go against them.

Scripture tells us that being human is a fragile affair. As we face tribulations and trials, we are forced to rely more on God's power than on our own strength. The apostle Paul puts it this way: "But we have this treasure in clay jars, so that it may be made clear that this extraordinary power belongs to God and does not come from us. We are afflicted in every way, but not crushed; perplexed, but not driven to despair; persecuted, but not forsaken; struck down, but not destroyed" (2 Cor 4:7-9).

Being a first-generation immigrant is not easy. But as my lay leader, Esther, continually reminds me, God "gives power to the faint, and strengthens the powerless. . . . But those who wait for the LORD shall renew their strength, they shall mount up with wings like eagles, they shall run and not be weary, they shall walk and not faint" (Is 40:29-31).

This chapter is about the first-generation immigrant experience, and the sorrows, joys and changes involved in coming to America. The chapter focuses on recent research about modern immigrants—who they are and why they come—and also shares the personal journeys of several members of my congregation.

The New Americans

One of the most useful resources I have found for discovering who modern immigrants are and why it is they come to America is a book by Alejandro Portes and Ruben G. Rumbaut entitled *Immigrant America: A Portrait.* The authors argue that recent debates on immigration have focused on the plight of undocumented workers, but this focus has resulted in an unfair and unbalanced presentation on the pros and cons of immigration. The xenophobes in the immigration debate paint a picture of a country being overrun by largely undocumented, poor and uneducated immigrants. This scenario is just not accurate. In fact, the international poor have never represented significant numbers of immigrants—the poorest people cannot afford to immigrate.[1]

One of the interesting statistics Portes and Rumbaut point out is that the proportion of "professionals and technicians among occupationally active immigrants consistently exceeds the average among U.S. workers."[2] From 1980 to 1990, they say, "immigrant professionals represented around 25 percent of the total, at a time when professionals and technicians amounted to no more than 18 percent of the American labor force."[3]

They have found that the motivating force behind recent immigration waves is not escaping poverty or destitution but rather the gap that exists between "life aspirations and expectations and the means to fulfill them in the sending countries."[4] For skilled workers, for example, they say, "migration is the means to stabilize family livelihoods and meet long-desired aspirations—a car, a TV set, domestic appliances. . . . For urban professionals, it provides a means of reaching life standards commensurate with their past achievements and to progress in their careers."[5] Immigration, then, may be directly traced to the "successful" exportation of Western culture abroad, creating an appetite for the lifestyle the United States represents, which may only be satisfied by immigrating here.[6]

Portes and Rumbaut list four primary categories that make up the modern immigrant: (1) manual laborers, (2) professional and skilled workers, (3) entrepreneurs and (4) refugees and asylum-seekers. The first category, manual laborers, sparks much of the debate over immigration. This category comprises foreign workers who come in search of low-paying jobs. These persons tend to represent the mass of undocumented immigrants. And corresponding to stereotype, these workers are drawn to the United States because of the higher wages offered here compared to those in their countries of origin.

Unlike the stereotype, however, not all manual-labor immigrants are poor or uneducated. Many people in this category, say Portes and Rumbaut, are educated and skilled but are willing to accept menial jobs well below their abilities because the wages offered are still lucrative compared to what they can receive at home. Many of the jobs these persons take may involve harsh and difficult conditions, but "to them, the trek to the United States and the economic opportunities associated with it often represent the difference between stagnation or impoverishment and attainment of their life's goals."[7] Besides, argue Portes and Rumbaut, "immigrants could not come if there were not a demand for their labor [and] that demand is strong and growing. Employers value immigrant workers' diligence, reliability, and willingness to work hard for low pay."[8]

Joey Valdez and his wife, Lily, and their two daughters, Jayzel and Jaylyn, arrived from the Philippines in 1991, just after Joey's retirement from the merchant marines. They came to the United States with a nonimmigrant status, as temporary workers, a status that applies to a large number of persons in Portes and Rumbaut's first category. They feel very fortunate that they have good employers sponsoring them for their visas. Coming to the United States has provided them with an opportunity to make a new beginning for their family.

Since they arrived in this country, Joey says, issues have emerged that have posed special challenges to his family. Joey notes that the materialism of this culture overwhelms the senses. He thanks God that many economic opportunities are available to him here. He is grateful that God has brought him to a place that is bountiful and provides for his needs. But he also recognizes dangers. The message he and his family receive is "Buy things that enable you to define your success here." An ever-present temptation is to spend money before you have it and to go into debt. Life in the Philippines didn't hold as many temptations. There they had a much more frugal and simple life.

Hand in hand with the materialism are the number of hours one must put in at work to afford an American lifestyle. Joey is a diligent and hard worker, but the amount of work and the expectations of it in the United States represent a change in values. Although people put in long hours back in the Philippines, for example, making time for family and friends was a high value. Here there is time only for work and sleep.

Joey is not alone in his feelings about how time is spent in the United States. Another member of the congregation from another region of the world remarked about how, for her, the greatest struggle in her cultural adaptation has been loneliness. Back home, in her opinion, people were more family-oriented than they are in urban America. Back home you could socialize at any time, but here it is not so easy. One is either working, going to school or chauffeuring the children to their activities. There is just no time. Church, she notes, is one of the places that can bring great personal satisfaction. She notes that even when you work very hard at your job, all your efforts sometimes go unappreciated. The Christian fellowship of church at least gives you a chance to go where people appreciate you.

Joey would "amen" that sentiment. He found Culmore in the yellow pages, listed under "Filipino Ministries," after searching long and hard for a congregation that might accept him. First and foremost, he felt welcomed as a Filipino. But he was also glad that the church had activities in which he could immediately involve his daughters, especially choir and youth ministry. Because of the importance of the family bond, Joey is grateful that in this new land he and his family are growing together in the Lord and are maturing spiritually. Joey was elected as lay leader of our Filipino Fellowship and recently began a home-based Bible study in the apartments near us, which is now drawing twenty-five to thirty unchurched Filipinos every Friday night. He serves as Pastor Max's right hand in ministry, and he is beginning to explore his own call to ministry. He is very certain of one thing: God has called him here. Joey believes that God places people in the proper places and provides for their needs.

The second category of immigrant is the professional and skilled worker. Unlike those in the first category, say Portes and Rumbaut, these immigrants are "not destined to the bottom layers of the American labor market."[9] Frequently called the "brain drain" by their home countries, these trained and well-educated immigrants come to increase their career opportunities. As the authors point out, though, "they tend to enter at the bottom of their respective occupational ladders and to progress from there according to individual merit. This is why, for example, foreign doctors and nurses are so often found in public hospitals throughout the country."[10] One important characteristic of this group is its inconspicuousness. As the authors point out, one seldom hears "reference to a Filipino or an Indian immigration 'problem,' " even though the total numbers of these ethnic communities are quite large. The reason is, they say, that these professionals tend not to attract a great deal of attention, because they "seldom form tightly knit ethnic communities."[11]

An example of this second immigrant group in my congregation is Ely Ty and her family. In her home country of the Philippines, Ely worked in the government as a computer programmer. Her siblings are also professionals, including a banker, a teacher, a musician, a missionary and an engineer. All of the immediate family members have now immigrated. The origin of their exodus was the Philippine political unrest of the 1980s. Edmund, Ely's brother, was the first to come, arriving in 1983, the year Benigno Aquino was assassinated. The immigration process for Ely and her family was helped by the fact that her grandfather had served in the

U.S. navy in World War I. At that time the Philippines was under U.S. jurisdiction. Her grandfather was considered a U.S. national, and he later came to Norfolk, Virginia, to file his letter of intention for U.S. citizenship, which he was granted. He then returned to the Philippines to live out his life. His citizenship gained renewed importance as the family planned to emigrate. Though it took more than three years for Edmund to trace their grandfather's documentation, his persistence resulted in most of the family's qualifying for citizenship.

Ely says that she is actually a very nationalistic Filipina. As her family departed for the United States, she told them, "You all can go the United States if you want, but I am staying here! After all, someone has to!" When I asked her what changed her mind, she said that political instability was the deciding factor. Also, as her family settled in northern Virginia, she became increasingly convinced that opportunities for her were more plentiful there than in the Philippines. She said that her country has more barriers in the workplace. Age discrimination, for example, is a frequent issue. For some jobs, if you are older than twenty-five you need not apply.

A great advantage in adapting to this new culture, Ely says, was being from the Philippines. Because English was taught as a second language in her country, she didn't face a communication barrier on arriving in the United States. Also, the Philippines has been very westernized through the heavy influence of American culture, especially with the large U.S. military presence there in recent decades.

Still, being an immigrant here has involved growing in humility. Ely says that no matter how high a position you may occupy in your home country, you are not guaranteed an equivalent position here, especially at first. You have to be willing to start at the bottom and work your way up. In a sense you have to swallow your pride and become a student again, learning new job skills. You cannot let yourself fall into thinking, *If only I was in my old position*, because that will result in resentment and dissatisfaction. Fortunately for Ely, she has been able to continue in the same field of work here as in the Philippines, and she is especially grateful that she has been able to work for the federal government. Ely now works for the U.S. Securities and Exchange Commission. Since starting there, Ely has risen rapidly, due to her job performance.

In many ways Ely and her family are the model success story of the professional immigrant class. Each of her siblings has found a good job.

When I first visited her in 1991, sixteen adults plus children were living in a small house, which they rented together. Today they own three homes in the suburbs. They have done very well indeed.

The third type of immigrant is the ethnic entrepreneur. Many cities have concentrated ethnic enclaves known by names such as Koreatown, Little Saigon or Chinatown. In our own immediate area is an aging shopping center that has been completely renovated and is filled with Vietnamese businesses. The Eden Center, as it is known, is now the largest Vietnamese business district on the East Coast.

Portes and Rumbaut say that the emergence of the entrepreneurial immigrant community has depended on three conditions: "First, the presence of a number of immigrants with substantial business expertise acquired in their home countries; second, access to sources of capital; third, access to labor. The requisite labor is not too difficult to obtain because it can be initially drawn from family members and then from more recent immigrant arrivals."[12]

The Chinese community in northern Virginia, as elsewhere, has been recognized for its entrepreneurial abilities. Like the Vietnamese in our community, many Chinese have moved into dilapidated stores and shopping centers, bringing economic revival to those areas. One especially well-known business is a Chinese restaurant down the street from Culmore, where the famous and near-famous dine. The restaurant gained its reputation during the Reagan and Bush administrations, when George Bush frequently came for Chinese food. The rumor was that Bush, a former ambassador to China, found this restaurant to have the most authentic Chinese food in the metropolitan area. Now, as you arrive, as you wait for a table you can gaze at pictures of the restaurant's more famous patrons: presidents, administration officials, members of Congress, ambassadors and local politicians.

Of the four immigration categories delineated by Portes and Rumbaut, they say that the significance of the entrepreneurial class "is that they create an avenue for economic mobility unavailable to other groups. This avenue is open not only to the original entrepreneurs, but to later arrivals as well."[13] Because of a shared ethnicity and cultural heritage, the relationship between employer and employee "often go[es] beyond a purely contractual bond."[14]

The fourth and final category of immigrant is the refugee or asylum-seeker. A refugee is someone who goes to a consulate or embassy abroad because of fear of persecution and asks for the protection of the U.S. government. An asylum-seeker is someone who is already in the United States when he or she applies for protection. The numbers and types of immigrants considered for this category increased after President Carter signed into law the Refugee Act of 1980. As Portes and Rumbaut note, this legislation was intended to help eliminate the then-common practice of "granting asylum only to escapees from Communist-controlled nations. Instead, it sought to bring U.S. policy into line with international practice, which defines as a refugee anyone with a well-founded fear of persecution or physical harm, regardless of the political bent of his or her country's regime."[15] Under the current statutes, refugees have legal status and the right to work. If their claim is rejected for some reason, they are classified as undocumented.

As the new immigration laws passed by the 104th Congress become effective, organizations offering immigration legal assistance have seen a swelling number of asylum-seekers. This increase is due in part to a backlog of asylum cases at the Immigration and Naturalization Service. Many of these cases are several years old. The Culmore neighborhood is largely Central American, and many who seek asylum in our area come from that region, the largest number from El Salvador and Guatemala. Many of them belong to a special group of asylum-seekers called "the ABC class"—a reference to a class-action suit that was brought by the American Baptist Church on behalf of Central Americans who had fled the civil wars of their homelands. This suit was filed in the late 1980s, when the U.S. government did not want to acknowledge the wars in Guatemala and El Salvador. The suit filed by the American Baptists alleged that these persons were being denied asylum for political reasons, even though they had valid claims. The result was a settlement with the INS and the creation of a new immigration category. These cases are only now being heard, and those who initially fled persecution, settling in this country and contributing to its prosperity, still face an uncertain future.

Assimilation American-Style

Immigrants who arrive here tend to follow a well-trod developmental path of assimilation, or acculturation, as they they seek to find their place in their new home. Bernard Adeney, drawing on the work of Anthony J.

Gittins and Arnold van Gennep, presents three different stages of assimilation one may experience when arriving as a stranger in a new culture. He cautions that these stages are not necessarily linear and distinct from one another. An immigrant may, in fact, move back and forth between these stages as circumstances change in his or her life.

The first stage Adeney cites is the *preliminary stage*. This stage, he says, is the stage of exploration and "is marked by formality and tentativeness." During this period the immigrant "may be treated with exaggerated politeness and respect" by those of the host culture.[16]

The second stage is the *transitional stage*. The immigrant may no longer feel like or be treated as an "honored guest." Reality begins to set in. "If you have made it this far without fleeing the culture shock, you are now accepted as a normal part of the local scene. You are still a foreigner, but no longer noteworthy."[17] This stage is still a time of exploration, but it is driven less by fascination with the new culture and more by the question of who you are in relation to this culture. What is most important in this stage is to cultivate both flexibility and commitment.

Adeney says that one of three things can happen in the transitional stage: (1) a person can become stuck in this stage and remain on the periphery until such time as he or she may leave; (2) a person can become "liminoid," or alienated from the new culture while remaining within it; or (3) a person can begin to find his or her place and be "adopted" into this new culture, thus moving on to the third stage.[18]

The third stage of transition is *incorporation*. An immigrant is incorporated, Adeney says, "when she or he is fully accepted and integrated into the culture. Both sides have made a long-term commitment to the other which will not be terminated even if the stranger (immigrant) leaves. When you are incorporated, you have internalized the culture to the extent that it has become part of you."[19]

Portes and Rumbaut offer a word of caution on the virtues of cultural assimilation. They argue that whereas in the past assimilation has been viewed by the host culture as having only beneficial results for the immigrant, as well as for the host culture, recent studies show that rather than alleviating stress in the transition, some aspects of assimilation actually may increase stress. The components of cultural assimilation include mastery of the language, development of new job skills and a growing familiarity with the culture. These qualities in and of themselves may be helpful, but they do not automatically eliminate the strain of adaptation.[20] Portes and Rumbaut argue that there is no "simple solution to the traumas of immigration because it can itself be a traumatic process."[21] For immigrants with less education, they say, rates of drug abuse and mental illness are higher.

Doug Ruffle, a pastor of a multicultural congregation in Teaneck, New Jersey, has recognized a similar phenomenon among his parishioners, reflecting the trauma of acculturation. He calls this an "adjustment disorder." Some immigrants may unknowingly experience emotional trauma due to the stress of their adaptation, which can result in atypical social behavior. One factor Ruffle has recognized is difficulty in coping with the greater sense of personal freedom in this culture, as well as the overwhelming number of choices to be made—far greater than most immigrants would have had available at home.[22] Ely Ty notes how individualistic America is. All decisions are based on the individual. She says that here someone may say, "I am going over to my cousin's house to visit." In the Philippines one rarely refers only to oneself; one is more likely to say, "We are going over to our cousin's house to visit." And in fact that person probably would not go alone but would take someone else along.

Portes and Rumbaut say that the acculturation stresses for better-educated immigrants involve confronting the realities of life in America versus the idealized expectations they may have held previously, and the resulting need to reaffirm their cultural identity by reestablishing ties with their ethnic community.[23] When Moses led the children of Israel from captivity in Egypt toward the Promised Land, he told them that they would be entering a land "flowing with milk and honey." When they finally came near this Promised Land and sent spies to check it out, most of them came back terrified, telling the Israelites that the land was filled with giants, who made the Israelites look like grasshoppers in comparison. How could they possibly hope to make this land their home? Scripture says that after this report, "then all the congregation raised a loud cry, and the people wept that night" (Num 14:1). For many immigrants expecting "milk and honey," the United States may also seem forbidding, causing them to wonder whether it can really ever be their home.

Many studies have been done on the assimilation process. The results from one study, which Portes and Rumbaut mention (primarily involving Indochinese refugees), are reflected in my own congregation. The results also support Adeney's three-stage hypothesis. The study shows that the first year here is "a relatively euphoric period, and the lowest depression scores and highest levels of well-being are usually reported during this time." The second year tends to be the period of greatest stress and danger, with the highest levels of depression and hopelessness reported. The term frequently used for this period is "exile shock." During the third year and beyond, adaptation seems in full swing, with greater personal confidence emerging and a "psychological rebounding" seeming to take place. Levels of depression and other expressions of stress seem to decrease significantly in this period and following.[24]

In the remainder of this chapter, I share with you the journeys of two women in our congregation who have moved through the process of cultural assimilation. Their stories reflect many of the findings of the studies just mentioned.

Singing the Lord's Song

Won-Hee Kang's story begins in Seoul, South Korea. She was serving as a church musician and operating a music institute while her husband served as a pastor in a Presbyterian congregation. They wanted to come to the United States in order to study. The decision was not easy to make. Both she and her husband, See-Eun Sul, had long discussions, but more important, they entered into a period of fasting and prayer to discern what God's will was for them about this matter.

One day after a prolonged period of prayer, she says, her mind was torn the decision of whether to stay or to leave. Won-Hee says that she really suffered in her struggle to decide. During this prayer time, she turned to the Bible. As she read, it seemed as if God was speaking directly to her. Suddenly her despair lifted and her mind was filled with joy. It became clear to her that it was God's will for her family to come to America. What else could she say but "Yes, Lord"?

Though she was certain the decision to emigrate was the correct one, Won-Hee says, actually doing so was very painful. To leave Korea meant giving up her music institute, as well as the congregation See-Eun served. More important than that, it meant leaving family. Won-Hee is the oldest daughter in her family, and See-Eun is the only son. These are two very important roles in the Korean family: the parents have greater dependence on these children. In addition, Won-Hee and See-Eun are very close to their families, and to move so far away was heartbreaking. But a mitigating factor was that See-Eun's father, who was a pastor also, had, before his death, encouraged See-Eun to continue to study. He felt that studying in Korea was not enough. And since the Korean Christian revival of the twentieth century was based on the missionary work of many Americans who came to share the gospel, the United States seemed an obvious place to go.

The move to America cost them not only emotionally but also financially, especially the first year. As they settled into the new culture, they seemed only to be spending money without actually earning money. They primarily drew on savings they had accumulated over the years until they could get jobs here. They settled in northern Virginia initially because of family ties. Soon See-Eun was pastoring a small Presbyterian congregation, and Won-Hee began to teach in a Korean-language school on Saturday mornings, instructing second-generation children in their mother tongue.

Won-Hee says that her initial impressions of America were very scary. In just a few weeks she went from being an esteemed music teacher (in Korea, being a teacher of any subject is a highly respected position) to, in her words, "feeling like a baby." All her self-confidence melted away. She was unsure of American etiquette and was very afraid of doing something that would be viewed as inappropriate. And then there were all the new skills she had to learn. For example, the extensive public transportation system in Seoul meant that she had never had to drive a car. If she wanted to go anywhere in northern Virginia without having to ask her husband to chauffeur her, however, she needed to learn to drive a car. Even after she passed the test, she still felt "stuck" in her apartment, not knowing where to go.

The biggest hurdle for Won-Hee was learning a new language. She had taken English classes in high school and college, but actually having a conversation in English was very different. Won-Hee says that for quite some time she seemed to be living in two worlds: one American and the other Korean.

Portes and Rumbaut note that one of the factors in successful adaptation is the ability to master the new language:

> With few exceptions, newcomers unable to speak English in the Anglo-American world face enormous obstacles. Learning English is a basic step to enabling them to participate in the life of the larger

community, get an education, find a job, obtain access to health care or social services, and apply for citizenship. Language has often been cited as the principal barrier initially confronting recent immigrants, from the least educated peasants to the most educated professionals.[25]

Won-Hee certainly found this to be true. The language barrier became most real for her initially after she registered her oldest daughter, Sharon, in preschool. Soon she was told that school personnel were having great difficulties with Sharon, particularly on the bus. The bus driver had complained that Sharon would yell and scream from the moment she got on until she left the bus. Won-Hee was completely puzzled. She had never before had trouble with Sharon. What was causing her to yell? She asked her. Sharon told her that she did not mean to be bad. When she got on the bus, all these other children were speaking words she did not understand. Not only was the air full of strange sounds, but no one approached her and she was left to herself. But when she screamed her isolation always ended. People recognized her for the first time when she made herself known. When Won-Hee explained that this was not the right way to have people notice her, Sharon said that she would not yell again.

A second problem was aired at dinner one evening. Sharon told her mom that her teacher was calling her "He-Kai." Won-Hee asked her why. That was not her name—it sounded like a Japanese name, not a Korean one! Sharon's Korean name is Hye-Kyoung. As it turned out, Sharon's teacher could not pronounce her Korean name, and since Won-Hee did not have the confidence at that time to correct the teacher (a very un-Korean thing to do anyway), she chose instead to give her daughter an American name. So Hye-Kyoung became Sharon, named after the "rose of Sharon" in the Bible. By the time the youngest daughter went to school, though, Won-Hee's confidence had grown, so she took time to help the teacher learn to pronounce Hye-jin's name. Hye-jin never received an American name.

After these experiences Won-Hee committed herself to mastering English. She began taking English classes at Culmore, which she found to be not only informative but great fun. Her teacher, Diane, and she became great friends. Won-Hee was greatly impressed that all the ESL teachers were volunteers. In Korea people would pay a great deal of money to take English classes. For a time her husband had paid more than one thousand dollars a month to be tutored in English. Yet here were teachers *volunteering* their time—and they were *good* teachers, not bad ones! She was shocked. What was going on here? Volunteer work is not popular in Korea. If someone is volunteering their time, you do not expect to receive much from them. But that was not the case here. She came to the conclusion that, in her words, "this is real ministry—this must surely come from God."

Won-Hee joined our staff in 1993 as church musician. This was the first time she had been employed by or participated in a church outside the Korean community. At first she was terrified. She says the first year was especially traumatic. Not only was she anxious about performing well, but she had a difficult time understanding what people were saying in the service. Fortunately the choir helped her out by telling her when to play. Interestingly, most of her Korean friends had discouraged her from taking the position at Culmore. They argued that because of the language difference she would be overwhelmed and would fail. Won-Hee, however, saw it as a challenge. Here was a chance to be with Americans and learn more about them—precisely the kind of opportunity she had hoped to have in coming to America in the first place. As a result, Won-Hee mischievously observed, what she has learned is that Americans are people "just like Koreans and are not monsters after all!"

Won-Hee has been a blessing to this congregation in countless ways. As a result of her courage in coming to America and accepting the music position at Culmore, we are joyfully singing the songs of Zion.

An American Too!

Ileana Rosas, our Latin American pastor, first came to the mainland United States more than a decade ago from her home in Puerto Rico. Like Won-Hee, she came seeking opportunities that were not available to her at home. She also wanted a different kind of future for her children. She wanted them to have the kinds of educational opportunities available in the United States. Particularly she wanted them to grow up bilingual. Though English is an official language of Puerto Rico, most people grow up learning English in the way that many Americans learn Spanish—a few classes in high school and that's it. She also wanted her daughters to grow up where there is less crime. Why then, I asked, did she come to northern Virginia? She said that even with the urban problems here, it still seems much safer. In Puerto Rico people live in houses behind large walls on top of which shards of glass are cemented to keep out intruders. Here, she said, you can go outside and play on the grass and not be fenced in by your fear.

In Puerto Rico Ileana had worked as a journalist for a number of years; later she worked in the senate, where she was employed for five years, rubbing elbows with many of the important political and business leaders of her country. In addition, she had been very active in her church, holding most of the leadership positions at one time or another. By the time she prepared to leave Puerto Rico, she had been certified as a candidate for ordination.

Then Ileana came to the United States. Her identity changed overnight: she went from being a respected person to being an unemployed mother of three daughters. All of a sudden, no titles defined her. Like Ely, she notes that it was a tremendous lesson in humility. For the first time in her life, she had to learn who she was apart from any job or position she held. This was the beginning of her spiritual journey toward the discovery of her own self-worth.

English mastery was also a problem for Ileana. Though she had studied English, she had never spoken it conversationally. She could read English fairly well but did not have the confidence to engage others in conversation. She decided that this situation had to change. If she was going to live here, she needed to be able to communicate with others. She began to strike up conversations with strangers on the bus or at the grocery store. She would apologize for her English, but to her surprise, people began to tell her not to apologize, because she spoke English very well. These comments helped enormously in boosting her confidence. Nonetheless, because of language, it was six or seven months after her arrival before she was able to get a job.

She says that three particular areas caused her the most frustration in adjusting to this new culture. The first area concerned her own identity as a U.S. citizen. Having grown up in a U.S. territory, she did not need a passport to come to the mainland, and since she had not traveled to other countries, she had had no need of a passport. When she first arrived, she went to sign up for English classes at a local adult education center, where they asked for her passport or visa. She told them that she did not have either. They said that she would not be allowed to take the classes. Being new to this country, she assumed that they must be right. Then she went to the bank to open a checking account, and they asked for the same documentation. Again she told them that she did not have it and was turned away.

How could she expect to make it in the United States if she wasn't even allowed to register for English classes or open a bank account? She waited for a few weeks and then asked some American friends at her church what she should do. They told her that because she was a citizen, she had every right to what she had applied for. Bolstered by these Christian friends, she went back to the bank with her driver's license in hand and a new attitude. She told them that she wanted to open an account. This time when they asked for identification, she handed them her driver's license and said she was a citizen. Who were they to tell her no? There were no problems this time, and they quickly opened her account.

The second area of adjustment was her cultural education about what is normative in America. Ileana said that she had to change the way she perceived things, that is, what was appropriate and inappropriate. One day during that first year in the United States, she went shopping for clothes for her daughters. Afterward she returned to the car with her three girls, only to realize that she had forgotten something. She told them to stay in the car and keep the doors locked; she would be back soon. Not ten minutes later she returned to the car, only to find a police officer standing there talking to her daughters. He asked her if they were her children, and when she said yes, he began to lecture her about neglecting her children by leaving them in the car alone. She asked if that was wrong. He told her that "of course" it was wrong. Didn't she know that? No, she didn't know, but she did not tell him. Instead she accepted the lecture and promised not to do it again.

This episode reminded her how different life is here from life in Puerto Rico. Back home, Ileana says, everyone watches out for other people's children, whether you know the person or not. There it is safe to leave them in the car, knowing that adults passing by will check on them if something seems wrong. Even here, other Latin American women will hand Ileana their babies to watch while they run an errand, although they may have only just met her. She misses that kind of trust and community.

The third area of adjustment had to do with her own attitude as a Hispanic woman. She says that one of the first things you must deal with as an immigrant is your own prejudice, particularly about who you think Americans are. Some people in her home country have very negative feelings about Americans; they view Americans as imperialistic conquerors. They believe that America is imposing its will on the countries of the Caribbean, not to mention taking advantage of its territories, such as Puerto Rico. These folks are a minority, but their views do influence how many Puerto Ricans see Americans. The majority, on the other hand, tend to put Americans on a pedestal, feeling that Americans are somehow more special and better than they are. Though many would like to relate to Americans, many Puerto Ricans think Americans are untouchable, and do not reach out to them for friendship out of a fear of rejection.

After coming to the United States, Ileana found, much to her surprise, that Americans were more than willing to reach out to her and her family, to accept her, to love her. She expected to have to fight for her rights and to be faced with overwhelming discrimination, but that was not the case. She was welcomed with open arms. She is glad that she came to the United States. She says that this is a wonderful country, beautiful and clean. Even in urban northern Virginia, she finds it much more peaceful and quiet—at least here there are no roosters to wake you before the dawn! And she has found community in the church. The loneliness that seemed to almost overwhelm her at first has now subsided. She has felt the love of God embracing her through her brothers and sisters in Christ. Now she has a sense of familiarity, that this new land is becoming home.

The prophet Jeremiah gave this advice to the exiles living in a land not their own:

Thus says the LORD of hosts, the God of Israel, to all the exiles whom I have sent into exile from Jerusalem to Babylon: Build houses and live in them; plant gardens and eat what they produce. Take wives and have sons and daughters; take wives for your sons, and give your daughters in marriage, that they may bear sons and daughters; multiply there, and do not decrease. But seek the welfare of the city where I have sent you into exile, and pray to the LORD on its behalf, for in its welfare you will find your welfare. (Jer 29:4-7)

11
Into the Fiery Furnace

••

PRINCIPLE: A multicultural church is composed of God's pilgrim people.

Hear the word of the LORD, O nations, and declare it in the coastlands far away; say, "He who scattered Israel will gather him, and will keep him as a shepherd a flock." . . . Then shall the young women rejoice in the dance, and the young men and the old shall be merry. I will turn their mourning into joy, I will comfort them, and give them gladness for sorrow. JEREMIAH 31:10, 13

V*eronica Barrell is both a nurse and a full-time missionary.* Until just recently, she was working at a nearby church, helping to develop Latin American ministries. I have known Veronica for some time, but I had the opportunity to get to know her much better when we both served as teachers at a mission school. The reason we had this opportunity to share was not just that we were both attending the school but also that I recently had had surgery on my shoulder and needed daily physical therapy. Veronica, in her capacity as a trained nurse, willingly helped me with my exercises. As she pulled my arm in directions it did not want to go, we chatted about race, ethnicity, cultural identity and other such light topics.

Veronica looks like a middle-class, blue-eyed, blond Anglo woman. She has no noticeable accent in English. If I had not met Veronica in her capacity as missionary, I never would have guessed she was of Hispanic origin. Yet Veronica was born in Uruguay, speaks Spanish fluently and has a strong call from God to work in the Latin American community. During our time together, I decided to investigate these seeming incongruities between racial appearance and cultural identity.

"Veronica, do you consider yourself a Latina?" I asked her.

She replied, "Oh yes, very much so." She said I was not the first to ask about her identity. Although she was born in Uruguay, she emigrated to the United States with her parents at the age of twelve. They established a new home in Chester, Virginia, where few Hispanics resided at the time. Veronica grew up bilingual by choice. Her brothers, however, opted to speak English only. Unlike many Hispanic immigrants, her family spoke primarily English in the home, not Spanish. The reason for this also explains Veronica's racial identity. Her grandfather was British and emigrated from England to Uruguay just after World War I. There he married her grandmother, who was a Uruguayan of Swedish descent. Because of the influence of her grandfather, English was always spoken in their home. She learned Spanish primarily in Uruguayan schools, where subjects were taught in both Spanish and English.

Veronica's family's experience is typical of that of most Uruguayans. Even more than the United States, Uruguay is known as a land of immigrants and has virtually no indigenous Indian population. For that reason many, if not most, Uruguayans are of European descent and may appear racially white. In the twentieth century Uruguay became a safe haven for many Europeans who fled the wars of their continent. As a result, Uruguay has come to be known as "the Switzerland of Latin America." Veronica's family still maintains ties with Great Britain. Veronica herself possesses British citizenship, even though she was born in South America, has grown up in North America and has never resided in England!

As Veronica and I talked, I thought about how interesting it was that both of us had a heritage rooted in the British Empire: one a redheaded, blue-eyed descendant of Scotch-Irish immigrants in the 1700s, the other a blond, blue-eyed descendant of English-Uruguayan immigrants from the 1900s. One of us is considered an Anglo, yet the other is considered Hispanic. Go figure.

Well . . . Who *Am* I?

"Who am I?" is a difficult question for any adolescent or young adult to ask, but it is especially so for those who were born abroad to immigrant parents but have grown up in the United States (called 1.5, or "one-and-a-half," generation). It is also true for the American-born children of first-generation immigrants (called second-generation). Tim Stafford, in an article for *Christianity Today* entitled "Here Comes the World," writes that although the first generation continues to be "preoccupied with their home culture, speaking its language in their churches, proudly asserting their ethnic heritage at home, protecting their children from American decadence, and often dreaming of return to their native land," their children, 1.5- and second-generation, are somewhere "in between—bilingual and bicultural." The third generation, says Stafford, "often knows very little of their grandparents' language and culture; they are fully Americanized (though they often become extremely interested in their roots)."[1] But, he says, between these generations "there is heartache—grave disappointment from the elders, frustration and rebellion from the youth. Korean-American Christians speak of the 'silent exodus of young people from their churches.'"[2]

Sociologists note that although much is known about the large and diverse wave of first-generation immigrants in the latter half of this century, much less is known about their children. One reason for this lack of information is, demographically speaking, a change in the method of collecting census data. The 1970 U.S. census represents the last comprehensive tracking of immigrants' children.[3] Another reason that little is known about these youth and young adults is that they frequently follow a more fragmented or segmented path in their cultural adaptation than their parents did. Alejandro Portes observes that the second generation is "the key to establishing the long-term consequences of immigration, but the course of adaptation is uncertain at present." Language and ethnicity, in his opinion, are one piece of a much larger puzzle, a puzzle that will determine whether "today's children of immigrants will follow their European predecessors and move steadily into the middle-class mainstream or whether, on the contrary, their ascent will be blocked and they will join children of earlier black and Puerto Rican migrants as part of an expanded multiethnic underclass."[4]

One thing of which we may be certain is that the question "Who am I?" will be answered very differently by the 1.5- and second-generation population from the way it was by their parents. As Ruben Rumbaut, in his essay "The Crucible Within," argues,

"Becoming American" takes different forms, has different meanings, and is reached by different paths. But the process is one in which all children of immigrants are engaged: defining an identity for themselves—which is to say, finding a meaningful place in the society of which they are the newest members. To be sure, the process is complex, conflictual, and stressful, and profoundly affects the consciousness of immigrant parents and children alike. The process also is shaped within a much larger historical context, of which the participants may be no more conscious than fish are of water, and within an American crucible that has been shaping identities since the origins of the nation. In the final analysis, it is the crucible without that shapes the crucible within.[5] This chapter is an exploration of both the internal crucible of cultural identity of the 1.5 and second generations and the external crucible of the larger society. The latter influences and shapes the paths of cultural adaptation of the youth and young adults in the multicultural church.

Caught in the Web

In the fall of 1991 I attended a symposium at the Korean United Methodist Church of Greater Washington, the oldest and one of the largest of the Korean congregations in the metropolitan area. The symposium was a celebration of their fortieth anniversary as a congregation. Rather than this occasion's being simply a time to reflect back on their history, they used the anniversary to ponder the meaning of their future. The symposium was called "Roots and Wings," and it focused on issues of 1.5- and second-generation Korean ministry. Though Culmore at the time had no Korean members, we did have a large number of immigrant youth and young adults who fell into this generational category. I attended in the hope of gleaning something about the experience of the children of immigrants from the Korean perspective, wondering whether it might have implications for non-Korean children as well.

The name of the symposium itself reveals the poignant nature of second-generation ministry. As Daniel Shin, one of the pastors at that time, noted, roots signify the part of the immigrant experience that digs deep in the collective past shared as ethnic Americans, and wings represent the future of unnamed possibilities. Both aspects, the past and the future, are to be treasured, and yet an unspoken tension exists between the two.

A lecture delivered by Dr. Young Pai, titled "Caught in the Web: A Perspective for Socio-cultural Understanding of Korean-American Youth," spoke directly to the dilemma of the second generation: they are caught in a web between two cultures, two languages and two worldviews.

A web, it was said, can be the place where one is caught and is the victim, or it can be the place where one lives. Like a web, the "complex network" of the world of second-generation youth and young adults is filled with "different strands (streams) of cultural norms" and expectations that "intersect, overlap, and interact with each other," including the cultural norms of adolescents in general, as well as in school, in the larger society, in the first-generation community, and in the second-generation community.[6]

While noting the positive achievement orientation of Korean-American youth in general (a stereotypical image of the "model minority" that many resent), Pai also describes a deep-felt alienation among many second-generation youth. Particularly distressing was the high percentage of Korean-American youth who said they very often wished they had different parents, as well as the unwillingness of many second-generation youth and young adults to turn to others (parents, friends or clergy) when needing help to solve problems. An alarming number responded that if they faced difficult choices they would probably turn to no one rather than to traditional supportive relationships. In this respect second-generation immigrants share an "aloneness factor" with their American generational counterparts, Generation X, an age group for whom "aloneness" (that is, dependence only on oneself) is increasingly becoming normative.

Even Youths Shall Fall Exhausted

Dr. Pai's words proved to be prophetic in my own ministry with second-generation members of Culmore. As I suspected, many of the issues of the Korean-American community also applied to other immigrant communities. In the fall of 1993, an incident occurred in our congregation that revealed a deeper alienation within our second-generation community than I had previously suspected. The setting was a children's party, which the church was hosting as an outreach to neighborhood kids. Many of our youth and young adults were helping that night. Near the end of the evening, two young girls from the youth group came to the party, bringing with them two fifteen-year-old male friends. Three young men from our congregation, ranging in age from eighteen to twenty-three, became very jealous. Within a short time a fight erupted at the rear of the social hall. Our three young adults descended on the fifteen-year-old boys, and a brawl ensued.

After the fight was broken up, I called the police to make an incident report. Though the two boys were not seriously injured, our young adults had instigated a unprovoked fight against two minors. Nothing in my experience with these boys had prepared me to anticipate such violence from them. In fact, just the opposite was true. They came from very strong and supportive Asian families. They are close to and respectful of their parents. They attended church every Sunday and most Friday nights.

Over the course of the next several months, ripples from this incident continued to spread through the congregation. It revealed a generational chasm not previously acknowledged. The incident forced not only the immediate families involved but also the young men's friends and me to ask ourselves how we could have missed the anger, frustration and alienation that must have been lurking under these boys' easygoing exteriors.

Over the course of those months, people within the congregation reached out to them in many ways. Though progress and healing began to take place with one of the boys in particular, I felt we were losing the others. Gil was the oldest of the three, and as the months passed, his anger seemed only to increase. Because I was the one who had called the police, he effectively severed his relationship with me and quit coming to church. By spring, I wondered if Gil would ever return.

As it happened, we planned a Good Friday service of healing using the anointing of oil. Though this ritual was familiar to many in the congregation, I had never before used the anointing of oil in congregational worship. Given the deep sense of brokenness in our congregation at that time, however, it seemed most appropriate.

After the sermon that night, we held a time of congregational prayer for confession of sins. As we lifted up our petitions to God, a hammer struck a nail in a wooden cross, and the words "Lord, have mercy" were spoken. This prayer of confession lasted several minutes, the hammer continued to strike the nail, and "Lord, have mercy" was repeated. The spiritual intensity of this prayer of confession was deeply moving. People began to weep and mourn for their sins, asking God's forgiveness. We ended the prayers with the words of pardon: "In the name of Jesus Christ, you are forgiven."

We had planned to conclude this service with persons coming forward to the altar rail and receiving the anointing of oil and a blessing. They could remain, if they wished, for prayer at the altar. Since this was my first healing service, I did not know quite what to expect. I thought it might be something like receiving Communion by intinction: persons would come forward, stand in front of me, be anointed and depart—all in a very orderly fashion. When the time came, I invited all who had repented of their sin and desired God's healing in their lives to come forward. Won-Hee played praise choruses softly as I stood at the altar rail. A stillness filled the sanctuary that night—a holy stillness. It was if we were waiting for something, or, more appropriately, Someone!

I stood for what seemed like several minutes, and no one came forward. Anxiously I once again announced the invitation. Finally a figure from the rear of the dimly lit sanctuary rose and came forward. It was Gil! This was the first time he had returned to church since the fight in October.

As Gil approached me, I smiled with deep joy and asked him why he needed God's healing. Gil began to make confession. For several moments he poured out his heart and asked for God's forgiveness. Then I, the one who had reported Gil to the police, reached for the bottle of scented oil and with my thumb began to make the sign of the cross on his forehead: "Gil, I anoint you in the name of the Father, and of the Son and of the . . ."

Before I could say "Holy Spirit," Gil was spiritually and emotionally overcome, falling face-forward to the floor, knocking both Pastor Max and me to the ground.

Never before had I seen such an ecstatic experience in worship. I was not quite sure what to do. Gil was clearly unconscious at my feet—and I mean he was out cold! The service suddenly became much more animated, with emotions and prayers growing in intensity. My very first thought was *What am I going to tell the bishop?* Sure, such things may have happened to John Wesley, but we modern Methodists are not known for such outbreaks of the Holy Spirit. My second thought was *This is absolutely real!*

I knelt down and made sure that Gil was physically all right. Soon several Filipina women came to him, praying and watching over him until he awoke. Needless to say, these women were far more experienced at this than I and were much more composed. For twenty minutes or so Gil lay quietly, with the women ministering to him. Later Gil said that in those moments as he lay unconscious on the floor, he experienced the deep healing presence of God as never before.

Since Gil seemed to be taken care of, I decided to keep my place at the altar, and I continued to invite persons for anointing. That night many of the young adults in our congregation came forward, made confession, acknowledged the brokenness in their lives, admitted the depth of their alienation and asked for God's healing in their own lives. The service ended an hour and a half later, with mourning and weeping turning into joyful laughter and singing. The prodigal had returned! Gil had come home, and because he did, a door opened for us to minister to the deeper spiritual issues of our young adults.

Gil, as well as one of the other boys in the fight, later enrolled in Bible college and is still wondering whether God may be calling him to ministry. At twenty-six, he is about to get married to a young 1.5-generation Filipina in the congregation. What could have been a tragic turn of events in his life leading to further alienation was transformed by God into an experience that drew him deeper into his knowledge and love of God.

Mind you, "resting" or, as some say, being "slain in the Spirit" is not the most conventional approach to young adult ministry, but in this case God knew better than I what was needed to bring Gil home.

The psalmist says:

To you, O LORD, I cried,
  and to the LORD I made supplication:
"What profit is there in my death,
  if I go down to the Pit?
Will the dust praise you?
  Will it tell of your faithfulness?
Hear, O LORD, and be gracious to me!
  O LORD, be my helper!"

You have turned my mourning into dancing;
  you have taken off my sackcloth
  and clothed me with joy,
so that my soul may praise you and not be silent.
  O LORD my God, I will give thanks to you forever. (Ps 30:8-12)

The Lions' Den

The Bible has a powerful story of four 1.5- and second-generation young adults and the way they faced adversity and cultural adaptation while remaining faithful to God. It is the story of Daniel, Hananiah, Mishael, and

Azariah—the last three better known by their Babylonian names: Shadrach, Meshach, and Abednego. Daniel, in particular, was among the first captives taken to Babylon. Scripture tells us that God honored him in his exile, and enabled him to rise from slave to counselor to the kings of Babylon.

From the very beginning, the story of Daniel is a story of cultural assimilation. King Nebuchadnezzar instructed his palace master, Ashpenaz, to bring before him some of the brightest and best young Israelite captives for service in his court. He instructed Ashpenaz that they should be "young men without physical defect and handsome, versed in every branch of wisdom, endowed with knowledge and insight, and competent to serve in the king's palace; they were to be taught the literature and language of the Chaldeans" (Dan 1:4).

Note the intentionality of the cultural assimilation of these young adults. First, Daniel and the others are taught Aramaic, the language of their new cultural home. Second, because they are intellectually bright, they are instructed in Babylonian culture and academics. Third, they are given new and more culturally appropriate names. Daniel, which means "God is my judge," receives the name Belteshazzar, which means "the one whom Bel favors" (Bel, of course, being the foremost god in the Babylonian pantheon). Hananiah and Mishael are given names honoring the moon god, Aku; and Azariah's new name means "the one who serves Nebo," who was the fire god. These name changes were meant not only to reflect new cultural identities, but, more important, a new religious orientation and allegiance. That, of course, would not be the case for Daniel and his friends, but it was the intention. Finally, the young adults were also commanded to eat the food provided to them by the royal court. Of all the things asked of Daniel and the others, this violation of the dietary laws was the most serious. Daniel and the others chose to stand their ground and not defile themselves by eating the food given to them.

Daniel sought a nonconfrontational approach to this problem by asking permission from his master to keep the Jewish dietary laws. At first the master balked, fearing that Daniel and the others in his care would appear unhealthy and he would be punished. Daniel persuaded him, however, to permit them simply to eat vegetables and drink water for ten days. At the end of that time, Daniel said, the palace master could judge for himself whether they were any worse for the wear, and, depending on their appearance, could then instruct them differently. They surrounded themselves with prayer, and at the end of this period, Scripture says that they appeared "better and fatter than all the young men who had been eating the royal rations" (Dan 1:15). As a result, the palace master continued to let them observe the Jewish dietary laws.

The example of Daniel, Hananiah, Mishael and Azariah is an important one as we consider what the Bible has to say to 1.5- and second-generation young adults. In this passage cultural assimilation is an accepted fact of entering and becoming a part of a new culture. Cultural assimilation, however, is also portrayed as not always conforming to the purposes of God. God intended to use Daniel and his friends for God's purposes in that culture. Not all the cultural adjustments mentioned were considered bad. But God enabled the young men to faithfully navigate the issues that would have forced them to so accommodate themselves to culture as to be disobedient to God.

The story of Daniel is ultimately a story of the triumph of faithfulness in a land and culture not one's own. Questions we might ask as Americans include the following: How much of our own cultural assimilation of immigrants and their children comes perilously close to asking them to so accommodate themselves as to be disobedient to God? Do we ask Christians from other countries to compromise their faith through adaptation to a materialistic American lifestyle? Do we require persons to choose cultural loyalty before fidelity to God?

Daniel and the three others faced imprisonment, the lions' den, even a fiery furnace. Today's 1.5- and second-generation young adults also face great threats of their own. But through the perseverance and faithfulness of Daniel and the others, God blessed and used these young immigrants of another era. So too will God bless and use the young immigrants of today. The Bible says that "to these four young men God gave knowledge and skill in every aspect of literature and wisdom; Daniel also had insight into all visions and dreams" (Dan 1:17). Wherever and whenever young men and women listen attentively to the voice of God, their eyes will be opened and their ears will hear, and they will dream of God's purposes for the world.

The prophet Joel says, "I will pour out my spirit on all flesh; your sons and your daughters shall prophesy, your old men shall dream dreams, and your young men shall see visions" (Joel 2:28). What follows in this chapter comes from the visions, experiences and wisdom of three young adults in

Culmore, who told me how they have navigated the fiery furnace between the culture and expectations of first-generation parents and their own acculturation to American society.

A Cultural Interpreter

Manny is a thirty-one-year-old Filipino-American who came to the United States with his adoptive parents when he was sixteen. His adoptive mother is, in fact, his mother's sister. When Manny was growing up in the Philippines, his aunt Evelyn lived with his family. She later married a Filipino man, Jesse, who was serving in the U.S. navy. Because Manny had been very attached to Evelyn when he was growing up, Evelyn asked her sister, Doris, if she might adopt him and take him with her when she and Jesse moved to the United States. Doris approved, and although it took more than two years to complete the adoption process, Manny eventually joined his new family in San Diego, California.

Manny said that one of his first adjustments after arriving in the United States had to do with language. Though English was a second language to him, he still found himself continually translating from Tagalog to English in his mind before speaking. In addition, Manny was very shy to begin with. As he made friends at school, however, his fluency rapidly increased. Manny now speaks primarily English, though he uses Tagalog with family and Filipino friends.

More than language, the change in coming to a new country was somewhat scary. It was like starting over. His own experience in cultural adaptation was clearly different, however, from his parents' experience. They continued to hold on to much of their cultural heritage and identity. For example, his mother never learned to drive. Many women do not drive in the Philippines. After arriving here, she and her husband decided that she would still leave the driving to him.

If Manny had difficulty initially with English, his parents struggled all the more. Tagalog is still the preferred language in the home. Manny's parents have a harder time if someone is speaking to them in English. They tend to become intimidated, because they might not understand what is being said. They do not want to embarrass the person speaking, nor do they want to be embarrassed themselves by seeming not to understand. When Manny lived at home, his parents frequently asked him to come along on errands, especially those of a business nature, such as going to the bank. As with many children of immigrants, one of Manny's responsibilities in the family was to serve as a translator.

Some of the 1.5-generation youth in our church seem to resent this responsibility at times. One year Pablo (mentioned earlier in the book) and his mother came to our house for Christmas dinner. At this time Pablo's mother still had little comprehension of English. For an hour or so he translated back and forth between Spanish and English. When the conversation was over, he—with great dramatic flair—collapsed on the sofa, as if to demonstrate how much energy it took for him to translate.

I asked Manny if he ever resented serving as a translator. He said no. In fact, he was glad to be his parents' translator. It was one concrete way he could help them, so he was glad when they asked. He did admit that at moments natural exhaustion took its toll, but for the most part it was not a burden. It gave him a defined role in the family and a responsibility. In many ways it made him feel protective of his parents. Translating for them was a way to make sure his parents were treated fairly by others.

When I asked Manny how he identified himself culturally and racially, he said that he prefers to identify himself as a Filipino-American. When he fills out forms requiring him to identify his ethnic identity, he checks "Asian" because of his physical features. In many ways, Manny says, he has two identities: "I have both worlds in me. There is still much of the Philippines in who I am, but on the other hand, I am also very American-ized." His transcultural nature becomes more obvious to him when he is with his brothers, who are older and came to the United States as adults. Because of his Filipino identity, he can understand where they are coming from. It is easy to see how they arrive at conclusions based on their Filipino thought processes. On the other hand, when he is with Americans, he also feels that he understands where they are coming from and how they think.

Manny continues to serve as a translator for his family, but now, instead of language, it is culture he interprets. Misunderstanding occurs in many areas of crosscultural communication, Manny notes, such as the directness of Americans versus the indirect way most Filipinos communicate. He tries to stand between the two worlds to help bridge the gap, enabling his brothers and sisters to understand Americans, and vice versa.

This role of cultural interpreter also now extends to Manny's own immediate family. Four years ago he married Lisa, an Anglo young adult who had grown up in Culmore. Though cultural miscommunication has not been an issue for them, there are moments when Manny has to interpret customs and ways of thinking and perceiving between Lisa and her American family and his Filipino family. One such instance was shortly after they were married. In the Philippines many families have a child in the first or second year of marriage. The expectation is that following the wedding, the husband and wife will immediately begin planning to expand their family. So, at least for Manny, it was not surprising when family members began to ask Lisa when she was going to have a baby.

At first it seemed like gentle teasing, but increasingly she began to be bothered by the comments. On one level she was worried that she might disappoint her new relatives, because she was not planning to have a baby immediately. She wanted to be accepted by them, to be a part of the family. On the other hand, she wanted to be clear that having a child right after getting married was not in the plan. Manny was able to help her understand where his relatives were coming from and also help her feel confident about expressing herself honestly to the family members in ways they would understand.

Manny and Lisa recently did have a child. Her name is Hope Victoria. This name reflects their belief that her life is a sign of hope from God in their lives and that victory always comes from trusting in God. Her name represents the Christian hope of all new beginnings. Their daughter is among the growing number of multiracial Americans who will challenge the traditionally inflexible notions of racial identity in America and may represent the dream of a truly color-blind society.

Born in the U.S.A.

Paul was born in 1978 in Washington, D.C., to a father from Sierra Leone and a mother from Nigeria. Paul, however, readily identifies himself as an African-American. When I asked what this term means for him, he said that it means his parents are African but he was born in the United States. He feels great affinity with the historic African-American community, which was descended from slaves. Initially he identified with this community because of skin color, an obvious factor that they held in common. Growing up, Paul made friends with other African-American youth because of this shared experience of color. And because he was growing up in an international community, he was far from being the only American-born child of African immigrants. He had friendships stemming from both the historic black American community and the African-immigrant experience. His friends, however, have not been limited to these communities. He considers himself a part of a multicultural community of friends, including Asian Indians, Chinese, Japanese, Korean, Anglos and those of interracial heritage.

The question of African-American identity also has another layer for Paul. Some of his friends who were born abroad but have grown up here still strongly identify with Africa. At the same time they may struggle with their heritage, asking, "Am I African, American or both?" For Paul, the answer is clearly the middle way—he is both! He is grateful that his parents have shared his African heritage with him, and he is also glad that their approach was low-key. His awareness of his cultural background has been shaped largely by trips back to his parents' homelands of Sierra Leone and Nigeria. His parents have encouraged his American identity as well. He feels that he is fortunate to know about both heritages.

Paul talks about the distinctive aspects of being the American-born child of immigrants. When he was in elementary school, he found that he fit in quite nicely but his parents stood out. His classmates would ask, "Where are your parents from? They sure talk funny." In recent years Paul has gotten a kick out of being with other American-born youth with African parents by identifying mannerisms, attitudes and approaches to life that their parents have in common. One thing that seems to stand out most is the common approach of African parents when you get in trouble—the lecture!

Paul is especially grateful for the many gifts his parents have given him. Because of who they are, he has been taught to have a strong work ethic, to cherish family, to value education and to develop a moral purpose in his life. Paul says that he has been taught to lead a good life in order to be happy and satisfied with the decisions he makes. Religion has played an important role in his development, largely because it also played a guiding role in his parents' development and in their parents' lives before them. Far from being an empty tradition that has been handed down to him, faith has been a personal decision. For Paul the community of faith gives him a sense of security in this world. It serves as a safe haven, a place of warmth and help. It is the rock he knows will always be there for him.

As for racism, Paul says that in recent years his eyes have been opened to the fact that not everyone is color-blind. In many ways, before he went to college Paul was sheltered and protected by his parents from the worst effects of racism. He has now experienced racism personally—from both blacks and whites. Paul is very clear in articulating his belief that racism comes from ignorance. The prejudice he has experienced from other African-Americans comes in part from their ignorance about Africa. He has discovered that many hold misperceptions about Africa and its people. Some are even unaware that many of the cities of that continent are industrialized. Though their biases hurt, Paul seems to take it in stride, because "they just don't know what they are talking about." As for the racism he has experienced from whites, Paul finds it curious that many whites cannot seem to understand that being a black man in America does not necessarily mean leading a life of crime—black men can and do go to college and succeed! Paul wants other second-generation young adults to know that it has been a blessing for him to have immigrant parents. He rejoices in his dual identity as both African and American. For Paul the middle way has proved to be the right way.

Acting White

Gabrielle is a 1.5-generation eighteen-year-old Filipina who goes by her nickname, Maoi. She received her nickname from her family. Her mother went to Hong Kong just after Maoi was conceived, and when she came back to Manila and announced that she was pregnant, everyone in the family joked that the baby must have been Chairman Mao's. The teasing only increased after Maoi was born and, in the words of her mother, she seemed to have Chinese features. But of course, so did others on her father's side, because they were descended from Chinese immigrants to the Philippines.

Maoi came to the United States when she was only two years old. She lived in Houston, where her parents immigrated, until five years ago, when they moved to northern Virginia. The reason for their move was that her father received a job offer in the federal government. In addition, many of their relatives already lived here, and they thought it would be good to be with their extended family again.

Even though Maoi could be considered second-generation, she still identifies herself as a Filipina. Maoi is just about as American as teenagers get, so I asked her why she identifies with her parents' culture. Her answer was much like Manny's—because she looks ethnically Asian. The irony,

Maoi points out, is that if she went back to the Philippines she would not fit in. Maoi does not like Filipino food. She prefers to eat at McDonald's and Bennigan's. She does not speak Tagalog, only English. And yet because of physical racial characteristics, she continues to identify with a culture of which, for all practical purposes, she has never been a part.

Since moving to northern Virginia, Maoi has been exposed to more 1.5-generation Filipinos than she was in Texas. One of the most surprising reactions from them has been that they think she is "white," both culturally and racially. One of the comments she overheard about herself was, "What is she doing acting white? Doesn't she know where she comes from?" Her mannerisms, her accent, the way she carries herself all set her apart culturally from young Filipinos who immigrated at a later age.

She tends to experience more bias from other Filipinos than from Americans. In her own words, Americans do not seem to make a big deal over her race; they treat her as if she were white. This phenomenon is not uncommon for those who came to the United States at a very young age, because they do in fact have more in common culturally with Americans than with those from their home culture.

Racially speaking, even though Maoi does have Asian features (yes, the Chinese characteristics are present), she does not appear to be a pure Filipina. Some Filipinos ask her, "Are you pure?" Actually Maoi is of a mixed-race heritage. Her grandmother was a white Spaniard, and her great-grandmother was Norwegian. Maoi does appear more light-skinned than other Filipinos—hence the comment about her being white.

In a sense Maoi is a multicultural and multiracial person. And she is not alone in this designation. Although the exact number of persons of multiracial identity is unknown, the 1990 census counts two million persons under the age of eighteen whose parents are of different racial backgrounds. Michel Marriot writes in *The New York Times* that "increasingly, multiracial people are arguing—and many scientists agree—that race is a social construct, not a biological absolute." In addition, Marriot notes, "Many historians and social scientists . . . believe that the notion of race was largely invented as a way to assign social status and privilege."[7] Thus "acting white" is also a way of expressing resentment that a person is seeking to transcend his or her given social position.

Maoi is unfazed by any attempts to define her racially or ethnically. She says that she values her multiracial identity—she likes looking distinctive.

Her strong self-esteem is clear. She likes who she is, and no one can make her think differently.

When asked about what sets her apart from other American teenagers, she readily responds that it is the relationship with her parents. They are much stricter than American parents. For example, at age eighteen she has yet to be allowed to sleep over at a friend's house. If that was the case, I asked, why was her youngest sister, Danielle, allowed to have a sleepover with my daughters? Maoi said, "Because you're the pastor. My parents trust you." She also notes the difference between the types of punishment given by her parents and other American parents. Her American friends, when they get in trouble, are likely to be grounded. When she gets in trouble, like Paul, she prepares herself for the lecture. Maoi says that her parents lecture and lecture and lecture—until they are sure the message has gotten through. Interestingly, she prefers the lecture to being grounded. She thinks that it helps her learn to do the right thing, unlike just being punished for doing the wrong thing.

Maoi says that she does not resent her parents' strictness. In fact, she sees it as positive. She respects them for it. It is a sign to her that they love her and want to protect her. Maoi is willing to give her parents the benefit of the doubt: she knows they have her best interests at heart. She points out that the Bible says to listen to your parents if they are seeking God's will. She trusts that her parents are indeed seeking God's will for her life. Maoi believes that God is teaching her parents so that they may teach her.

One of the things that she believes also sets her family apart from other American families is that her parents are still married. She observes that most of her American friends come from divorced families but that almost none of her Filipino friends' parents are. Recent research supports Maoi's conclusion. Rumbaut notes that "all Asian-origin groups have a higher proportion of families with both natural parents at home; the somewhat higher incidence of father absence among the Hmong, and especially the Cambodians, is due not to divorce but to the death of the father prior to the family's arrival in the United States." He also points out that "research literature has pointed to the high levels of familism—a deeply ingrained sense of obligation and orientation toward the family. . . . These collectivist obligations to the family contrast with the individualistic values in the American milieu."[8]

One other significant difference Maoi observes, and one that bothers her, is that many of her American friends take church very lightly. She, on the other hand, takes church very seriously and makes it a focal point in her life. When I asked why this was, Maoi responded that this was the way she was brought up. As with Paul, faith is not just tradition; it is a personal relationship with God. God, says Maoi, is the most important thing in her life. God has guided her through everything. She is not sure where she would be without God's guidance. She considers herself to have a very close relationship with God. In many ways God is her best friend. She says that whenever something significant happens in her life, whether it is good or bad, she and her mom look up a verse in Scripture about that matter to give them guidance. Maoi never misses church. Her American friends have come to understand its importance in her life, and they never ask her to skip church so that they can go out together. Instead they now schedule their activities around Maoi's involvement in church. "Worship," Maoi says, "is not an obligation. It is where I go to find peace and answers and to relieve the stress in my life."

The writer of Proverbs says:

My child, keep your father's commandment,
> and do not forsake your mother's teaching.
Bind them upon your heart always;
> tie them around your neck.
When you walk, they will lead you;
> when you lie down, they will watch over you;
> and when you awake, they will talk with you. (Prov 6:20-22)

A Pilgrim People

At the symposium mentioned at the beginning of the chapter, one of the speakers, Sang Hyun Lee, presented a paper titled "Called to Be Pilgrims." He said that all Christians are, in fact, called to be pilgrims. Like Abraham, we journey through the wilderness of this world, never completely at home in any one culture. Nor are Christians merely "wandering, aimless nomads"; rather, we are a "pilgrim people who are on a sacred journey."[9]

Particularly for immigrants and their children, Dr. Lee says that the "alien predicament [of being 'strangers and exiles'] is something [to be turned into] a sacred vocation."[10] Much as Daniel turned his experience as a slave and exile in Babylon into an opportunity to be God's voice to that nation, so it is with God's pilgrim people in all cultures, who can use their circumstances to witness to the will of God.

Although the marginality of 1.5- and second-generation persons may pose a threat, living on the margin or edge, in Lee's words, "is wilderness enough for anybody."[11] Nonetheless, this marginality may pose an opportunity as well. Lee says:

> A pilgrim is willing to leave the security of home and to enter the wilderness of homelessness in order to be open to the higher horizon of the purposes of God. Viewed in the light of this understanding of Christian existence, the religious meaning of our marginality (in the sense of bicultural existence) can only be this: that we are called to appropriate or use our marginal existence as the path of pilgrimage. The life in a wilderness seems to be a training ground for all those who are called to be God's special servants.[12]

12
Every Knee Shall Bow
& Every Tongue Confess

•••

PRINCIPLE: A multicultural church is eschatological.

After this I looked, and there was a great multitude that no one could count, from every nation, from all tribes and peoples and languages, standing before the throne and before the Lamb, robed in white, with palm branches in their hands. They cried out in a loud voice, saying,
  "Salvation belongs to our God who is seated on the throne, and to the Lamb!"
REVELATION 7:9-10

*E*ach Sunday morning during worship, Pastor Max steps up to the lectern and says to the congregation in his rich baritone voice, "Well—praise the Lord!" Immediately and joyfully, the congregation roars back, "Praise the Lord!"

The children who sit in the first two pews absolutely cannot wait for Pastor Max's portion of the service. Their faces beam whenever he speaks. They are not alone in their adoration of Max Francisco. His sweet and gentle spirit has endeared him to every member of the congregation, not just to the Filipino Fellowship.

Pastor Max's gentleness and humility arise out of his spirituality. Like the desert fathers and mothers of the early church, Max has endeavored to live his life as a never-ending prayer. Arising at four a.m. every day, he spends several hours lifting up the congregation—one by one—in prayer. Throughout the rest of the day, as he makes his way to the homes of members, he can be heard to utter under his breath prayers of gratitude: "Thank you, Jesus. Praise the Lord. Amen." His whole day is, in effect, spent in prayer.

Max's prayer life has caused me to reconsider the practicality and plausibility of Paul's admonition to "rejoice always, pray without ceasing, give thanks in all circumstances; for this is the will of God in Christ Jesus for you" (1 Thess 5:16-18). And its not Max only—his wife, Esperanza, is also said to have a direct line to the Lord. If anyone needs effective and expedient prayer at Culmore, we know where to turn.

I will not forget when I first met Max. Soon after I arrived, my district superintendent, Bob McAden, encouraged our church to bring Max on staff in an official capacity. Bob's suggestion grew out of his previous discussions with Filipinos about how to reach more Filipinos in northern Virginia. As I mentioned in chapter five, this was a time of great fiscal austerity for our congregation, but we willingly found the seed money to begin Max's ministry.

As we sat in my office, I announced the good news that he would be the new associate pastor for Filipino ministries at Culmore. Then I had to offer an apology: we did not have enough money to bring him on full time, just part time. I told him how sorry I was, but I hoped the situation would change in the future. His response was immediate and gracious: "Brother Steve, you may only pay me part time, but I want you to know that I always work full time for the Lord."

The Filipinos have a saying about Max: "He lives with one foot planted on earth and the other one in heaven." Phillip, Max's nephew, comments that Max just doesn't seem to live on the same plane as we ordinary mortals. What Phillip means by this, of course, is Max's intimacy and friendship with God. Phillip remembers a time earlier in Max's ministry, when he was still in Manila. He had no money at that time, and the food pantry was empty. Rather than being depressed and asking why God was not blessing his ministry so that he could provide for his family, he pulled out his guitar and began singing praises to the Lord. Not very long thereafter, one of the members of his congregation brought by enough food to last them a week.

Max lives a frugal life economically, but he has always considered himself rich in God's grace. A Filipino member once apologized to Max for not being able to help him more financially. Max quickly responded, "Please, do not worry yourself. Are you my employer? No! My employer is the Lord, whom I trust to provide for all my needs."

In worldly terms Max's life may not seem very successful. Success, however, is not the most useful way of measuring Max's life. Max is far more concerned with victory than with success. In that sense Max bears much resemblance to Abraham. Like Abraham, he "was called to set out for a place that he was to receive as an inheritance; and he set out, not knowing where he was going" (Heb 11:8).

When his family emigrated to the United States, Max trusted that it was God's will for him to go with them, even though it meant leaving behind not only a homeland but also a congregation he had pastored for thirty-five years. He left with no assurance of a job, no place to live, no visible way to support himself or his immediate family. He came to the United States with nothing but the promises of God to go on. And for more than seven years he has made a new home and new ministry in this country.

But I am quite certain that this is not yet the fulfillment of Max's immigrant journey. As with Abraham, the fulfillment of God's promises for Max Francisco may lie just past life's horizon. The writer of Hebrews notes that Abraham and other faithful pilgrims "died in faith without having received the promises, but from a distance they saw and greeted them. They confessed that they were strangers and foreigners on the earth" (Heb 11:13). It is not uncommon for Max to talk about his "home-going" to the Lord. He says that he trusts God more than he fears death. He is, in his words, "just passing through" in this world, on his way to a greater glory with God.

As Max's faithfulness continues to demonstrate, the multicultural church is composed of a pilgrim people, making their way as immigrants in this world, longing for that "better country" (Heb 11:16). Obedience to the promises of God does not necessarily guarantee success, but it does give victory. And because of the humble admission that much of life is beyond our grasp and that we can only live by faith, the writer of Hebrews says, "God is not ashamed to be called their God; indeed, he has prepared a city for them" (Heb 11:16).

Max Francisco does truly appear to live with one foot on earth and the other in heaven. Then again, maybe both of his feet are already firmly planted in God's kingdom, where our citizenship truly belongs.

Last Things

As one century comes to an end and another is given birth, many people are asserting that we are living in the "last days." I could not agree more. We are living in the last days of a century marked by wars of racial and ethnic animosity, unparalleled in their destructive capacity in the history of humankind. We are living in the last days of an era when communities could isolate themselves from other peoples of the world, if they so chose. We are living in the last days of a cultural Christianity that has taken its cues far more from Caesar than from Scripture. We are living in the last days of a denominational hegemony that asks only for organizational loyalty, not sacrificial obedience. We are living in the last days of the idolatry of success, in which Christians bow before the false god of homogeneous church growth instead of throwing the church doors wide open to all God's children.

Yes, we are living in the last days. But then, where else should we be living? As God's pilgrim people, we are called to live on the margins not only of culture, society and ethnicity but also of time itself. We are an eschatological people, living on the very margins of history. Like Pastor Max, we are a people with our feet planted both on earth and in heaven, in the present and in the future, in human history and in God's eternal kingdom.

Recalling the words of Paul that "salvation is nearer to us now than when we became believers; the night is far gone, the day is near" (Rom 13:11-12), Lesslie Newbigin comments:

> The New Testament evidently envisages a goal, one toward which we can make progress. . . . The eager expectation of a real end is vibrant on almost every page. The Bible ends with the vision of the city of God from which all that is evil will have been excluded and into which all the nations will bring their treasures. . . . The vision of a real horizon, a real goal toward which we move, is what gives the whole New Testament its most distinctive character, the character of hope which is both alert and patient.[1]

What's more, says Newbigin, the consummation of history itself will once and for all heal the division between "the public and the private worlds which death creates."[2] The public hope Newbigin mentions is the yearning for human progress and accomplishment that places our hope in the future—a hope that is most assuredly a human one, not a divine one. The private hope is the denial of public responsibilities and the placing of hope in a "personal immortality in a blessed world beyond this one."[3] Yet it is the vision of the holy city as portrayed by the apocalyptic writer John that represents the unification and reconciliation between the human accomplishments of culture and civilization and the eternal life created out of the loving purposes of the almighty God. Out of this synthesis is created a holy city, "not made with hands, [but] eternal in the heavens" (2 Cor 5:1).

Newbigin says:

> If I ask what in all my active life is the horizon of my expectations, the thing to which I look forward, the answer, it seems to me, cannot be some social utopia in the future and cannot be some personal bliss for myself; it can only be, quite simply, the coming of Jesus to complete his Father's will. He shall come again. He is the horizon of my expectations. Everything from my side, whether prayer or action, private or public, is done to him and for him.[4]

Newbigin reminds us that no amount of human action builds the eternal city. Our work in this world is but a living prayer for what God has promised us will be.

Happy We Are Here

When we gather to worship as God's children, we recognize that the praise of God comes in many languages, colors, expressions, emotions and styles, but out of all this diversity, the Spirit of God is creating the holy harmony of heaven, enriching our lives beyond measure. This act of worship serves both as witness to the world of the plausibility of God's promises, and as our own living prayer: "Our Father in heaven, hallowed be your name. Your kingdom come. Your will be done, on earth as it is in heaven" (Mt 6:9-10).

Multicultural congregations are not God's kingdom come on earth, but they are the foretaste of that kingdom. The way Christians live out God's story in these congregations "makes the kingdom visible."[5] Charles Van Engen says that all such congregations are "branch offices" of God's kingdom in this world, the anticipatory sign, the "eschatological heralds of that which is coming."[6]

When I think of worship in the multicultural church, I cannot help but think of the eschatological imagery of worship in Revelation 7:

> There was a great multitude that no one could count, from every nation, from all tribes and peoples and languages, standing before the throne and before the Lamb, robed in white, with palm branches in their hands. They cried out in a loud voice, saying, "Salvation belongs to our God

who is seated on the throne, and to the Lamb!" And all the angels stood around the throne . . . and they fell on their faces before the throne and worshiped God, singing, "Amen! Blessing and glory and wisdom and thanksgiving and honor and power and might be to our God forever and ever! Amen." (vv. 9-12)

At one of our Friday-night praise celebrations, during testimony time, Rich Ploch, a lay member of our congregation, stood to tell about his daughter's first-grade birthday party. Christy, like any six-year-old, waited anxiously by the window for the first of her friends to arrive. When the first one came, she burst through the front door, rushing out to greet her friend, and they hugged one another, jumped up and down, and then together came in to sit by the window to wait for the next guest. When the next car pulled up, Christy and the first child rushed out together, and all three children danced for joy, hugging one another, and then came inside. This pattern of happy hospitality continued until the eighth and last guest arrived, when all the children ran out to greet her, and the whole party hugged, screamed and jumped up and down together.

Rich said that as he watched this unfold, he remarked to his wife, Carol, "I've been looking for this kind of feeling all my life. How neat it must feel to arrive at a party and to have everyone run out to welcome you, happy that you are there!" Rich concluded his testimony with this observation: "It wasn't until I came to this congregation that I felt as warmly and happily accepted as Christy and her friends must have felt that day."

The Reverend Dave Zuchelli, a guest pastor who was leading testimony time that Friday night, followed up Rich's comment with this observation:

Whenever heaven is depicted, it's always described as this lonely image of St. Peter waiting by the gates, checking to see whether you are on the guest list or not. But I think heaven is far more like Christy's party, when all the saints will rush out to greet us, joyfully jumping up and down, hugging us, happy that we are there.

Multicultural congregations are the foretaste of this heavenly hospitality. "So then you are no longer strangers and aliens, but you are citizens with the saints and also members of the household of God" (Eph 2:19). Let the party begin!

Notes

Introduction

[1]Leonard Sweet, *FaithQuakes* (Nashville: Abingdon, 1994), p. 176.

[2]Penny Loeb et al., "To Make a Nation," *U.S. News & World Report,* October 4, 1993, p. 54.

[3]Throughout this book I refer to non-Hispanic whites as Anglos, though this is by no means a precise use of the word. At this point in our culture's racial identification of subgroups, I am not sure there is a better word to use.

[4]Tom Sine, *Cease Fire* (Grand Rapids, Mich.: Eerdmans, 1995), p. 92.

[5]Arthur M. Schlesinger Jr., *The Disuniting of America* (New York: W. W. Norton, 1992), p. 10.

[6]Ibid., p. 11.

[7]Maria Puente, "Immigration Backlash in the Land of Liberty," *USA Today,* July 14, 1993, p. 1.

[8]Ruben G. Rumbaut, "The Crucible Within: Ethnic Identity, Self-Esteem and Segmented Assimilation Among Children of Immigrants," in *The New Second Generation,* ed. Alejandro Portes (New York: Russell Sage Foundation, 1996), p. 121.

[9]More than 95 percent white and of Scotch-Irish ancestry.

[10]Stanley J. Grenz, *A Primer on Postmodernism* (Grand Rapids, Mich.: Eerdmans, 1996), p. 18.

[11]Ibid., p. 14.

[12]Ibid., p. 12.

Chapter 1: With Their Own Languages, Families & Nations

[1]The Christian population in Cambodia is less than one percent, and it is highly unusual to have a Cambodian intentionally seek out the church unless he or she has had a previous experience with the church.

[2]Terence E. Fretheim, "Genesis," *The New Interpreter's Bible,* ed. Leander E. Kech (Nashville: Abingdon, 1994), 1:409.

[3]Walter Brueggemann, *Genesis,* Interpretation Series (Atlanta: John Knox Press, 1982), p. 91.

[4]Lesslie Newbigin, *The Gospel in a Pluralist Society* (Grand Rapids, Mich.: Eerdmans, 1989), p. 82.

[5]Brueggemann, *Genesis,* p. 99.

[6]Ibid., p. 100.

[7]Fretheim, "Genesis," 1:414.

[8]Stanley Hauerwas, *Christian Existence Today: Essays on Church, World and Living in Between* (Durham, N.C.: Labyrinth, 1988), p. 49.

[9]Fretheim, "Genesis," 1:413.

[10]Brueggemann, *Genesis*, p. 103.

[11]George Weigel, "The Christian Citizen and Democracy," in *Reinventing the American People*, ed. Robert Royal (Grand Rapids, Mich.: Eerdmans, 1995), p. 183.

[12]As cited by Sine, *Cease Fire*, p. 97.

[13]Arthur M. Schlesinger Jr., *The Disuniting of America* (New York: W. W. Norton, 1992), p. 112.

[14]Ibid.

[15]Ibid., p. 113.

[16]Ibid., p. 16.

[17]Ibid., p. 42.

[18]Ibid., p. 74.

[19]Michael Lind, *The Next American Nation* (New York: Free Press, 1995), p. 12.

[20]Ibid.

[21]Ibid.

[22]Ibid., p. 98.

[23]Ibid., p. 123.

[24]Ibid., p. 124

[25]Ibid., p. 135.

[26]Ibid., p. 359.

Chapter 2: To Bless the Nations

[1]Fretheim, "Genesis," 1:424.

[2]Brueggemann, *Genesis*, p. 116.

[3]Walter Brueggemann, *The Land* (Philadelphia: Fortress, 1977), p. 15.

[4]Hauerwas, *Christian Existence Today*, p. 49.

[5]Brueggemann, *Genesis*, pp. 105-6.

[6]Galatians 3:8: "And the scripture, foreseeing that God would justify the Gentiles by faith, declared the gospel beforehand to Abraham, saying, 'All the Gentiles shall be blessed in you.' "

[7]Brueggemann, *Genesis*, p. 113.

[8]Brueggemann, *Land*, p. 18.

[9]Stanley Hauerwas and William H. Willimon, *Resident Aliens* (Nashville: Abingdon, 1989), p. 57.

[10]Sweet, *FaithQuakes*, p. 209.

[11]Newbigin, *Gospel in a Pluralist Society*, p. 72.

[12]Lesslie Newbigin, "Mission in the World Today," in *A Word in Season* (Grand

Rapids, Mich.: Eerdmans, 1994), p. 128.

[13]Ibid.

[14]Ibid.

[15]J. Richard Middleton and Brian J. Walsh, "Facing the Postmodern Scalpel," in *Christian Apologetics in the Postmodern World*, ed. Timothy R. Phillips and Dennis L. Okholm (Downers Grove, Ill.: InterVarsity Press, 1995), pp. 148-49.

[16]Brueggemann, *Genesis*, p. 119.

[17]Charles Van Engen, *God's Missionary People: Rethinking the Purpose of the Local Church* (Grand Rapids, Mich.: Baker Book House, 1991), pp. 103-4.

[18]Hauerwas and Willimon, *Resident Aliens*, p. 43.

[19]Stanley Hauerwas, *A Community of Character* (Notre Dame, Ind.: University of Notre Dame Press, 1981), pp. 84-85.

[20]Zan Holmes, *Encountering Jesus* (Nashville: Abingdon, 1992), p. 37, as cited in Leonard Sweet, "Double Dutch," *Homiletics*, April-June 1993, p. 33.

[21]Quoted in Edith Draper, ed., *Draper's Book of Quotations for the Christian World* (Wheaton, Ill.: Tyndale House, 1992), p. 200.

[22]Leonard Sweet, "From a Distance," *Homiletics*, July-September 1992, pp. 23-25.

[23]Gary Smalley and John Trent, *The Blessing* (New York: Pocket Books, 1986), p. 29.

[24]Fretheim, "Genesis," 1:425.

[25]Quoted in *Draper's Book of Quotations*, p. 201.

Chapter 3: Just Give Them Jesus

[1]Fanny is first mentioned in chapter one as a participant in our Friday-night revival.

[2]Hauerwas and Willimon, *Resident Aliens*, p. 121.

[3]Hauerwas, *Community of Character*, p. 51.

[4]Roberta Bondi, "Friendship with God," *Weavings*, May-June 1992, p. 8.

[5]Walter F. Taylor, "Unity/Unity of Humanity," in *The Anchor Bible Dictionary*, ed. David Noel Freedman, 6 vols. (New York: Doubleday, 1992), 6:746.

[6]Ibid., p. 748.

[7]Ibid., p. 749.

[8]Hauerwas, *Community of Character*, p. 106.

[9]Newbigin, *Gospel in a Pluralist Society*, p. 14.

[10]Ibid., p. 22.

[11]Allan Bloom, *The Closing of the American Mind* (New York: Simon & Schuster, 1987), p. 26, as quoted by William Lane Craig, "Politically Incorrect Salvation," in *Christian Apologetics in the Postmodern World*, ed. Timothy R. Phillips and Dennis L. Okholm (Downers Grove, Ill.: InterVarsity Press, 1995), p. 76.

[12]Craig, "Politically Incorrect Salvation," p. 76.

[13]Newbigin, *Gospel in a Pluralist Society*, p. 7.

[14]Ibid.

[15]Ibid., p. 25.

[16]Middleton and Walsh, "Facing the Postmodern Scalpel," pp. 148-49.

[17]Newbigin, *Gospel in a Pluralist Society*, p. 159.

[18]Ibid., p. 158.

[19]Ibid., p. 182.

[20]Susanne Hargrave, "Culture, Abstraction and Ethnocentrism," *Missiology* 21, no. 1 (January 1993): 5.

[21]Ibid., p. 9.

[22]Ibid.

[23]Ibid., p. 10.

[24]Ibid., p. 8.

[25]Hauerwas, *Community of Character*, p. 105.

[26]Bernard T. Adeney, *Strange Virtues* (Downers Grove, Ill.: InterVarsity Press, 1995), p. 21.

[27]Ibid., p. 24.

[28]Newbigin, "Mission in the World Today," pp. 130-31.

[29]Ibid., p. 131.

[30]Alister McGrath, *Evangelicalism and the Future of Christianity* (Downers Grove, Ill.: InterVarsity Press, 1995), p. 162.

[31]Ibid.

[32]Lesslie Newbigin, "The Cultural Captivity of Western Christianity," in *A Word in Season* (Grand Rapids, Mich.: Eerdmans, 1994), p. 72.

Chapter 4: Be My Witnesses

[1]Quoted by Leonard Sweet, "God's Missionary People," *Homiletics*, April-June 1993, p. 37.

[2]John Killinger, *Letting God Bless You* (Nashville: Abingdon, 1992), pp. 111-12, as quoted by Leonard Sweet, "Double Dutch," *Homiletics*, April-June 1993, p. 33.

[3]Sweet, *FaithQuakes*, p. 209.

[4]William H. Willimon, *Acts*, Interpretation Series (Atlanta: John Knox, 1988), p. 30.

[5]Ibid., p. 37.

[6]Hauerwas, *Christian Existence Today*, p. 50.

[7]Ibid., p. 53.

[8]George A. Lindbeck, *The Nature of Doctrine: Religion and Theology in a Postliberal Age* (Philadelphia: Westminster Press, 1984), p. 118.

[9]Hauerwas and Willimon, *Resident Aliens*, p. 97.

[10]Ibid., p. 24.

[11]Adeney, *Strange Virtues*, p. 126.

[12]Willimon, *Acts*, p. 42.

[13]Adeney, *Strange Virtues*, p. 40.

[14]Harvey Cox, *Fire from Heaven* (New York: Addison-Wesley, 1995), pp. 14-15.

[15]Ibid., p. 47.

[16]Ibid., p. 58.

[17]Ibid.

[18]Ibid., p. 63.

[19]David F. D'Amico, "Evangelization Across Cultures in the United States: What to Do When the World Comes to Us?" *Review & Expositor* 90 (1993): 95.

[20]Quoted by McGrath, *Evangelicalism and the Future of Christianity*, p. 100.

[21]Van Engen, *God's Missionary People*, p. 110.

[22]Ibid., p. 55.

[23]Thom Hopler and Marcia Hopler, *Reaching the World Next Door*, rev. ed. (Downers Grove, Ill.: InterVarsity Press, 1993), p. 78.

[24]Willimon, *Acts*, p. 65.

[25]Van Engen, *God's Missionary People*, p. 26.

[26]D'Amico, "Evangelization Across Cultures," p. 94.

Chapter 5: Choosing Life

[1]One notable exception was Good Shepherd United Methodist Church in Durham, North Carolina, which actually began as a multicultural church.

[2]Michael D. Yapko, *Breaking the Patterns of Depression* (New York: Doubleday, 1997), p. 55.

[3]Milton Erickson, as quoted in ibid., p. 56

[4]Ibid., p. 22.

[5]I asked Bill if he was related to the great evangelical orator; he said no, but he is related to Dallas's famous Bryan's Barbecue!

[6]Hopler and Hopler, *Reaching the World Next Door*, p. 119.

[7]David Howard, quoted in David L. Ripley, "Reaching the World at Our Doorstep," *Evangelical Missions Quarterly*, April 1994, p. 146.

[8]Ripley, "Reaching the World at Our Doorstep," p. 146.

[9]Newbigin, "Cultural Captivity," pp. 66-67.

[10]S. D. Gaede, *When Tolerance Is No Virtue* (Downers Grove, Ill.: InterVarsity Press, 1993), pp. 63-64.

Chapter 6: No Partiality

[1]Newbigin, *Gospel in a Pluralist Society*, pp. 87-88.

[2]Richard J. Mouw and Sander Griffioen, *Pluralisms and Horizons: An Essay in Christian Public Philosophy* (Grand Rapids, Mich.: Eerdmans, 1993), p. 168.

[3]C. J. H. Wright, "Family," *Anchor Bible Dictionary*, 2:762.

[4]Ibid., p. 769.

[5]Adeney, *Strange Virtues*, p. 16.

[6]Lesslie Newbigin, *Foolishness to the Greeks* (Grand Rapids, Mich.: Eerdmans, 1986), p. 3.

[7]Ibid.

[8]Ibid.

[9]Ibid.

[10]Adeney, *Strange Virtues*, p. 16.

[11]Hopler and Hopler, *Reaching the World Next Door*, p. 14

[12]Ibid.

[13]Ibid., pp. 14-15.

[14]Ibid., p. 15.

[15]Newbigin, *Foolishness to the Greeks*, p. 4.

[16]Newbigin, *Gospel in a Pluralist Society*, p. 95

[17]Ibid., p. 184.

[18]Ibid.

[19]Ibid., p. 186.

[20]Ibid., p. 195.

[21]Schlesinger, *Disuniting of America*, p. 93.

[22]Adeney, *Strange Virtues*, p. 15.

[23]Newbigin, *Gospel in a Pluralist Society*, p. 124

[24]Willimon, *Acts*, p. 96

[25]Ibid., p. 97

[26]Ibid., p. 96.

[27]Ibid., p. 99.

[28]Newbigin, *Gospel in a Pluralist Society*, p. 168

Chapter 7: The Alien Among You

[1]Parker J. Palmer, *The Company of Strangers* (New York: Crossroad, 1983), pp. 56-57.

[2]Willimon H. Willimon, *Clergy and Laity Burnout* (Nashville: Abingdon, 1989), p. 89.

[3]Ibid., p. 91.

[4]Palmer, *Company of Strangers*, p. 59.

[5]The legislation I am specifically referring to includes the Illegal Immigration Reform and Immigrant Responsibility Act (IIRIRA), the Anti-terrorism and Effective Death Penalty Act (AEDPA) and portions of the Welfare Reform Law, all of which were adopted in 1996 following the popular response to Proposition 187.

[6]Joe Maxwell, "The Alien in Our Midst," *Christianity Today*, December 13, 1993, p. 48.

[7]S. E. Wheeler, "John Wesley and 'Social Ethics' " (lecture given at the Wesley Studies Institute, Hagerstown, Penn., 1995).

[8]Ibid.

[9]Ibid., p. 5.

[10]Walter C. Kaiser, Jr., "Leviticus," *New Interpreter's Bible*, 1:1136.

[11]Middleton and Walsh, "Facing the Postmodern Scalpel," pp. 146-47.

[12]Israel's sensitivity to the "stranger" actually precedes slavery in Egypt, as is evidenced by the Abrahamic narrative.

[13]"You shall not wrong or oppress a resident alien, for you were aliens in the land of Egypt" (Ex 22:21).

[14]"Thus says the LORD: Act with justice and righteousness, and deliver from the hand of the oppressor anyone who has been robbed. And do no wrong or violence to the alien, the orphan, and the widow, or shed innocent blood in this place" (Jer 22:3).

[15]"Does not oppress anyone, but restores to the debtor his pledge, commits no robbery, gives his bread to the hungry and covers the naked with a garment, . . . does not wrong anyone, exacts no pledge, commits no robbery, but gives his bread to the hungry and covers the naked with a garment" (Ezek 18:7, 16).

[16]Kaiser, "Leviticus," 1:1135.

[17]John R. Spencer, "Sojourner," *Anchor Bible Dictionary*, 6:104.

[18]Kaiser, "Leviticus," 1:1136.

[19]Hauerwas, *Community of Character*, pp. 83-84.

[20]Stanley Hauerwas, *Against the Nations: War and Survival in a Liberal Society* (Minneapolis: Winston, 1985), p. 117.

[21]Hauerwas and Willimon, *Resident Aliens*, p. 24

[22]Ibid., p. 51.

[23]Ibid., pp. 42-43.

Chapter 8: Someone to Guide Me

[1]Fred B. Craddock, "Preaching," Candler School of Theology (Nashville: Abingdon, 1986), videocassette.

[2]Eusebius *Historia Ecclesiastica* 2.2, as quoted in Willimon, *Acts*, p. 72.

[3]McGrath, *Evangelicalism and the Future of Christianity*, p. 59.

[4]Ibid.

[5]Stanley J. Grenz and Roger E. Olson, *20th-Century Theology* (Downers Grove, Ill.: InterVarsity Press, 1992), p. 284.

[6]Ibid.

[7]Newbigin, *Gospel in a Pluralist Society*, p. 65.

[8]Hauerwas, *Community of Character*, p. 149.

[9]Ibid., p. 50

[10]Adeney, *Strange Virtues*, p. 79.

[11]O.G. stands for "original gangster." It can refer to the founder of a gang, the oldest member, or serve as a deferential term of respect for someone who has been in the gangster life for a while.

Chapter 9: Ambassadors for Christ

[1]Duane Elmer, *Cross-Cultural Conflict* (Downers Grove, Ill.: InterVarsity Press, 1993), p. 118.

[2]Ibid.

[3]Carol Hoffman-Guzman, "Cross-Cultural Leadership and Participation in the Local Church" (working paper, Miami Urban Ministries, Miami, Fla., 1995).

[4]Willimon, *Acts*, pp. 129-30.

[5]Ibid., p. 130.

[6]Leonard I. Sweet, "Be an Engergizer Bunny," *Homiletics*, January-March 1995, p. 12.

[7]Desmond Tutu, *The Rainbow People of God* (New York: Doubleday, 1994), p. v.

Chapter 10: By the Rivers of Babylon

[1]Alejandro Portes and Ruben G. Rumbaut, *Immigrant America: A Portrait* (Berkeley: University of California Press, 1990), p. 12.

[2]Ibid., p. 10.

[3]Ibid.

[4]Ibid., p. 12.

[5]Ibid., p. 13.

[6]Ibid., p. 14.

[7]Ibid., p. 16.

[8]Ibid., pp. 16-17.

[9]Ibid., p. 18.

[10]Ibid., p. 19.

[11]Ibid., pp. 19-20

[12]Ibid., p. 21.

[13]Ibid.

[14]Ibid.

[15]Ibid., p. 23.

[16]Adeney, *Strange Virtues*, p. 133.

[17]Ibid., p. 134.

[18]Ibid., p. 135.

[19]Ibid., p. 136.

[20]Portes and Rumbaut, *Immigrant America*, p. 167.

[21]Ibid., p. 171.

[22]Ibid.

[23]Ibid.

[24]Ibid., p. 161.

[25]Ibid., p. 181.

Chapter 11: Into the Fiery Furnace

[1]Tim Stafford, "Here Comes the World," *Christianity Today*, May 15, 1995, p. 23.

[2]Ibid.

[3]Leif Jensen and Yoshimi Chitose, "Today's Second Generation: Evidence from the 1990 Census," in *The New Second Generation*, ed. Alejandro Portes (New York: Russell Sage Foundation, 1996), p. 83.

[4]Alejandro Portes, introduction to *The New Second Generation*, ed. Alejandro Portes (New York: Russell Sage Foundation, 1996), p. 3.

[5]Rumbaut, "Crucible Within," p. 168.

[6]Young Pai, "Caught in the Web: A Perspective for Socio-cultural Understanding of Korean-American Youth," *Roots and Wings: An Invitational Symposium on the Future Ministry for the Korean-American Community* (Washington, D.C.: Korean United Methodist Church of Greater Washington, 1994), p. 25.

[7]Michel Marriot, "Multiracial Americans Ready to Claim Their Identity," *The New York Times*, July 20, 1996, p. 1.

[8]Rumbaut, "Crucible Within," p. 144.

[9]Sang Hyun Lee, "Called to Be Pilgrims: Toward an Asian-American Theology from the Korean Immigrant Perspective," *Roots and Wings: An Invitational Symposium on the Future Ministry for the Korean-American Community* (Washington, D.C.: Korean United Methodist Church of Greater Washington, 1994), p. 41.

[10]Ibid.

[11]Ibid, p. 42.

[12]Ibid., pp. 43-44.

Chapter 12: Every Knee Shall Bow & Every Tongue Confess

[1]Newbigin, *Gospel in a Pluralist Society*, p. 110.

[2]Ibid., p. 115.

[3]Ibid., p. 113.

[4]Newbigin, "Cultural Captivity," p. 78.

[5]Stanley Hauerwas, *The Peaceable Kingdom* (Notre Dame, Ind.: University of Notre Dame Press, 1983), p. 97.

[6]Van Engen, *God's Missionary People*, p. 111.

Bibliography

Adeney, Bernard T. *Strange Virtues: Ethics in a Multicultural World*. Downers Grove, Ill.: InterVarsity Press, 1995.

Augenbraum, Harold, and Ilan Stravans, eds. *Growing Up Latino: Memoirs and Stories*. Boston: Houghton Mifflin, 1993.

Augsburger, David W. *Conflict Mediation Across Cultures: Pathways and Patterns*. Bethesda, Md.: Alban Institute, n.d..

Beck, Roy. *The Case Against Immigration*. New York: W. W. Norton, 1996.

Bernstein, Richard. *Dictatorship of Virtue: How the Battle over Multiculturalism Is Reshaping Our Schools, Our Country, Our Lives*. New York: Vintage, 1995.

Brimelow, Peter. *Alien Nation: Common Sense About America's Immigration Disaster.* New York: Random House, 1995.

Brueggemann, Walter. *The Land: Overtures to Biblical Theology.* Philadelphia: Fortress, 1977.

Chun, Sang E. "A New Immigrant Church." In *Center City Churches: The New Urban Frontier.* Edited by Lyle E. Schaller. Nashville: Abingdon, 1993.

Cose, Ellis. *Color-Blind: Seeing Beyond Race in a Race-Obsessed World*. New York: HarperCollins, 1997.

————. *A Nation of Strangers: Prejudice, Politics and the Populating of America*. New York: William Morrow, 1992.

Cox, Harvey. *Fire from Heaven: The Rise of Pentecostal Spirituality and the Reshaping of Religion in the Twenty-first Century.* Reading, Mass: Addison-Wesley, 1995.

Daniels, Roger. *Coming to America: A History of Immigration and Ethnicity in American Life.* New York: HarperCollins, 1990.

Decker, Scott H., and Barrik Van Winkle. *Life in the Gang: Family, Friends and Violence.* Cambridge Criminology Series. New York: Cambridge University Press, 1996.

DeYoung, Curtiss Paul. *Coming Together: The Bible's Message in an Age of Diversity.* Valley Forge, Penn.: Judson, 1995.

D'Souza, Dinesh. *The End of Racism: Principles for a Multiracial Society.* New York: Free Press, 1995.

Dyson, Michael Eric. *Between God and Gangsta Rap: Being Witness to Black Culture.* New York: Oxford University Press, 1996.

Elmer, Duane. *Cross-Cultural Conflict.* Downers Grove, Ill.: InterVarsity Press, 1995.

Foster, Charles R. *Embracing Diversity: Leadership in Multicultural Congregations.* Bethesda, Md.: Alban Institute, 1997.

Foster, Charles R., and Theodore Brelsford. *We Are the Church Together: Cultural Diversity in Congregational Life.* Valley Forge, Penn.: Trinity Press International, 1996.

Gaede, S. D. *When Tolerance Is No Virtue.* Downers Grove, Ill.: InterVarsity Press, 1995.

Gaukroger, Stephen. *Your Mission, Should You Accept It . . . : An Introduction for World Christians.* Downers Grove, Ill.: InterVarsity Press, 1997.

Glazer, Nathan. *We Are All Multiculturalists Now.* Cambridge, Mass.: Harvard University Press, 1997.

Goldberg, David Theo, ed. *Multiculturalism: A Critical Reader.* Cambridge, Mass.: Blackwell, 1994.

Gonzales, Justo L., gen. ed. *Each in Our Own Tongue: A History of Hispanic United Methodism.* Nashville: Abingdon, 1991.

Grenz, Stanley J. *A Primer on Postmodernism.* Grand Rapids, Mich.: Eerdmans, 1996.

Guillermo, Artemio R., ed. *Churches Aflame: Asian Americans and United Methodism.* Nashville: Abingdon, 1991.

Hacker, Andrew. *Two Nations: Black and White, Separate, Hostile, Unequal.* Rev. ed. New York: Ballantine, 1995.

Hauerwas, Stanley. *Against the Nations: War and Survival in a Liberal Society.* Minneapolis: Winston, 1985.

————. *Christian Existence Today: Essays on Church, World and Living In Between.* Durham, N.C.: Labyrinth, 1988.

————. *A Community of Character: Toward a Constructive Christian Social Ethic.* Notre Dame: University of Notre Dame Press, 1981.

————. *The Peaceable Kingdom: A Primer in Christian Ethics.* Notre Dame: University of Notre Dame Press, 1983.

Hauerwas, Stanley, and William H. Willimon. *Resident Aliens.* Nashville: Abingdon, 1989.

Hoffman-Guzman, Carol. *Cross-Cultural Leadership and Participation in the Local Church.* Miami: Miami Urban Ministries, 1995.

Hollinger, David A. *Postethnic America: Beyond Multiculturalism.* New York: BasicBooks, 1995.

Hong, Maria, ed. *Growing Up Asian American: Stories of Childhood Adolescence and Coming of Age in America from the 1800s to the 1990s.* New York: Avon, 1995.

Hopler, Thom, and Marcia Hopler. *Reaching the World Next Door: How to Spread the Gospel in the Midst of Many Cultures.* Downers Grove, Ill.: InterVarsity Press, 1993.

Hunsberger, George R., and Craig E. Van Gelder, eds. *The Church Between Gospel and Culture*. Grand Rapids, Mich.: Eerdmans, 1996.

Hunter, James Davison. *Culture Wars: The Struggle to Define America*. New York: BasicBooks, 1991.

Jankowski, Martin Sanchez. *Islands in the Street: Gangs and American Urban Society*. Berkeley: University of California Press, 1991.

Kim, Elaine H., and Eui-Young Yu. *East to America: Korean American Life Stories*. New York: New Press, 1996.

Korem, Dan. *Suburban Gangs: The Affluent Rebels*. Richardson, Tex.: International Focus, 1994.

Lind, Michael. *The Next American Nation: The New Nationalism and The Fourth American Revolution*. New York: Free Press, 1995.

Lindbeck, George A. *The Nature of Doctrine: Religion and Theology in a Postliberal Age*. Philadelphia: Westminster Press, 1984.

Loury, Glenn C. *One by One from the Inside Out: Essays and Reviews on Race and Responsibility in America*. New York: Free Press, 1995.

Magida, Arthur J., ed. *How to Be a Perfect Stranger: A Guide to Etiquette in Other People's Religious Ceremonies*. Vol. 1. Woodstock, Vt.: Jewish Lights, 1996.

Mahler, Sarah J. *American Dreaming: Immigrant Life on the Margins*. Princeton, N.J.: Princeton University Press, 1996.

Matlins, Stuart M., and Arthur J. Magida, eds. *How to Be a Perfect Stranger: A Guide to Etiquette in Other People's Religious Ceremonies*. Vol. 2. Woodstock, Vt.: Jewish Lights, 1996.

McGrath, Alister. *Evangelicalism and the Future of Christianity*. Downers Grove, Ill.: InterVarsity Press, 1995.

Middleton, J. Richard, and Brian J. Walsh. *Truth Is Stranger Than It Used to Be*. Downers Grove, Ill.: InterVarsity Press, 1995.

Millman, Joel. *The Other Americans: How Immigrants Renew Our Country, Our Economy, Our Values*. New York: Viking, 1997.

Newbigin, Lesslie. *Foolishness to the Greeks*. Grand Rapids, Mich.: Eerdmans, 1986.
———. *The Gospel in a Pluralist Society*. Grand Rapids, Mich.: Eerdmans, 1989.
———. *Truth to Tell: The Gospel as Public Truth*. Grand Rapids, Mich.: Eerdmans, 1991
———. *A Word in Season*. Grand Rapids, Mich.: Eerdmans, 1994.

Ortiz, Manuel. *The Hispanic Challenge: Opportunities Confronting the Church*. Downers Grove, Ill.: InterVarsity Press, 1993.

Palmer, Parker J. *The Company of Strangers: Christians and the Renewal of America's Public Life*. New York: Crossroad, 1983.

Phillips, Timothy R., and Dennis L. Okholm, eds. *Christian Apologetics in the Postmodern World*. Downers Grove, Ill.: InterVarsity Press, 1995.

Portes, Alejandro, and Ruben G. Rumbaut. *Immigrant America: A Portrait*. Berkeley: University of California Press, 1990

Portes, Alejandro, ed. *The New Second Generation.* New York: Russell Sage Foundation, 1996.

Reed, Ismael, ed. *MultiAmerica: Essays on Culture Wars and Cultural Peace.* New York: Viking, 1997.

Roots and Wings: An Invitational Symposium on the Future Ministry for the Korean-American Community. Washington, D.C.: Korean United Methodist Church of Greater Washington, 1994.

Royal, Robert, ed. *Reinventing the American People.* Grand Rapids, Mich.: Eerdmans, 1995.

Salins, Peter D. *Assimilation American Style.* New York: BasicBooks, 1997.

Schinto, Jeanne. *Huddle Fever: Living in the Immigrant City.* New York: Alfred A. Knopf, 1996.

Schlesinger, Arthur M., Jr. *The Disuniting of America: Reflections on a Multicultural Society.* New York: W. W. Norton, 1992.

Sowell, Thomas. *Race and Culture.* New York: BasicBooks, 1994.

Takaki, Ronald. *A Different Mirror: A History of Multicultural America.* Boston: Back Bay, 1993.

Tutu, Desmond. *The Rainbow People of God.* New York: Doubleday, 1994.

Ungar, Sanford J. *Fresh Blood: The New American Immigrants.* New York: Simon & Schuster, 1995.

Van Engen, Charles. *God's Missionary People: Rethinking the Purpose of the Local Church.* Grand Rapids, Mich.: Baker Book House, 1991.

West, Cornel. *Race Matters.* New York: Vintage Books, 1994.

White, Randy. *Journey to the Center of the City.* Downers Grove, Ill.: InterVarsity Press, 1997.

Wicker, Tom. *Tragic Failure: Racial Integration in America.* New York: William Morrow, 1996.

Wilkerson, J. Haire, III. *One Nation Indivisible: How Ethnic Separatism Threatens America.* Reading, Mass.: Addison-Wesley, 1997.

Willimon, William H. *Acts.* Interpretation Series, ed. James Mays. Atlanta: John Knox, 1988.

Subject Index

Scripture Index